MW01002120

The African Wars

Warriors and Soldiers in the Colonial Campaigns

Chris Peers

Pen & Sword
MILITARY

First published in Great Britain in 2010 and reprinted in this format in 2021 by
Pen & Sword Military
an imprint of
Pen & Sword Books Ltd
47 Church Street
Barnsley
South Yorkshire
S70 2AS

Copyright © Chris Peers 2010, 2021

ISBN 978 1 39901 314 7

The right of Chris Peers to be identified as Author of this Work has been
asserted by him in accordance with the Copyright, Designs and Patents
Act 1988.

A CIP catalogue record for this book is available from the British Library.

All rights reserved. No part of this book may be reproduced or transmitted in
any form or by any means, electronic or mechanical including photocopying,
recording or by any information storage and retrieval system, without
permission from the Publisher in writing.

Typeset in Ehrhardt by Phoenix Typesetting, Auldgirth, Dumfriesshire

Printed and bound in the UK by CPI Group (UK) Ltd, Croydon, CR0 4YY

MIX
Paper from
responsible sources
FSC® C013604

Pen & Sword Books Ltd incorporates the imprints of Pen & Sword Aviation,
Pen & Sword Maritime, Pen & Sword Military, Wharncliffe Local History,
Pen and Sword Select, Pen and Sword Military Classics, Leo Cooper,
Remember When, Seaforth Publishing and Frontline Publishing.

For a complete list of Pen & Sword titles please contact
PEN & SWORD BOOKS LIMITED
47 Church Street, Barnsley, South Yorkshire, S70 2AS, England
E-mail: enquiries@pen-and-sword.co.uk
Website: www.pen-and-sword.co.uk

Contents

Acknowledgements

The author especially wishes to thank the following for assistance with illustrations, and for their advice and encouragement: John Catton, Alan Colquhoun, Mark Copplestone, David Le Breton and the staff of the Birmingham City Reference Library. Also my wife, Kate, who has not only supplied some of the photographs but, as always, supported the entire project well beyond the call of duty. Of course none of the above are responsible for any of the opinions expressed in these pages.

Introduction

The theme of this book is warfare in sub-Saharan Africa during the nineteenth century. During that century European involvement in the affairs of the continent, which began with no more than a handful of enclaves and trading posts around the coast, gradually became the most important factor in the lives of its people, culminating in the 'scramble for Africa' of the 1880s and 1890s and the incorporation of the bulk of the continent into the empires of the European powers. This period also coincided with the Industrial Revolution in Europe, and the development of ever more sophisticated rifles, steamships and other materials of war. Native African armies, which had developed their own methods of fighting against similarly equipped opponents, now had to adapt to deal with enemies whose technological superiority increased almost year by year. The varying success with which they did this, and the adaptations which they and the African environment forced on the invaders in their turn, makes this a fascinating story. It is also, of course, an immense subject, and popular military history has traditionally concerned itself only with a few of the highlights. So in the English-speaking world the Anglo-Zulu war of 1879 and the Sudan campaigns of 1885 and 1898 are among the best-known episodes of the colonial era, while most of the smaller-scale 'bush wars' which raged across the continent remain in obscurity. In a book of this size it has still been necessary to concentrate on a few subjects which are of particular interest from a historical or tactical point of view. But many of these campaigns may be unfamiliar, while it is to be hoped that a discussion of the better known ones will benefit from being placed in a wider context.

In recent years archaeology, genetics and other scientific disciplines have confirmed what had been suspected since the days of Charles Darwin: that Africa was the original home of the human race, and that until the last few thousand years most of the people living on earth have been Africans. There is a paradox here, because no other inhabited continent appears so hostile to human life. Most of the interior is a vast, elevated plateau cut off from the narrow coastal plain by mountains and escarpments. To the north, access from Europe is cut off by the Sahara Desert, an obstacle as formidable as any ocean. South of the Sahara the coast has few useful harbours, and formidable rapids make most of the rivers unnavigable. Deserts and jungles cover huge areas, while elsewhere the soil is often too poor to support a dense agricultural population, or alternating droughts and floods make farming a precarious business. Malaria and a host of other endemic diseases affect people and their live-stock, and in places make life impossible for newcomers without the benefit of natural immunity or modern medicines.

Like the malarial mosquito, the tsetse fly has had a profound influence on the course of African history. It can carry sleeping sickness in some areas, but in most of its range it is not harmful to humans. It does, however, transmit a parasite which is fatal to unacclimatized cattle and horses. Even in the tropics its distribution is patchy, and elevated areas such as the Kenya Highlands are generally free from its ravages, but in most of tropical Africa north of the Zambezi River its presence severely restricted the use of horses for transport and warfare. South of the Zambezi white settlers found it possible to employ ox-drawn wagons, but elsewhere the small native breeds of cattle, the only ones which could survive the tsetse fly, were unsuitable for use as draught animals. Military expeditions were therefore forced to rely on human muscle to transport their food and munitions. In some places, especially in East Africa, whole tribes specialized in this carrying trade, but all too often it was necessary to conscript reluctant porters from the local population at gunpoint, and to maintain a constant watch to keep desertion down to manageable proportions.

These adverse environmental factors placed a variety of constraints on human societies and forced them to adapt in different ways, so that over thousands of years of relative isolation a staggering diversity of lifestyles evolved, ranging from centralized kingdoms and well-organized city states to nomadic herdsmen and hunter-gatherers with no organization beyond the family group. They also combined to ensure that the armies which operated in most parts of Africa were very small by European standards. Even when external invaders or powerful native kingdoms did manage to muster large forces, supply problems restricted their move-ments. In many areas supplies of either food or water (often both) were chronically scarce, and the unpredictable climate did not permit local farmers to build up the sort of food reserves which might have been commandeered for the benefit of military expeditions. Writing in the 1880s, the missionary W P Johnson remarked on the strain which even a small party could place on local resources, since, even if it was prepared to pay its way, there would often be nothing to buy. Therefore in East and Central Africa a military or exploring expedition of 400 or 500 soldiers and 1,000 porters would be a very large one indeed, and even lightly equipped native armies seldom exceeded 2,000–3,000.

Inland from the west coast, travel was even more difficult. The long-range trade routes of the east were lacking here, as each tribe was accustomed to trade only with its immediate neighbours. So there were no professional long-distance carriers such as the Swahilis and Nyamwezi who provided manpower for caravans coming from the east coast, but only an endless succession of communities linked by poor tracks, many of them with a vested interest in obstructing attempts to penetrate beyond them and possibly cut them out of the trade. Here most long-distance movement had to be by river, but it was often necessary to interrupt a journey to negotiate land routes around the ubiquitous rapids. Even the steam-driven gunboats which became such a potent symbol of European power had frequently to be dismantled into manageable loads and carried round impassable stretches of the rivers on the heads of local labourers, to be reassembled further upstream.

But in the eyes of the outsiders, the conquest of Africa promised advantages which more than compensated for the difficulties. The mysterious continent was popularly associated with fabulous wealth in gold, in ivory or in fertile land waiting for farmers capable of realizing its potential. Ever since the Portuguese had circumnavigated the continent at the end of the fifteenth century, Europeans had established trading posts and settlements at selected locations along the coasts. At first the focus was on the coastline of West Africa, between the Senegal and Niger rivers. Here the Portuguese, Dutch, British and others traded with the local kingdoms for goods such as gold, ivory, palm oil and slaves. The prevalence of diseases such as malaria and yellow fever made the area unsuitable for white settlers, however, and so for almost four centuries the interior remained unexplored.

The east coast seemed at first more promising, but the Arabs expelled the Portuguese from the north-eastern quarter of the Indian Ocean during the seventeenth century, and their attempts to penetrate inland via the Zambezi valley were thwarted by rapids, fever and native resistance. Although there were healthy and fertile highlands ideal for European farmers within a few hundred miles of the coast in what was to become Kenya, they were not discovered until the 1880s. The only easy access was via the southern tip of the continent, where the Dutch had set up a supply base at Cape Town in 1652. Gradually it was realized that here the conditions were perfect for settlers from Europe. The climate was equable and tropical diseases were less virulent, while the local people – the Khoikhoi pastoralists and San hunter-gatherers – were too few, too technologically primitive and too politically divided to mount any effective opposition. At first the settlers were mainly 'Boers' or farmers of Dutch origin, but during the Napoleonic Wars Britain seized the Cape from the Dutch, and the British government was soon promoting it as an ideal destination for its surplus population.

So in 1800 the European presence in sub-Saharan Africa comprised a few trading posts on the west coast, and a wave of settlement spreading gradually north and east from the Cape of Good Hope, still not much more than a couple of hundred miles from the sea. Except in South Africa, where the Boers had advanced as far as the Limpopo River, the northern border of today's South Africa, a map of 1880 would have shown little change. A few African powers – notably the Zulus and the Ashanti, whose wars with the Boers and British are discussed in Chapters 2 and 3 – had clashed with the outsiders, but even these were wars about trade and spheres of influence rather than over territory per se. Over most of the continent native kings and chiefs still ruled their own people, and fought their own wars, without regard to the white man. Even then the process of exploration was a slow one. Not until David Livingstone returned from his expedition to the Zambezi in 1856 was it realized that the centre of the continent was not a vast uninhabited desert. The lakes at the sources of the River Nile, whose lower reaches had been the home of great civilizations for 5,000 years, were not fully explored until the 1870s. It was not until 1888 that Europeans set eyes on the Mountains of the Moon, rumours of which had first been reported by Ptolemy.

The situation changed dramatically in the 1880s, and especially after the Berlin Conference of 1884–85, which allocated 'spheres of influence' to the various powers and encouraged them to put into effect what was known as 'effective occupation'. From the point of view of European political history the causes of the 'scramble' are complex. The French were looking to compensate for their loss of influence in Europe after the Franco-Prussian War of 1870–71, and so revived an old scheme to colonize the River Niger and create an empire to rival British India. The British had taken over Egypt in order to secure the Suez Canal and found themselves dragged into a war in the Sudan, which focused their attention on the sources of the strategically vital Nile. King Leopold II of the Belgians, who had been looking as far afield as New Guinea for a country which he could seize and exploit for his personal gain, decided to stake a claim in the newly discovered Congo Basin. Portugal, which had clung onto its coastal settlements in Angola and Mozambique since the sixteenth century, felt compelled to expand inland to prevent other powers from occupying territory which the Portuguese believed to be theirs by ancient right, even though they had never occupied it. Germany and Italy joined the rush for African colonies to ensure that they did not miss out on their shares of the wealth which they were expected to generate. Even the hardened explorer Henry Morton Stanley was shocked by the rapacity of the affair, comparing the partition of Africa to the way in which his hungry porters used to 'rush with gleaming knives' on game which he had shot for them. But the most important reason why Europeans partitioned Africa at this point in history was that they now had the capability to do so. And among the many material advantages which they now enjoyed over their prospective victims, the most obvious was the breech-loading rifle.

Chapter One

'Sultan of Africa': The Impact of Firearms

Guns manufactured in Europe had been important trade items on the coast of West Africa since the seventeenth century, when they had been exchanged for slaves as part of the infamous 'triangular trade' with the West Indies. Native powers such as Ashanti and Dahomey adopted them with enthusiasm, and by the middle of the nineteenth century they were spreading to other areas of the continent. By then the trade was assuming huge proportions: according to the explorer Richard Burton, in the early 1860s a single company was importing 13,000 guns a year through East African ports alone. By way of trade among the Africans themselves, guns had infiltrated into the heart of the continent even before the first explorers arrived. In 1862 John Hanning Speke, the first European to explore the shores of Lake Victoria, found that the people living there were already familiar with flintlock muskets brought by Arab traders, and when Stanley sailed down the Congo in 1876, the first clue that he was approaching the Atlantic and 'civilization' came when the Bangala opened fire on him with muskets instead of the spears and arrows which he had encountered so far. All these weapons were smoothbore muzzle-loaders of the type which had equipped the armies of Europe during the Napoleonic Wars. Many of them were army surplus pieces which may well have seen service at Waterloo, though others were manufactured specifically for the African market. But by the 1870s, just at the time when Europeans were beginning to contemplate the military conquest of large areas of the continent, it was realized with some alarm that more modern weapons were also getting into the hands of Africans.

The second half of the nineteenth century saw an unprecedented revolution in small arms technology. Before 1850 European armies still relied on the single-shot, smoothbore muzzle-loading muskets which had served them for 300 years. After 1900 the latest development, the magazine-fed repeating rifle, remained in front-line service for another half-century. But between those two dates the armies of the industrially

6

developed powers adopted and discarded with bewildering speed a succession of improved weapons, each of which promised a decisive advantage over those it replaced. First came the muzzle-loading rifle of the 1850s, not much quicker to load and fire than the old smoothbores, but far more accurate at long range. Rifles such as this – the French Minié, British Enfield and American Springfield, for example – equipped most of the combatants in the Crimea and the American Civil War. Faster-firing breech-loaders had already begun to make an impact in the latter conflict, but it was not until the late 1860s that they became the standard infantry weapon of most major powers. Typical of the first generation of breech-loaders were the British Snider and the American 'trapdoor' Springfield. These were both conversions of older muzzle-loading rifles, but by the 1870s purpose-built breech-loaders were appearing, of which the best known was the Martini-Henry. As the term 'breech-loader' suggests, they were loaded not through the muzzle but by opening and closing a breech at the rear of the barrel. Not only did this do away with the laborious process of ramming powder, bullet and wadding down the muzzle, so increasing the rate of fire, but it was now possible for a soldier to reload from a prone position without exposing himself unnecessarily to enemy fire. He could also load and fire more easily while advancing.

It was the breech-loader which gave the regular soldier the first decisive advantage over a traditionally armed African opponent with spear and shield, because he could now shoot so much quicker – perhaps ten rounds a minute compared to the musket's two. But each round still had to be extracted from its container and loaded individually, and even faster rates of fire could be achieved by fitting the rifle with a magazine containing five or more rounds, each of which could be fitted into the breech by operating a bolt or lever. The American Civil War had also seen the debut of early repeaters like the Henry, and the famous seventeen-shot Winchester followed soon afterwards, but these weapons were not widely adopted by European armies, even though explorers were using them in Africa as early as the 1870s. Stanley preferred the Winchester over his heavy and slow-firing hunting rifles for 'defensive' purposes, and took one on his famous expedition in search of Livingstone in 1871. However, they were not always reliable, and the early models used low-power cartridges which gave poor long-range performance. It was also believed – with some reason – that ever faster-firing guns would lead to the demand for impossible quantities of ammunition. But in 1886 the French introduced the Lebel, the first of the bolt-action service rifles which most infantrymen carried through two world wars. The British equivalent, the Lee-Metford, was in service early in the 1890s.

At the same time two more innovations were introduced. The traditional gunpowder or 'black powder' gave way to new smokeless versions, which avoided the clouds of white smoke which used to give away a rifleman's position, and also gave the bullet greater velocity and hence better range and accuracy. Simultaneously, and partly as a result, the heavy old-fashioned lead slugs were replaced by smaller calibre bullets – typically .303in. or 7.9mm, compared with .450in. or 11mm for single-shot breech-loaders. These were lighter and a soldier could carry more of them, largely avoiding the supply problem. Magazine rifles were capable of even more rapid fire than the single-shot breech-loaders – by 1914 the British regulars were achieving the staggering rate of thirty rounds a minute – but their impact on African warfare was less decisive than might have been expected. If an opponent was obliging enough to charge a firing line in the open, as the Dervishes did at Omdurman in 1898, they would be slaughtered, but Sniders and Martini-Henrys were usually more than adequate in such circumstances. In small-scale 'bush warfare', where the main threat came from ambushes launched from cover at close range, many observers felt that the new smaller rounds lacked the power to knock a man down quickly enough to stop him getting to close quarters. And the concealment afforded by smokeless powder was less useful against an enemy who did not return fire, but attempted to charge to contact with cold steel.

Each stage in this progression saw European and American armies discard hundreds of thousands of obsolete weapons, many of which found their way to Africa. In 1871 Stanley had found the Arabs of Tabora already in possession of 'German and French double barrels, some English Enfields, and American Springfields', as well as obsolete muzzle-loading flintlocks (Stanley, 1872). Already by this date military and exploring expeditions were arming their local recruits with Sniders and similar breech-loaders; these men often kept their weapons after they were discharged, and it was not long before traders were buying them up and selling them in the interior. In 1884 the imperial pioneer Harry Johnston visited a chief on Mount Kilimanjaro who maintained a force of 400 warriors, half of whom were armed with Sniders. In other cases weapons were deliberately sold by European merchants in areas where their governments hoped to make trouble for a rival power. The Zulus obtained many of their guns from the Portuguese in Mozambique. Others acquired them by defeating invaders in battle. In the Sudan in 1875, for example, the Bari massacred an Egyptian patrol and captured thirty-three Sniders and Remingtons. The presence of even this small number of guns in the hands of a hostile tribe caused the Egyptians considerable alarm, although it turned out that the Bari could not make use of them because they had not captured any cartridges.

In 1888 the British consul general at Zanzibar reported to London on the implications of this influx of breech-loaders, which were replacing the 'cheap and worthless' old trade muskets. Unless checked, he concluded, this meant that 'the development and pacification of this great continent will have to be carried out in the face of an enormous population, the majority of whom will probably be armed with first-class breech-loading rifles' (Beachey). So in the Brussels Treaty of 1890 the European powers agreed to ban imports of all rifles and percussion smoothbores into Africa between 20 degrees north and 22 south. This agreement has been regarded by some historians as a major factor in the suppression of African resistance, but in practice it had little effect on the lucrative gun-running business. Arab caravans transported firearms smuggled in via the east coast as far north as the Sudan, and were the main means by which King Kabarega of Bunyoro kept his armies supplied in his wars against the British. Officials in German East Africa happily sold guns to the warring factions in British Uganda, as did Charles Stokes, a renegade lay employee of the Church Missionary Society. The Ethiopians re-equipped much of their army with breech-loaders captured from the Egyptians or supplied by France, Italy and Russia, while Samori Touré, who led the Mandinka of West Africa in their wars against the French in the 1880s and 1890s, is said to have sent spies to work in French arsenals in Senegal, then set up his own workshops to manufacture rifles and ammunition, with considerable success.

Altogether around a million guns – most of them breech-loaders – were sold in Africa between 1885 and 1902 alone, but on the whole the consul's fears proved unfounded. There were occasions, however, when his prediction seemed all too plausible. Many African warriors proved to be poor marksmen, but some armies did win firefights even against European-trained troops, especially when they had the benefit of cover.

The Mahdist victory over Hicks Pasha in 1883 was partly due to the accurate shooting of the 'Jihadiyya' defectors from the Egyptian army (though later on the marksmanship of the Mahdist armies seems to have deteriorated). At Adowa in 1896 the Ethiopian army overwhelmed the Italians with close-range fire from modern rifles, and in Angola in 1904 Kwamatvi riflemen firing from the cover of the bush massacred a Portuguese column which included cavalry and artillery, as well as infantry armed with bolt-action rifles.

But more often the standard of African musketry was abysmally low. Charles Gordon complained that even the trained Egyptian soldiers whom he led against the Bari in the Sudan in 1872 were 'not a match for a native with spear and bow; the soldier cannot shoot, and is at the native's mercy, if the native knew it' (Hill). The missionary J H Weeks, writing with thirty years' experience of the Congo, put it even more forcefully: 'I have seen the native make war with both kinds of weapons, and I would prefer to fight twenty natives with guns than two armed with spears.' The reasons for this failure to make the most of the new weapons were complex. Many of the cheaply manufactured 'trade guns' were of very poor quality, and customers unfamiliar with guns were often deliberately cheated. In the 1830s the South African traders supplying muskets to the Zulu king Dingaan routinely removed some vital component, such as the spring which powered the flintlock mechanism, before delivering the guns. At first the Zulus did not realize that their new weapons were useless, though a newspaper article published in 1837 warned that Dingaan had 'at last' discovered the trick.

It is likely that many similar deceptions went undetected, since one writer believed that guns were frequently purchased for display only, and that many of those to be seen in African villages had never been fired and never would be. Even those weapons which were theoretically functional were not always reliable in practice. In 1845 a writer in Birmingham had condemned the city's gunsmiths for exporting 'horribly dangerous' weapons made of poor iron, and pointed out that while a good-quality musket cost sixteen shillings to make, 'African guns' were being sold at a profit for a third of that price (White). Later in the century cheap and inferior copies of more modern weapons were also manufactured specifically for the undiscerning African market, and by the 1890s, according to Hiram Maxim, a factory in Spain was even producing counterfeit

Winchesters. Furthermore the gunpowder supplied for these guns, Weeks reported, 'is generally adulterated, and is warranted to make more noise and smoke than do damage'.

Not only were their weapons often inferior, but African warriors seldom received proper training in the use of the sights, and shared the usual tendency of inexperienced shooters to fire too high. As Colonel J W Marshall reported after a battle in Sierra Leone in 1898: 'A large number of rifles were used by the enemy, but the bullets whistled harmlessly over-head. A native can seldom use a rifle at short range, for he thinks the higher the sights are put up, the more powerfully does the rifle shoot.' However, Samuel Baker, who led native troops in the Sudan, believed that their main problem was an inability to estimate range. Aiming high was in any case a perennial failing with shooters accustomed to the curving trajectories of spears and arrows, and was no doubt still necessary with the low muzzle velocities which poor-quality gunpowder produced. But when this habit was carried over to more modern cartridge weapons with a flatter trajectory, it must have made the tendency to fire over the enemy's heads even worse.

Africans often tried to compensate for the inadequacies of their muzzle-loaders by ramming in enormous charges of powder. Not only did this risk bursting the barrels, but the recoil made it difficult and dangerous to hold the gun to the shoulder. In Gabon in 1856 the explorer Paul du Chaillu watched his companions load their muskets, and 'wondered why the poor cheap "trade" guns do not burst at every discharge. They put in first four or five "fingers" high of coarse powder, and ram down on this four or five pieces of iron-bar or rough broken iron, making the whole charge eight to ten fingers high' (du Chaillu, 1861). The Austrian explorer Ludwig von Hohnel once borrowed a porter's gun to finish off a wounded zebra, and was nearly killed by the recoil. He later swore that he would never again use a weapon which he had not loaded himself. According to Weeks the firing method used on the Congo was as follows:

he holds the butt of the gun against the palm of his half-extended right hand, and, without taking aim, he pulls the trigger with a finger of his left hand. By this mode of firing he guards his eyes from the sparks of the powder as it flashes in the pan, and his head from being blown off should the barrel burst from the excessive charge of powder.

Not surprisingly the results of shooting in this manner were unimpressive. On one occasion during F D Lugard's campaign in Bunyoro, for example, an estimated 1,000 rounds were fired at his marching column with both muskets and breech-loaders from the far side of the Semliki River, a distance of about 100 yards, but no one was hit.

Even troops in European employ were often inadequately trained, because ammunition was too expensive to be wasted on target practice. Commander Verney Cameron, who took thirty-five African 'askaris' with Sniders on his trip across the continent in 1873, once had each of them fire three rounds at a roughly man-sized packing case set up 100 yards away. 'Although there were no hits,' he remarked resignedly, 'the firing was fairly good.' Another British officer, Captain Wellby, once saw two of his men firing repeatedly (against orders) at a friendly Turkana tribesman who was walking slowly towards them, obviously not appreciating the danger. Luckily they missed him completely, leaving Wellby unsure whether to be more angry about their disobedience or their marksmanship. W D M 'Karamoja' Bell, who made his name as an elephant hunter in the Karamojong country of northern Uganda in the first few years of the twentieth century, was once forced to issue .450in. calibre cartridges for his men's .577in. rifles; the poor fit naturally meant that the trajectory of the rounds was completely unpredictable once they left the barrel, but Bell claimed that the men's aim was so wild that if anything their accuracy was improved. On the other hand Paul du Chaillu (who had made his fortune from a previous book on Africa) took with him on his 1864 expedition 35,000 rounds of ammunition, most of which was intended for target practice before setting out for the interior. This stood him in good stead when he and seven of his men were attacked by hostile tribesmen, and du Chaillu is one of the very few African campaigners who does not complain about his men's poor shooting.

Another potential problem was that the world view of many Africans encouraged them to think of shooting skill in magical terms, and countless European soldiers and explorers were asked for charms that would make the locals' musketry as effective as that of the invaders. Speke encountered a classic statement of this attitude from King Mtesa in Uganda:

The king turned to me, and said he never saw anything so wonderful as my shooting in his life; he was sure it was done by magic, as my gun never missed, and he wished I would instruct him in the art. When I denied there was any art in shooting, further than holding the gun straight, he shook his head. (Speke, 1863)

Given these disadvantages, it might seem strange that Africans did not prefer their traditional weapons to the expensive imported firearms. Certainly not all the reasons for the popularity of guns are explicable in terms of technical performance. They no doubt included questions of prestige (firearms being associated with wealth), and simple fashion. But there were also practical considerations. Most traditionally armed warriors carried shields made of animal hide, which were effective against spears and arrows but could usually be penetrated by a musket ball. Guns were also popular because of their usefulness for hunting. Even large antelopes were seldom killed outright by spear or arrow wounds, even if poisoned, and usually had to be followed on foot for miles before they succumbed. A musket ball, however, with its much greater velocity and penetrating power, would bring the game down much more quickly, saving the hunter hours of walking. In the same way, if a man was hit by a bullet he seldom got up and carried on fighting as would often be the case with a superficial arrow or spear wound.

The musket, despite its poor long-range performance compared with more modern firearms, may also have had a greater effective range than traditional missile weapons: most African bows were designed for hunting in dense cover rather than for distance shooting, and the arrows rapidly lost hitting power at more than a few dozen paces, as well as being easily deflected by intervening vegetation. Firearms could therefore be an effective counter to skirmishing tactics. Among tribes such as the Ila of present-day Zambia, who specialized in throwing their spears, a show of bravado in the face of enemy missiles was much admired. The Ila took this to an extreme by doing without shields, relying instead on flourishing an elephant's tail, or a stick ornamented with a bunch of feathers, to distract an opponent's aim. But they had no effective counter to the guns adopted by their Barotse and Matabele enemies, whose balls travelled too fast to be seen and avoided, and they suffered a series of crushing defeats.

'When guns are pointed at you,' one warrior complained helplessly to a missionary, 'what can you do?' (Smith and Dale).

The noise and smoke of gunfire could have a decisive moral effect on opponents who were not used to it, and there are numerous examples of spearmen who refused to face firearms, even though theoretically they should have defeated them easily. Richard Burton recorded that the Tuta tribe, who terrorized the region south of Lake Victoria, had 'a wholesome fear of firearms' (Burton, 1860). They would avoid contact with a caravan carrying the red flag of Zanzibar, knowing that it would be accompanied by men with guns. According to the account of the not always reliable Portuguese explorer Major Serpa Pinto, when he was attacked in his camp on the Zambezi by an overwhelming force of Barotse spearmen, one of his askaris accidentally loaded his Snider with explosive rounds filled with nitroglycerine (presumably brought along for use against elephants). After firing a few rounds the gun inevitably burst, but by then several of the enemy had been literally blown to pieces. The Barotse, faced with this gruesome spectacle, quickly retreated, even though the weapon which had done the damage was now out of action.

Spears Versus Guns

Of course it should not be forgotten that not all African warriors were afraid of guns, and their psychological effects might wear off quickly. In 1871 David Livingstone reported that a tribe on the Upper Congo which had been victimized by Arab slavers had recently 'learned that every shot does not kill, and they came up to a party with bows and arrows and compelled the slavers to throw down their guns and powder-horns' (Coupland, 1947). Ignorance might provide the motivation for men to face guns, just as much as familiarity. Bell says that the Karamojong at the time of his visit 'were then at a most dangerous stage of ignorance with regard to firearms. Their experience of them had been gathered on raids with the Swahilis, and they all firmly held the conviction that all you had to do to avoid being struck by the bullet was to duck when you saw the smoke.'

Most Africans who came into contact with firearms eventually adopted them. This included even successful warrior peoples such as the Zulus and Matabele, although they tended at first to incorporate them into their traditional close-combat tactics as a sort of superior throwing weapon, to be discharged just before closing with their stabbing spears. But there were those who never saw the need to make the transition. The best known of these conservatives were the Masai, who in one battle in 1895 speared around 900 Swahili and Kikuyu gunmen with minimal loss to themselves. Their neighbours the Hehe had begun to rely on guns in the 1870s, but by the time of their fight with the Germans at Lugalo in 1891 they seem to have fallen back on traditional methods. In this battle, a Hehe eyewitness said, they 'shot one gun (probably as a signal to attack); they all moved quickly and fought with spears' (Redmayne). Certainly the results vindicated their decision, as the German column was almost annihilated.

The ducking tactic described by Bell among the Karamojong was widely adopted as a counter to firearms by those who still relied on hand-to-hand fighting. It required agility and quick reactions as well as courage, but it was frequently successful, and it is worth examining the facts behind it. When a flintlock musket is fired there is an appreciable delay between the flash of the priming powder in the pan and the detonation of the main charge (though ignition by means of percussion caps, which had become commonplace in Africa by the late nineteenth century, does not produce the same highly visible flash, and so the situation is less clear-cut). Precise data on the muzzle velocities of African firearms is lacking, but we can assume that the low quality of the powder and the large amounts used would cancel out, so that when it left the muzzle a round from a smoothbore would be travelling at about the same rate as one from a contemporary British Army musket. This could be as high as 1,500 feet per second, but modern tests have suggested 800 feet per second as more reasonable, especially if the round does not fit tightly in the barrel. Even with a proper round ball the velocity falls to about half that after 200 yards, and the irregularly shaped pieces of scrap iron often used in Africa would lose speed more quickly because of increased air resistance. So, as a rough approximation, over the first 300 feet (i.e. 100 yards) the ball might average 600 feet per second. This would give an attacker half a second to dive for cover on seeing the smoke from an enemy's shot at that range, or a quarter of a second at 50 yards. Of course this whole calculation is very crude and the situation oversimplified, but it does indicate that the tactic is theoretically feasible.

However, it would only work in the manner suggested against a single opponent, or a unit firing a simultaneous volley on a word of command, which is unlikely to have happened with the undrilled troops who formed the bulk of African armies. A more likely scenario would be that one man would open fire and his companions would then follow suit, producing a scattered volley or ripple of fire over several seconds. Perhaps the main advantage of the tactic lay not in the physics but in the psychology: if a warrior believed that he could avoid being shot he would charge more determinedly, and the more determined he appeared the more nervous his opponent might be, making the attacker's confidence self-fulfilling.

The time taken to reload a muzzle-loading musket would vary according to the training and steadiness of the shooter, and whether prepared cartridges were supplied or – as was usually the case in Africa – loose powder had to be measured out for each shot. But there seems little reason to doubt the general assumption at the time that a man on the receiving end of a charge could expect to get off only one shot. None of these tactics would be much use against breech-loaders, which usually had higher muzzle velocities as well as being much quicker to reload – though the effect might be the same if the rifleman was too nervous or excited to lower the sights as the enemy got closer, as happened some-times even to the British regulars in the Zulu War. Almost invariably the firepower of the breech-loaders was sufficient to stop a charge by spearmen in the open, however great their advantage in numbers might be. Writing of his fight with the Banyoro at Masindi in 1872, Samuel Baker recalled 'how impossible it appeared for natives in masses to produce any effect against Snider rifles' (Baker, 1873). Most African successes against troops equipped with such weapons were the result of ambushes and surprise attacks, but there were occasional exceptions to this rule. The best known of these was at Isandlwana in 1879, where the Zulus minimized the advantages of the British Martini-Henrys by clever use of ground, even after the element of surprise had been lost. This achievement is justly regarded as the high point of nineteenth-century African warfare, and it is fitting that this survey should begin with the men who did it, and the system which produced them.

Chapter Two

'That Terrible Wandering Race':
The Zulus and Their Northern Cousins

Some time during the first millennium AD a group of cattle-rearing tribes from the north began to filter into the southern tip of Africa, a region hitherto occupied only by the San and Khoikhoi, the ancestors of the people whom nineteenth-century whites knew as 'Bushmen' and 'Hottentots'. The newcomers are generally known to historians by the collective name of Bantu, after the word for 'man' in their closely related languages. ('Bantu' remains a respectable term for this language family in anthropological circles, despite its pejorative use in apartheid-era South Africa.) By the fifteenth century these Bantu groups had coalesced into five major families. The southernmost of these was the Nguni, who inhabited the region inland from what is now the east coast of South Africa and included the ancestors of the Xhosa and the Zulus. Especially north of the Tugela River in present-day KwaZulu-Natal, the fertile and well-watered country supported a dense and growing population, which by the eighteenth century was organized into four distinct clans: the Ngwame, Mthethwa, Ndwandwe and Qwabe.

The Nguni grew maize and other crops and were accomplished iron-workers, but their main wealth was in cattle. Several elements of southern Nguni culture – especially the fundamental role of cattle, both economically and as symbols of wealth and power – are also to be found several thousand miles to the north, among apparently unrelated peoples speaking Nilo-Saharan languages. Also common to both was the 'age-set' system, in which an entire generation of young men was initiated together into adulthood with appropriate ceremonies, and then provided the manpower from which military units were raised. It may be of course that these similarities are mainly coincidence, or reflect practices which were once more widespread. After all, cattle herding was practised in most parts of the continent where the climate was suitable. We have no evidence of direct contact between the two regions in the nineteenth century. But further parallels suggest that a mystery remains to be solved: the broad-bladed stabbing spear, for instance, probably appeared in East Africa (see Chapter 7) at about the same time as it did among the Nguni (see below). This example also shows that traditional African warfare was not necessarily static, but was gradually evolving even without European intervention. Early in the nineteenth century, in this south-eastern corner of the continent, it was to undergo an almost revolutionary transformation.

The Rise of the Zulus

By the beginning of the century the Nguni country was primed for an explosion. With so many people penned into a relatively small area between the sea and the Drakensberg Mountains, competition both for grazing land and for access to European trade – principally with the Portuguese at Delagoa Bay – led inevitably to internal warfare and the rise of powerful military leaders. The spark was provided by a rootless young warrior named Shaka, who had lived for a time among the Qwabe before joining the army of the Mthethwa chief Dingiswayo. In 1816 Shaka murdered the rightful chief of a small tributary clan called the Zulus, and took over their tiny army of a few hundred men. Then in the following year Dingiswayo was killed by the Ndwandwe, and the Mthethwa federation which he had formed fell apart. The time was ripe for a ruthless adventurer to seize power, and growing numbers of chiefs gravitated to Shaka as the man most likely to provide the leadership they needed.

According to Zulu tradition, Shaka had already begun to train his warriors in deadly new tactics. One informant interviewed by James Stuart early in the twentieth century described how the Nguni had previously employed what they called 'kisi fighting', in which warriors 'threw assegais at one another as if they were boys', shouting 'kisi!' as they did so, as a warning to their opponents to take evasive action (Spring). These assegais were presumably of the type later known as *isijula*, which had small iron heads and long shafts and were designed mainly as missiles. Shaka prohibited the use of throwing spears and invented – or, more likely, popularized – a weapon of different design, the *iklwa*, a name which was supposed to be an onomatopoeic version of the sucking sound it made when withdrawn from a body. This had a shorter handle and a broader blade, and was intended not for throwing but for stabbing at close quarters. Experiments with modern reconstructions show that it might also be wielded with a chopping motion, in which role it could cut as effectively as a short sword. The traditional oval Nguni shield made of cowhide was retained, but Shaka's version was much bigger, less useful for the old-fashioned dodging and skirmishing tactics but capable of protecting a warrior's whole body as he moved in for the kill.

Shaka also introduced a special battle drill for this new weapons system: the warrior was supposed to use his shield to catch the edge of his opponent's smaller shield and hook it aside, which would have spun the victim round and left him vulnerable to being stabbed under the armpit. That this was the usual target is suggested by an account given to Stuart of the execution of a coward: 'Shaka used to order that a person should be seized, and his arm lifted up; he would then say, "Give him a taste of the assegai, the thing that he fears so much."' In fact it seems unlikely that a more lightly equipped and more mobile enemy would have allowed this to happen very often, but – like the drills taught for twentieth-century bayonet fighting – it was probably never expected to be a realistic simulation of every actual encounter. Shaka himself is said to have killed an enemy in single combat using this sweeping and stabbing manoeuvre, but it would have been less appropriate in a mass mêlée in which men did not necessarily line up for one-to-one combats with individual opponents. What probably mattered was that the Zulu was encouraged to charge by the belief that he was superior in close combat, and that an opponent who was not physically or psychologically equipped for it would either retreat or be overpowered, whatever the precise techniques employed.

It is often stated that the fighting methods which came to be associated with the Zulus were invented by Shaka, and that the decisive advantage which they gave over the more traditional skirmishing tactics led to their adoption over a wide area of South and East Africa. The truth, as always, appears to be less straightforward. The adoption of the stabbing spear does seem to date from Shaka's time, but it was not the only factor in the military superiority of his people. Equally important were the discipline and organization which were already features of Nguni warfare. Certainly the characteristic organization of the army into regiments based on traditional age-sets, or *amabutho*, was not a Shakan innovation, since early in his career Shaka himself served in a similar *ibutho* in the army of Dingiswayo. In pre-nineteenth-century Nguni communities the term *ibutho* seems to have had no specifically military connotation, but simply meant a 'gathering'. It was first applied to the festivals at which groups of freshly initiated boys would congregate. It is often suggested that Dingiswayo was the first to use these gatherings as the basis for organized regiments, but as we have no contemporary descriptions of warfare in the region before his time, the practice may well be even earlier.

So by about 1818 Shaka controlled an army which was well disciplined, equipped with new weaponry and trained to fight in a manner calculated to brush aside the traditional Nguni skirmishers. But more than any other factor it was his own personality which was decisive in elevating the Zulus – who by now incorporated many Mthethwa, Qwabe and others – to dominance over the whole of the northern Nguni. Contemporary European writers generally portray Shaka as a monster: in the words of Nathaniel Isaacs, 'an insatiable and exterminating savage, in peace an unrelenting and a ferocious despot' (Isaacs, 1836). Zulu oral tradition tends to confirm this view, emphasizing his arbitrary executions and his massacres of women and children, who had traditionally been spared in Nguni warfare. But at least at first these methods may have been a deliberate policy to spread terror among his enemies, and Shaka was also noted for his willingness to absorb defeated tribes rather than exterminating them – a policy which was obviously necessary if the tiny Zulu clan was to grow in strength. He was eventually assassinated by his own people, who had become tired of his cruelty, but not before they had benefited from his ferocious energy to become the greatest native military power in sub-Saharan Africa.

In 1818 and again in the following year the Ndwandwe invaded the Zulu country in an attempt to crush Shaka, but were defeated in a series of bloody battles. The Zulus counter-attacked and most of the Ndwandwe fled to the north, leaving their land and cattle in the hands of the victors. For the next decade, conquering Zulu armies campaigned in all directions, creating for themselves a centralized and relatively stable state, but spreading chaos beyond their borders as the defeated tribes fled in terror of Shaka's wrath. At the same time the Afrikaners – farmers of Dutch origin – were spreading north from the Cape of Good Hope, putting still further pressure on the native peoples and restricting their escape routes. This period was known in the Zulu language as the *mfecane* – meaning 'scattering' or 'crushing' – and it changed the map of southern Africa beyond recognition. Some modern scholars have tried to play down the extent of the disaster, but the movements of peoples whose descendants can still be traced tell their own story.

Some Nguni took refuge among the related Xhosa in the south, where they became the Mfengu or 'Fingoes', who eventually sided with the British against their hosts. Others escaped into the Drakensberg Mountains, where they joined with the local Sotho to form what became the Basuto nation under an outstanding leader of their own, Moshoeshoe. Many of the Ngwame clan went north, where they formed the nucleus of the emerging Swazi kingdom. Others fled over the mountains to the High Veldt of what later became the Transvaal (now the Gauteng, Mpumalanga and Limpopo provinces of South Africa). There they dispersed local Sotho-speaking tribes such as the Taung and Fokeng, who in turn spread the disorder still further afield. One group, who became known as the Kololo, migrated north-west to the Upper Zambezi valley, where in 1823 they conquered the local Barotse. Their king, Sebitwane, befriended the explorer David Livingstone in the 1850s and became famous in Europe as a result, but the fever-ridden climate gradually weakened the conquerors, and in 1864 the Kololo were overthrown by a Barotse revolt. Finally, in the wake of the Ngwame came two separate Ndwandwe hordes, the Ngoni and the Matabele. These two peoples travelled further and gained a more fearsome reputation than any of the other Nguni, and are treated in more detail below.

After Shaka's death in 1828, his successor, Dingaan, faced new challenges. Shaka had always been careful not to clash with the whites, but under Dingaan relations with the Portuguese at Delagoa Bay deteriorated, and in 1833 a Zulu army sacked the town, and captured and executed the governor. The British settlement at Port Natal (later Durban) was once temporarily evacuated for fear of Zulu attacks, and later, during the fighting of 1838, it was actually plundered by the Zulus, but the traders soon resumed their policy of mollifying Dingaan by supplying him with guns. These early encounters with Europeans gave Dingaan a poor impression of their fighting qualities, which was to lead him to the verge of disaster. The Afrikaners (or 'Boers') of the Cape resented the rule of the British, who had taken over from the Dutch in 1806, and especially the abolition of their right to keep slaves. Large groups therefore moved away into the interior with their herds and wagons in what was to become known as the 'Great Trek'. By 1837 some 5,000 Boers were established beyond British control north of the Orange River, from where they diverged in different directions. One group, led by Piet Retief, crossed the Drakensberg Mountains from the west and arrived in Natal, a fertile region south of the Tugela River which was claimed by both the British and the Zulus. In an attempt to establish peaceful relations he visited Dingaan, who promised him land in exchange for recovering some stolen Zulu cattle. But when he returned to claim his reward, Dingaan murdered Retief and the sixty or so Boers who had accompanied him. Subsequent events showed that the Zulu king was right to fear the consequences of allowing the Boers to encroach on his territory, but the massacre tarnished his reputation with the whites, and was to lead to a long legacy of hatred between his people and the Afrikaners.

Dingaan then sent his 'impis', as the Zulu armies were known, into Natal to wipe out the rest of the trekkers. They were not expecting an attack, and were camped in scattered camps or 'laagers', protected against marauders and wild animals only by their circled wagons. The campaign taught both sides valuable lessons. Many of the Boer camps were taken completely by surprise; hundreds of men, women and children were speared; and tens of thousands of cattle and sheep were captured. But where they had received even a brief warning, from fugitives or the distant sound of gunfire, the trekkers managed to load their guns and take up firing positions in or underneath the wagons. The Zulus suffered heavy losses charging these obstacles under fire, and were unable to break into the laagers. The defenders then mounted their horses and followed the Zulus up as they retired, inflicting further casualties and recovering at least some of their livestock.

The four-wheeled 'Cape wagons' used by the trekkers proved to be one of the decisive weapons of the Zulu wars. They were tall, heavy vehicles drawn by teams of oxen. Each wagon was about 15 feet long and 5 feet high to the top of the rear wheels, the front wheels being slightly smaller. The body was made of heavy wooden planks held together with iron fittings, and the upper part was canvas over a bamboo frame. Though designed principally for transportation over the rough roads of the Cape, its heavy construction also made it an effective mobile fortification. The role of the wagons in battle was not just to provide cover for the defenders firing from inside or underneath them, but to break up the impetus of an attack. For this purpose they were often protected from missiles with panels of rawhide, and thorn bushes were cut and stuffed into the gaps between the wheels to prevent attackers crawling underneath them. The normal practice was to arrange most of the wagons to form an outer perimeter, which in open country would usually be circular, but might vary in shape to conform to the terrain. At the Battle of Blood River, for example, the laager was 'D' shaped, with the straight side resting on a *donga* or gully. If enough wagons were available, another four would be drawn up in a square in the middle of the laager and roofed over with planks to protect the non-combatants.

At this date the Europeans were still using muzzle-loading firearms, many of them crude but powerful 'roers' or elephant guns of up to 1 inch calibre. These could be loaded either with massive 4 oz balls or with bags of buckshot which turned them into giant shotguns. Either way they were lethal weapons at close range. But they were slow to reload, and in the open their users could never have got off more than one shot before the fast-moving Zulus overwhelmed them. The wagon obstacles not only gave the defenders precious extra seconds to reload while the enemy tried to clamber over them: they were also a psychological weapon, providing those behind them with a sense of security, and the extra determination which men always seem to gain from holding a marked territory, however small. On the other hand the first attackers to reach the wagons were exposed to point-blank fire with no immediate means of retaliating. It was impossible to see whether the Boers, hidden inside the laager and wreathed in powder smoke, were still reloading or already taking aim, and only the bravest warrior would dare to take the risk.

The impregnability of the Boer wagon laagers was a vital factor in the war which followed Retief's death. It culminated at Blood River on 16 December 1838 – a significant date in the Afrikaner calendar ever since. A position held by nearly 500 Boers and over 100 black fighters from Natal (whose role has inevitably been omitted from the subsequent mythology), supported by three small cannon, was attacked by an impi of approximately 10,000 men. The Zulus surrounded the wagons and launched repeated charges throughout the morning, but failed to break in. At last they fell back, and were scattered by a mounted pursuit. Their losses may have amounted to 3,000 dead. No Afrikaners were killed. The British brokered a brief peace after this battle, but war broke out again in 1839, when a rival claimant to the Zulu throne, Mpande, enlisted a Boer 'commando' or war party in his support. The combined Zulu and Afrikaner army routed Dingaan, who fled into the mountains. Like Shaka, he was eventually killed by his own disillusioned subjects. Dingaan had once been about to execute Mpande, but was persuaded to let him live on the grounds that he was feeble-minded and so presented no threat. In fact he was a competent ruler who reigned for the next thirty-three years, effectively conciliating both his white neighbours and the dissident elements within the kingdom. Zulu armies continued to raid the Swazis and other tribes to the north, and in the 1850s a bitter civil war was fought between the followers of Mpande's favoured heir, Mbuyazi, and another of his sons, Cetshwayo. But Mpande's impis never clashed with the whites, and so in 1872 Cetshwayo inherited Shaka's kingdom substantially intact.

The Matabele

Like other tribes conquered by Shaka, many of the Ndwandwe had been incorporated into the Zulu army under their own commanders. In 1822 one such chief, Mzilikazi of the Kumalo clan, who was then in his mid-twenties, was sent to lead a raid against the Swazis. Mzilikazi was later to emerge as one of pre-colonial Africa's greatest leaders, admired even by many whites, and revered by his own people as 'Umdabuli we Sizwe', the 'maker of the nation'. But his first appearance in recorded history was less impressive. He captured a large herd of Swazi cattle, some of which he kept for himself, instead of sending them to Shaka as ordered. Aware that the penalty for this theft was death, he went to ground with his regiment and some of their families in the hills of his native Kumalo country. Eventually the Zulus found him, took him by surprise and scattered his impi, but Mzilikazi and a few hundred followers escaped across the Drakensberg Mountains and onto the High Veldt. Here they encountered scattered groups of Sotho, Tswana and other peoples, many of whom had already been impoverished by Nguni or Afrikaner encroachment, and whose traditional fighting methods were no match for the Zulu-style tactics introduced by the newcomers.

Gradually Mzilikazi's people rebuilt their strength by stealing cattle, and by incorporating survivors from weaker groups which they overcame by force or treachery. In 1826 they were joined by a larger group of Ndwandwe refugees, but by this time they also included a large proportion of Sotho, who had a considerable influence on their language and culture. The name Matabele (or Ndebele) is said to mean 'they disappear from sight', referring to the way in which their huge shields completely covered the warriors when they deployed for battle. Exactly when the name came into use is unclear, but certainly by the end of the 1820s they had become a cohesive and self-confident people under the leadership of Mzilikazi. The High Veldt, however, was dry and infertile, and they were forced to move continually from one base to another in order to find fresh grazing for their growing herds. In the process they defeated and absorbed many more of the local tribes, and began to create a class system which persisted long after the disappearance of the Matabele nation. The 'amaZansi' or 'those from the south', in other words the original Ndwandwe families, constituted the aristocracy. Below them came the 'abeNhla' or 'those from the road', who were absorbed during their time on the High Veldt. Later, when they moved north of the Limpopo River, the local Shona tribes were incorporated as a servile underclass under the name of 'Holi'.

At first Mzilikazi, as head of this hierarchy, enjoyed a reputation among many whites as a tyrant on the Shaka model. It was alleged that he ruled by terror, inflicting arbitrary executions by barbarous methods such as impalement, amputation and feeding offenders to crocodiles. It was inevitable that a ruler endowed in the Shakan tradition with the power of life and death, and forced to hold together a disparate people by rigid discipline and force of personality, should have used such methods when necessary. That frequent executions did take place is confirmed by eyewitnesses. But Matabele oral tradition does not describe Mzilikazi in the same terms as the Zulus did Shaka. William Cornwallis Harris, an Indian Army officer who visited him while he was still on the High Veldt, was warned against him by American missionaries based at Mosega, but felt that they exaggerated his crimes out of annoyance at his refusal to allow his followers to work for the mission. The Scottish missionary Robert Moffat, who also first met him during this period, was personally on good terms with Mzilikazi but was under no illusions about the nature of Matabele power. Their concept of responsible kingship did not preclude ruthless aggression against neighbouring peoples. Moffat's native informants described 'the desolation of many of the towns around us – the sweeping away the cattle and valuables – the butchering of the inhabitants' (Moffat). One of them spoke eloquently of 'the great chief of multitudes . . . the chief of the blue-coloured cattle', who was so confident of his strength that he refused to flee when the invaders approached. 'Stooping to the ground on which we stood, he took up a little dust in his hand; blowing it off, and holding out his naked palm, he added, "That is all that remains of the great chief of the blue-coloured cattle!"' Moffat ascribed the superiority of the Matabele not to armament or tactics, but to the fact that their experiences under 'the barbarous reign of the monster Shaka' had toughened them, in contrast to their victims, who 'had, from peace and plenty, become effeminate'. Something of the legend of Matabele ferocity remains to this day. Over a wide area of southern Africa the large, aggressive army ants, famous for their vicious wars against the local termites, are still known as 'Matabele ants'.

Nevertheless, Mzilikazi's people were not always the aggressors. Griquas and Koranas from the south – people of mixed white and Khoikhoi origin who already possessed horses and guns – joined with members of the local Taung tribe to steal Matabele cattle, only desisting when in 1828 an impi trapped the Taung against the Modder River and massacred them. Then in 1832 the Zulus caught up with Mzilikazi while many of his men were away on campaign, and inflicted severe damage before withdrawing after a drawn battle. The Zulus were the one enemy whom the king feared, and he decided to take his people out of their reach once and for all. They moved a hundred miles to the west into the Marico valley, where they established a new stronghold protected by a ring of fortified villages, which were in turn surrounded by a belt of depopulated countryside across which an invader could not advance without being observed. Then in 1836 the Boers began to arrive, the vanguard of the trekkers whose clashes with the Zulus have already been described.

Like Dingaan, Mzilikazi decided to strike first before the newcomers grew too strong to be removed, but also like Dingaan he failed to finish the job. The first onslaught caught the Boers by surprise and eliminated many of their small encampments, but most of the men escaped. The Matabele raised an impi of around 3,000 men and advanced on the now concentrated Boers, who had set up a strong wagon laager beneath a ridge which came to be known as Vegkop, or 'Battle Hill'. Among the children who reloaded muskets for the Boer defenders on that day was Paul Kruger, subsequently President of the Transvaal Republic and opponent of the British in two Boer Wars. Like many others, he never forgot what the Afrikaners saw as Matabele treachery. The warriors seem to have launched a single charge, which reached the wagons but was unable to penetrate the laager. They then tried to throw spears over the top of the wagons to hit the defenders behind, but when this too failed they retreated, leaving at least 150 dead behind them. They did get away with thousands of cattle and sheep, including the oxen used to draw the wagons, and the loss of their transport forced the Boers to withdraw temporarily. But early the next year their mounted commandos were back, launching hit-and-run raids on the Matabele kraals.

Then, with the Matabele already distracted by the war against the trekkers, the Zulus and Griquas both returned to the fray. After another fierce but indecisive battle in the Pilanesberg Mountains, the Zulus returned home with enough stolen cattle to enable Dingaan to claim a victory. Mzilikazi realized that he could not hope to stand his ground against such a concentration of enemies, and decided to lead his people north once again, this time across the Limpopo River into the country which was to become known as Matabeleland, in modern Zimbabwe. It has often been claimed that he did so on the advice of Robert Moffat, and even that Moffat personally guided the fugitives to safety. But there is no evidence that Moffat had ever been to the new country, though Matabele raiding parties probably had. The king eventually settled around the site of modern Bulawayo, a region formerly inhabited by a branch of the Shona people. A related band of Ndwandwe, the Ngoni, had passed through the area only a few years before, and disrupted the once powerful Rozwi confederation which controlled it. So the Matabele met with relatively little opposition at first, though it was not until 1866 that the last of the Rozwi chiefs was defeated. By this time Mzilikazi was in poor health, and in 1868 he died – the last of Shaka's contemporaries, and in many respects his equal as a nation builder.

The Ngoni

While the Matabele were escaping west across the High Veldt, other Ndwandwe bands were fleeing northwards into what is now Mozambique. Already they seem to have been a diverse group, including many Sotho as well as Nguni elements, and they soon split into different factions. One group subjugated the local Tsonga and other tribes and founded the Gaza Nguni kingdom, which dominated the south of Mozambique until it was conquered by the Portuguese in 1895. Another chief, Zwangendaba, who was a member of the Kumalo clan and thus a relative of Mzilikazi, invaded the territory of the Rozwi beyond the Limpopo. The Rozwi king, Mambo, was killed and his strongholds quickly taken, but Zwangendaba did not stay to exploit his victory. One tradition related to the German explorer Carl Wiese maintained that Zwangendaba sent a scouting party far to the east, where it reached the outskirts of the Portuguese settlement of Tete on the lower reaches of the Zambezi River. The people of Tete were celebrating a festival with salutes fired from their handful of artillery pieces, and the noise so intimidated the scouts that they returned to Zwangendaba with wildly exaggerated accounts of Portuguese strength. So instead of moving in their direction he continued northwards, and in November 1835 he crossed the mighty Zambezi. The crossing coincided with a solar eclipse, an omen which was long remembered in the traditions of his people. According to later tradition a medicine man named Mbelewele (who was still alive when Wiese met him in 1889) made the waters part by magic so that the people could cross. Only three years later, the Matabele followed in Zwangendaba's footsteps and occupied the Rozwi country.

By now the Ngoni, as they were beginning to be known, had absorbed large numbers of tribespeople from along their route, including prisoners of war, and others who had joined them voluntarily. North of the Zambezi they split into two groups which moved along opposite shores of Lake Nyasa. Zwangendaba himself led the western party, which eventually established a kingdom on a fertile plateau in Ufipa, near the southern tip of Lake Tanganyika. The unwarlike local tribes were quickly reduced to vassalage, and Zwangendaba lived there peacefully until his death in 1848. Their Zulu-inspired battle tactics, and even more importantly the psychological effect of their Zulu-style dress and equipment, gave the Ngoni a crucial advantage over the local tribes, most of whom fled into mountain refuges, were defeated and incorporated into the impis of the invaders, or eventually copied Zulu methods themselves. Livingstone described the terror which, decades later, still gripped the local inhabitants at the mere sight of the Zulu shields.

But after Zwangendaba's death his kingdom fragmented and the Ngoni armies resumed their wanderings. Some remained in Ufipa and turned to pillaging their neighbours. They became notorious as bandits under various names, including Mafiti, Maviti or Mazitu. Others returned to the western shore of Lake Nyasa, where they founded two large and two smaller kingdoms in which were preserved many of the institutions which they had brought with them from the south. The Gwangwara, led by a chief called Zulugama, moved east towards the Indian Ocean. Near Kilwa they encountered their relatives who had migrated up the eastern side of Lake Nyasa, a group now known as the Maseko, and attacked them, driving them back southwards. The Gwangwara traded on their military reputation by terrorizing the inhabitants of the Rovuma valley. They twice attacked the Arab town of Kilwa on the coast, and according to Livingstone only the presence of the tsetse fly, which killed their cattle, prevented them from settling there permanently.

Yet another Ngoni band took the name of Tuta (or Watuta) after their chief Ntuta, and migrated still further north into what was to become Tanganyika (now Tanzania). According to Burton they had been invited by a local chief to help him against his enemies, but were defeated. They retaliated by plundering the whole region and soon amassed large herds of cattle, but the shortage of pasture in the arid Tanganyikan bush obliged them to continue their semi-nomadic lifestyle. Some time in the early 1850s they arrived on the southern shore of Lake Victoria, the last and remotest ripple from the storm unleashed by Shaka nearly forty years earlier in Zululand. Several of the early explorers of East Africa admitted to going in fear of the Tuta – 'that terrible wandering race of savages', as John Speke (1863) called them – although they never clashed seriously with a European expedition. Speke's companion James Grant claimed that their armies often numbered several thousand, and were almost constantly in the field against one or other of their neighbours. They might besiege a village for months if they were unable to break in at once. The local tribes even had a special drum signal to warn of the approach of the Tuta, just as they had for man-eating lions. In 1876 H M Stanley found the country east of Lake Tanganyika entirely laid waste by Tuta raiding parties. He says (Stanley, 1879) that they were hated by all their neighbours, and that the Arabs regarded killing them as 'far more necessary than killing a snake' (though in practice the Arabs occasionally hired them as mercenaries).

Some of Zwangendaba's veterans were still to be found among many of these Ngoni bands well into the 1870s. In 1877 James Stevenson met old men among the Mazitu who 'began to talk about old Zulu-land in a very familiar way' (*Proceedings of the Royal Geographical Society*, vol. 22, 1877–78). Other groups, however, retained only a vague tradition of their origins in the south. As well as these 'genuine' Ngoni and their descendants, the bands roaming East Africa now included many local tribesmen who had been captured and assimilated, and others who had voluntarily adopted Ngoni dress and fighting methods. In the early 1880s the missionary W P Johnson came across settlements inhabited by Yao, Gindo and other local people, whom the Gwangwara had subdued and forcibly relocated to garrison distant parts of their territory, like 'miniature Babylonian conquerors'. To confuse things further, there were also gangs of entirely bogus 'Ngoni' bandits, who deliberately copied the costume of the southerners in order to trade on their fearsome reputation. A report to the Royal Geographical Society in 1881, for example, drew a distinction between the Maviti of Lake Nyasa, who were 'true' Ngoni, and the Maviti of the lower Rovuma valley, who, said the author dismissively, were 'really refugee Gindos who live by plunder', and as such were much less formidable. Some long-established peoples and states of local origin – notably the Fipa, Lungu, Bena and Mahenge, all from what is now southern Tanzania or northern Malawi – were also virtually indistinguishable from the Ngoni in their appearance by the time Europeans first encountered them in the 1870s. In many cases, however, the resemblance was confined to their outward appearance. Joseph Thomson, who visited the Mahenge in 1879, remarked that although they looked like Zulus, they had 'no more affinity to that tribe than a donkey in a lion's skin has to a lion', and were in fact 'a set of most arrant cowards'. Nevertheless, although there were no more than about 4,000 Mahenge altogether, they had depopulated an area twice the size of their own country, and their surviving neighbours lived in abject terror of them.

The Zulu and Matabele 'Art of War'

Among the Zulus and Matabele, as well as those Ngoni who retained the original Zulu system of organization, the basic military unit was the 'regiment' or *ibutho* (plural *amabutho*). These *amabutho* were commanded by senior military officials known as *izinduna* (the Zulu plural of the singular *induna*, often Anglicized as '*indunas*'). In theory at least, a Zulu king would raise a new regiment every few years by calling up all the boys in the kingdom who had reached military age since the last unit was formed. In practice local chiefs were sometimes granted exemptions, or took advantage of succession disputes or other causes of royal weakness to keep back some of the recruits for local defence. For these reasons regiments were not of a standard size even when they were first mustered, and some – especially those raised by a weak king or while the throne was disputed – were much smaller than the norm.

This system also meant that a regiment could not be brought up to strength by replacements, as all the young men not already serving would be held back to await the formation of the next *ibutho*. So as time passed a Zulu unit would inevitably dwindle away as a result of battle and other losses, until only a hard core of experienced veterans remained. Eventually an entire regiment would receive royal permission to marry, after which the men would disperse to form a sort of reserve, still liable to be called up in time of war but free from routine military obligations. One important difference in the Matabele system was that some regiments did eventually receive reinforcements in the form of the sons of the original recruits, who were drafted to serve alongside their fathers. So according to the authoritative modern study by Summers and Pagden, although most of the fifty-six regiments founded by Mzilikazi disappeared around thirty or forty years later – as would be expected if the original personnel had either been killed or grown too old to fight – those which remained then gained a new lease of life, and were still in action with new personnel in the 1890s.

Each regiment was divided into two wings, and further subdivided into *amaviyo* (singular *iviyo*) or companies, each under its own commander. Inevitably the companies would vary in size, but Ian Knight suggests a typical strength of between fifty and seventy men. Below this level there appears to have been no formal command structure, and a Matabele veteran interviewed in the 1940s denied that there had ever been an equivalent of the European non-commissioned officer, although men of known ability might be selected from the ranks to lead small detached task forces. The regiments did, however, cultivate their own *esprit de corps*, and encourage a sense of superiority over their neighbours which would have been familiar to the British soldier of the time. At the ceremonies held before an impi was sent on campaign, warriors from rival regiments would taunt each other in front of the king with boasts about their past deeds and those which they were about to perform. On some occasions this certainly influenced their conduct in combat. At the crisis of the Battle of Isandlwana in 1879 the uMcijo regiment had gone to ground under British fire, when an *induna* who belonged to the regiment ran up and reminded the warriors that this was not what they had promised the king they would do when they met the enemy. The officer was killed immediately afterwards, but uMcijo nevertheless rose and charged, followed by their comrades.

At least in theory, Zulu regiments were distinguished from each other by different coloured shields. This is a complicated subject, but as a general rule the more white there was on the shield, the more senior the regiment. The cowhide surfaces of the shields were left in the colour of the beasts from which they had been taken, so it is obvious that very large herds of similarly coloured cattle were necessary in order to maintain consistency in a batch of up to a thousand shields. Nguni cattle varied enormously in appearance, and over a hundred different names are known to have been used for specific colours or patterns. This no doubt explains the inconsistencies in regimental shields which are often apparent from photographs, especially later in the century when the proportion of cattle to people in Zululand had begun to decline. Among the Matabele, where cattle were even less numerous, the system may have been abandoned altogether before the end of Mzilikazi's reign.

The term 'impi', which is often used to denote a Zulu army, seems never to have had a precise organizational meaning, but could be used for a detached force of any size, from a small patrol to an army of several regiments. Summers and Pagden suggest that the nearest English equivalent would be 'task force'. Whatever its size, an impi would deploy in a standard crescent-shaped formation, usually described by analogy with the chest and horns of a buffalo. The centre or 'chest' was made up of older and more experienced men, with the younger warriors deployed on either side in extended wings or 'horns'. Behind the chest, if numbers permitted, would be a reserve formed of the steadiest veterans, known as the 'loins'. The task of the chest was to advance and pin the enemy, while the horns raced out to the flanks and swung inwards to encircle him. This was the nearest thing to a formal tactical doctrine in the Zulu army, though two recent writers, Sutherland and Canwell, have argued that it was not always well co-ordinated, and that the horns frequently wrecked the plan by charging too soon. In fact similar crescent formations and encircling tactics were not uncommon in Africa, being employed by the Azande and Ashanti among others, so the 'chest and horns' cannot in any case be regarded as a specifically Zulu innovation. It may have arisen as a natural consequence of veteran warriors seeking the most prominent central position in the battle line, relegating the younger men to the wings. Being fitter and more enthusiastic, the youngsters would naturally rush ahead and get behind the enemy's flanks while his attention was focused on the apparently greater threat from their seniors.

The aim of Zulu tactics was always to bring the individual warrior into hand-to-hand combat with his adversary. It is difficult to get a clear picture of what actually happened when these tactics were used against other traditionally equipped armies, but one of the few accounts which is detailed enough to be useful comes from Henry Fynn, who witnessed a battle between the Zulus and the Ndwandwe in 1826. As fellow Nguni, the Ndwandwe were armed with the same large shields and stabbing spears as the Zulus. The latter, Fynn tells us, advanced cautiously to within 20 yards of the enemy, when a musket was fired as a signal to charge, and 'both parties, with a tumultuous yell, clashed together, and continued stabbing each other for about three minutes'. Then they drew apart and paused to assess their losses. These seemed to be about equal, so neither side was prepared to give ground and the armies rushed together again. This time they fought for slightly longer than in the first clash, and when they again paused for breath it was obvious that the Ndwandwe had lost more men. This realization encouraged the Zulus and correspondingly demoralized their opponents, so that when battle was again resumed the Ndwandwe began to give ground, while Shaka's warriors fought more ferociously as they sensed victory within their grasp. Finally the Ndwandwe broke and fled, only to be massacred by the pursuing Zulus.

This account gives us an insight into several questions posed by Shaka's hand-to-hand combat tactics. First of all it is obvious that battles described as lasting for several hours did not involve men fighting continuously for that length of time. Fynn's three minutes is comparable to the length of a round in a boxing or wrestling match, and corresponds roughly to the time for which even a fit man can fight at close quarters before becoming tired and out of breath. Frequent pauses to rest and regroup were therefore essential, and these gave an opportunity to assess the relative strengths of the two sides and their chances of success. It is also significant that this appears to have been done by a rough assessment of the number of casualties. In classical Greek warfare – which similarly involved men fighting at close range with stabbing spears – it was generally believed that serious losses were not incurred until the men on one side dropped their shields and fled, and were cut down as they turned their backs to the enemy. However, the Greeks were better protected than the Zulus, with body armour and metal shields, and fought in very close formation with men partly sheltered by each other's shields. Not only was the Zulus' equipment much lighter, but they seem always to have fought in more open order, seeking out single combat rather than taking cover behind a wall of shields. We might therefore expect that a Zulu battle would be bloodier than its ancient equivalent, with more men falling in the actual fighting rather than during the pursuit, and this is what Fynn's account implies. We are not told here what methods were used to motivate men to face death on such particularly intimate terms, but later Zulu and Matabele armies employed rigorous training methods, which will be discussed below. A prominent part was also played by ritual purification ceremonies and even the administration of traditional drugs.

After Shaka's death Dingaan reintroduced the throwing spears which his predecessor had abandoned, though in essence tactics remained the same. Warriors now threw a volley of javelins to distract the enemy and damage his shields as they closed with the *iklwa*, in the same way as the Roman legions had combined the throwing spear, or *pilum*, and the short sword. This would seem to be an improvement on the unsupported charge to close quarters, so it is surprising to read the opinion of one of James Stuart's informants that Shaka's method was superior. But from a psychological point of view it is understandable. A man equipped only for hand-to-hand combat has no choice but to advance, because until he does so he is vulnerable to enemy missiles but has no way of replying. If he carries throwing weapons he may charge with less determination because he knows that he has an alternative, and even if he is keen to use his stabbing spear he will first have to slow his rush within about forty paces of the enemy in order to throw accurately. This gives him a chance to observe what is happening around him, and perhaps to be discouraged by the sight of friendly casualties. It may then be difficult for his officers to make him advance again.

In August 1838, for example, one of Dingaan's impis surprised a party of seventy-five Boer trekkers on Bushman's River. The Boers managed to form their wagons into a laager with one side protected by the river, but they still had too few men to hold the rest of the perimeter, and expected to be quickly overwhelmed. However, the Zulus did not launch the expected charge, but instead skirmished with muskets and throwing assegais, some of the latter being wrapped in burning straw in an unsuccessful attempt to set fire to the wagons. The defenders therefore had time to move a reserve from one threatened point to another, compensating for their lack of numbers. After an indecisive firefight the Zulus eventually withdrew. If they had still been equipped as in Shaka's day they would have had no alternative but to rush the wagons, and although Zulu losses would no doubt have been heavy, the Boers would certainly have been wiped out. The throwing spears were by no means useless, however, and we have several accounts of their deadly effects. Livingstone, who says that he had seen the Kololo throw them between 40 and 50 yards, examined one unfortunate casualty who had been struck on the shin by a spear which split the bone, and had stuck there so firmly that it had to be chopped out with an axe.

Summers and Pagden, in their work on the Matabele, remark that sketches of warriors made in the 1830s by Charles Bell and Cornwallis Harris show them with only a single stabbing spear, but that later artists such as Thomas Baines and A A Anderson, working in the 1870s, generally depict men carrying three weapons each. The authors conclude that when the Matabele began their migration to the north in the 1820s they were equipped like Shaka's impis with the *iklwa* alone, and that the *isijula* was probably reinstated after Mzilikazi's death in 1868 by his successor, Lobengula. However, Afrikaner accounts of the Battle of Vegkop in 1836 describe spears being thrown into the laager, so missile weapons may actually have reappeared at about the same time as Dingaan reintroduced them in the Zulu army. Summers and Pagden also observe that surviving examples of the *isika*, as the Matabele stabbing spear was known, tend to have smaller blades than the Zulu versions, and they suggest that these were the original Zulu weapons still in use up to seventy years later, having reverted to the king on the original owner's death and been re-issued to a young recruit. Their reduced size would be explained by their having been repeatedly resharpened.

Alongside them, late nineteenth-century Matabele warriors carried an odd assortment of spears of various origins, including hunting and fishing weapons taken from enemy tribes. Throwing spears were also prominent among the Ngoni in East Africa, although the stabbing version certainly remained in use. Perhaps there was always a tendency for men to supplement their issue *iklwa* or *isika* with extra throwing weapons, and it was only exceptionally strong leaders such as Shaka and Mzilikazi who could enforce standardization. European writers tend to obscure the issue by their inconsistent use of the term 'assegai', which originally had no connection with southern Africa but was a Berber word denoting a throwing spear or javelin. So, for example, Joseph Thomson tells us that the armament of the Mahenge of Tanganyika consisted of 'a spear [and] two assegais', the 'spear' being presumably a version of the *iklwa*, and the 'assegais' throwing weapons.

By Shaka's time guns had already been introduced into the region by European traders and hunters, and the Zulu and Matabele kings were always keen to acquire them. One reason for the success of both peoples, however, was their refusal to allow the influx of new weapons to change their basic tactics. Instead firearms seem to have been treated in most cases as a more technically advanced variety of *isijula*, with warriors discharging a volley before closing with the *iklwa* in the normal way. The big-game hunter F C Selous visited Lobengula not long after the battle which brought him to power in 1870, and was told by a hunter named Philips, who had treated the wounded after the battle, that although both sides possessed large numbers of muskets nearly all the wounds were caused by spears.

The training of the warriors could be extremely tough. In the 1870s Emil Holub collected accounts of the training regime of the Matabele armies, and claimed that although high-class 'Zansi' boys were raised in rather leisurely fashion in their fathers' kraals, perhaps relying on their natural sense of social superiority to motivate them in battle, the regime imposed on prisoners of war and other non-Matabele recruits was far more rigorous (Summers and Pagden). On one occasion only 117 out of

160 recruits survived the training period. This is not surprising if some of the more lurid stories are true. Holub says that, apart from fatigues, route marches and mock fights with clubs, one task involved killing a wild hyena with a stick. A former Shona captive quoted by Summers and Pagden adds that groups of young warriors would be sent to kill buffalos with clubs, and even to tackle lions bare-handed. In this context the story told by the elephant hunter William Finaughty, of Mzilikazi ordering one of his regiments to haul a man-eating crocodile out of a river and bring it to him alive, can be seen not as the whim of a capricious tyrant, but as part of a consistent if brutal policy of accustoming young warriors to hardship and bloodshed.

Of course there was a lot more to the Zulu system of warfare than a willingness to charge and stab the enemy, and on several occasions professional European officers were outgeneralled by Zulu *indunas*. Particularly impressive was the warriors' ability to take their enemies by surprise, even in apparently open country. After the Battle of Blood River in 1838 a mounted Boer commando was decoyed into pursuing what looked from a distance like a herd of cattle, only to find that it consisted of crouching warriors with their cowhide shields on their backs. And in January 1879 an impi at least 20,000 strong managed to get undetected within 5 miles of Lord Chelmsford's camp at Isandlwana, despite the presence of strong British mounted patrols. By that time the Zulus had learned to respect European firepower and adapted their tactics accordingly. At Gingindlovu, also in the 1879 campaign, Captain Edward Hutton wrote of his admiration for 'the perfect manner in which these Zulus skirmished. A small knot of five or six would rise and dart through the long grass, dodging from side to side with their heads down . . . . They would then suddenly sink into the long grass, and nothing but puffs of curling smoke would show their whereabouts.' And at Ulundi in the same year Major Ashe described the Zulu deployment in terms which we might more commonly associate with a regular European army, in 'half-open order . . . under cover of their strong lines of skirmishers'.

Summers and Pagden have suggested that local circumstances caused Matabele tactics to diverge somewhat from their Zulu prototypes. Matabeleland was on the whole more wooded than Zululand, so the warriors were more accustomed to making use of cover and less practised in exploiting the minor irregularities of open ground to protect them from fire. Furthermore, Summers and Pagden argue that the Matabele had a more unbroken record of success in war than the Zulus, and that this experience made them more brittle when they did finally meet with reverses against the British in 1893. This argument, however, is unconvincing. At Bembesi in the 1893 campaign, two Matabele regiments rallied and returned to the charge three times against massed machine guns before they finally retired – behaviour which can hardly be described as 'brittle'. Moreover, their previous record was by no means uniformly successful. Mzilikazi had spent the first sixteen years of his rule gradually withdrawing northwards in the face of Zulu and Boer pressure, and even in their final home his people met with occasional defeats at the hands of local tribes. Robert Moffat was told that some time during the reign of Sebitwane (between 1823 and 1854) the Kololo had resorted to a cunning trick to lure a Matabele raiding party onto an island in the Zambezi. They ferried some cattle across to the island but left a calf belonging to one of the cows on the west bank, where the raiders were camped. The cow called for her calf, which swam across to her in full view of the Matabele. Supposing that what they could see was the far bank where the main Kololo herds were kept, they commandeered some local canoes and paddled over to the island, only to be stranded when the Kololo returned after dark and took the canoes. Sebitwane's men waited until their enemies were weakened by hunger and thirst, then paddled back to the island and wiped them out. And in 1885 an impi sent against the Tawana of Lake Ngami was so soundly beaten that it abandoned its weapons and shields and returned home in disgrace. The Intemba regiment, in fact, lost so heavily in this debacle that it was still not fit for action in the war of 1893.

Ngoni Organization and Tactics

In the south at least, the Ngoni retained much of the original Zulu system of organization. In the Lake Nyasa chiefdoms the population was made up of four separate elements, reminiscent of the classes of Matabele society. These were: 'those from the south', the mainly Swazi leaders of Zwangendaba's army and their descendants; 'those from south of the Zambezi', who had joined them on their migration through Matabeleland; 'those from the march', or tribespeople incorporated after 1835; and 'those from the country', who were the most recently subjugated locals. The latter were usually slaves, but they were expected to fight alongside their masters and could receive their freedom if they showed courage. From their origins as a migrating army the Ngoni had inherited a very strong military tradition. In the words of their own historian, Y M Cibambo, 'To the Ngoni war was like work and his heart rejoiced to think of it. When the old men sat in the kraal the talk that roused discussion was of war and their journeyings. All the heroes of the tribe had received their praise-greetings through service in war.'

Most units were based on territorial divisions, and warriors tended to live in their villages and not in separate kraals as they did in the Zulu army, but some groups in late nineteenth-century Nyasaland still organized their warriors into regiments by age. Every few years their young men were formed en masse into a new regiment, known as a *libandla*, of which each large village or prominent chief might have several. Each *libandla* was divided into companies called *libuto*, which varied in strength up to a hundred men or more, and would be allocated to one of the two major divisions of the army – the younger men, or *amajaha*, and the veterans, *amadoda*. Each regiment and company was led by an officer with the Zulu title of '*induna*', who was responsible to the overall leader or 'war *induna*', appointed by the *Nkosi* or chief. Alongside him was a 'war-medicine doctor', whose job it was to prophesy the outcome of a campaign, as well as using magic to encourage and protect the warriors. Boys learned the basics of the art of war early on by fighting against their neighbours from other Ngoni villages, although spears were forbidden in these fights and the boys carried only shields and clubs.

There is little reliable information on the size of Ngoni armies, although it seems that in the fertile and densely populated country around Lake Nyasa they could be very large by African standards. The *British Central Africa Gazette* of December 1894 was certainly exaggerating when it claimed that the central Nyasaland kingdom could put 50,000 men into the field, but more plausibly W A Elmslie reported seeing a 10,000-strong northern Ngoni army in 1878. Like their Zulu and Matabele cousins, many Ngoni armies acquired large numbers of guns – Carl Wiese estimated that Mpezeni's tribe had 2,000–3,000 in the late 1880s – but were reluctant to rely on them in battle, preferring their traditional spears. The Tuta further north never adopted firearms, and perhaps because of ignorance of their limitations they tended to be very wary even of the

smoothbore muzzle-loaders employed by their neighbours. It is probably
this fear of guns which accounts for the fact that the exploring expeditions
led by Speke and Stanley both traversed the Tuta country at the height
of their depredations without having to fight.

Burton describes the Tuta using the Zulu tactic of enveloping their
enemies with two 'horns' extending out from the flanks of the main body.
He adds: 'Their thousands march in four or five extended lines . . . . There
is no shouting or war-cry to distract the attention of the combatants: iron
whistles are used for the necessary signals' (Burton, 1860). What signals
were actually given in battle we are not told, and Burton implies that there
was very little in the way of central control or discipline: 'During the
battle the sultan, or chief, whose ensign is a brass stool, sits attended by
his forty or fifty elders in the rear; his authority is little more than
nominal, the tribe priding itself upon autonomy. The Watuta rarely run
away, and take no thought of their killed and wounded.' Burton (1860)
and Grant both repeat a rumour that the Tuta women fought alongside
the men – with bows according to Grant, although Burton states that the
tribe never employed missile weapons. If true this would be a significant
departure from Zulu practice, but it is worth noting that neither of these
writers ever encountered the Tuta in battle (although Grant saw plenty
of their warriors around his campsites), and so they were both heavily
reliant on interviews with their Arab enemies.

According to Cibambo, a Ngoni army would march out to war very
slowly, sending out scouts in all directions. Boys and girls from the
warriors' households accompanied them to carry food and water, just as
Zulu boys did, with sections of men detailed to protect them from attack.
When they neared an enemy village the warriors would sit and rest while
their *indunas* carefully reconnoitred, meanwhile taking snuff or smoking
hemp, which 'maddened the warriors and gave them hearts without fear'.
Even if the enemy had detected them, preparations would not be hurried:
'In the enemy stockade the drums would be beating to show that their
enemies were angry, but the army of the Ngoni sat and rested as though
there were no enemy.' Such was their moral ascendancy over their victims
that they seem not to have feared the possibility of a pre-emptive attack.
Then their commander called them to arms by performing his own
praise-dance, and the companies deployed into their 'chest and horns'
formation, blowing horns and whistling to drown the sound of the

enemy's drums. Captain F D Lugard, who fought the Ngoni in Nyasaland in the late 1880s, refers to the 'unearthly yells, grunts, and groans with which they accompany their attack' (Lugard, 1893). At last the command was given: 'Utsho njalo yena, uti, Aziqwebane' – 'Let the bulls fight.' Then every warrior would race to be the first over the enemy's stockade and into the village, because to do so earned not only great prestige but the first choice of the captured livestock. After the fight each *induna* would report to the overall commander the names of those who had been first into action, as well as those of any other men who had especially distinguished themselves. These men were singled out for praise at the victory dance held before the *Nkosi* on their return.

By the last quarter of the century, though, even the 'genuine' Ngoni seem to have begun to rely as much on their reputation as on real fighting prowess. The reports of European observers suggest that they were actually fairly cautious, preferring ambushes and surprise attacks under cover of darkness. Under these circumstances the victims were usually too terrorized to offer any resistance. Lugard quotes a report of a night raid on Lake Nyasa in 1893, in which 'the Angoni came down to the lake shore in great numbers, and attacked the village of Kayuni. They entered the village silently, and each warrior took up his position at the door of a hut, and ordered the inmates to come forth. Every man and boy was speared as he emerged, and every woman was captured' (Lugard, 1893). Many of the tribes living along the shore were forced to build their huts on stilts out in the lake for fear of such raids.

Pitched battles in the open were rare, but Carl Wiese describes an attack on a 400-strong Arab caravan which took place in northern Mozambique in the late 1880s. For this battle the Ngoni were organized into three divisions: the first consisted of a newly formed regiment, the Kabaenda, made up of youths of between fourteen and eighteen years old; the Mahora and Mabema regiments, comprising men in their twenties, were brigaded together; and finally the Amadoda formed a reserve. (Elsewhere Wiese gives 'Madouda' as the title of a regiment, but it is more likely that the term referred to veteran warriors in general, as it did in Zulu usage.) The Ngoni were actually on their way to attack a neighbouring tribe, but on finding the trail of the Arabs decided to follow them in the hope of richer spoils. They discovered their camp, determined their direction of march from the tracks, and hurried ahead to set an ambush.

The Kabaenda opened the battle by charging from the cover of bushes and tall grass, but fled when the Arabs fired a volley from their muzzle-loaders. Wiese does not explicitly say so, but it is likely that this retreat was a deliberate tactic designed to lure the enemy out of position. Arab armies seem to have been particularly vulnerable to this sort of stratagem because of their excessive confidence in the moral advantage which their guns gave them: Burton describes the success of a similar feigned retreat by the Masai (see Chapter 7). Without stopping to reload, the Arabs broke ranks and recklessly pursued the youths into the bush, where they were ambushed by the Mahora and Mabema, who were lying in wait. The Kabaenda then returned to the attack and surrounded the enemy. The Amadoda had been stationed further along the road to intercept the Arabs in case they resumed their march after driving off the initial attack, but now they hurried up and joined in the fight. Very few Arabs survived the battle, and several of the leaders who escaped later committed suicide in disgrace. Most of the Ngoni casualties occurred among the boys of the Kabaenda, who were in military terms the most expendable.

A photograph of an 'Angoni' published in Harry Johnston's *British Central Africa* of 1897 shows that the traditional costume, including many elements of Zulu derivation, was still in use in Nyasaland at that time. Most observers agreed that the Ngoni very closely resembled the Matabele. Nevertheless, despite the psychological advantages of resembling their dreaded southern cousins, the Ngoni north of the Zambezi did gradually adopt items of local dress. The commonest distinguishing feature was a headdress of black cock's feathers, although Johnston adds that a 'circlet made of zebra mane' was a popular alternative. He also describes 'a huge kilt of animals' tails or of dressed cat skins', and a strip of red cloth worn around the waist. The latter was common among the warriors of the Tanganyika region, and apparently had magical significance. Married Ngoni men are sometimes mentioned wearing the head ring which denoted married status in Zululand, but this practice was less common after Zwangendaba's generation. W P Johnson, who visited the Gwangwara in 1883, found only 'a few old men' wearing this headdress, though Wiese describes it as still in use among Mpezeni's people in 1889. The Tuta were at the same time the most conservative of the descendants of Zwangendaba's people and the most diluted by local influences. They were equipped in a similar fashion to their southern relatives, but appear to have been less showily dressed, and often fought entirely naked.

All the Ngoni retained the Zulu cowhide shield, and the practice of keeping the original pattern of the animal from which the shields were made, but there seems to be no evidence that regiments were still distinguished by different shield colours or patterns. One photograph, for example, shows a large group of warriors carrying shields which vary in colour, from entirely black to almost completely white with a few scattered dark spots. The assimilation of large numbers of local recruits, and the relative poverty in cattle of the bands north of the Zambezi, probably made the maintenance of any kind of formal regimental distinctions impossible. Most Ngoni carried both stabbing and throwing spears; Johnston confuses the issue by describing a drawing of a typical small-bladed *isijula* as a 'stabbing spear', but also illustrates what is obviously a proper stabbing assegai or *iklwa*. Burton (1860) describes the Tuta carrying 'large' shields and two stabbing spears each, though unlike other Ngoni they never used the throwing versions.

The Fall of the Zulu Kingdom

There has been much debate about the causes and consequences of the Zulu War of 1879, but there can be no doubt that from a short-term perspective it was an unnecessary conflict provoked – against the wishes of the government in London – by British officials in South Africa. The principal culprits were the high commissioner, Sir Bartle Frere, and the Natal secretary for native affairs, Theophilus Shepstone. Their ultimatum to Cetshwayo over what was essentially a minor border incident demanded that he accept a British resident, disband his army, abandon traditional Zulu marriage customs, and in effect voluntarily dismantle his own kingdom. No sovereign ruler could accept such terms, and indeed Cetshwayo was not expected to: Frere and Shepstone clearly hoped that he would fight and be quickly defeated, thus forcing the Zulus to accept British control. But in the long term the prospects for an independent Zulu kingdom were in any case gloomy. In the late 1870s much of Africa north of the Limpopo River remained unexplored, or at least beyond the political or economic reach of the whites. The Berlin Conference of 1884, which partitioned the continent among the European imperial powers, was still in the future, and most African potentates continued to rule unaffected by any outside authority.

But for Cetshwayo, the greatest of all these rulers, the successor of the great Shaka, the situation was very different. Across the Tugela River to the south was the increasingly prosperous colony of Natal, which included many Africans once subject to the Zulus, while on the High Veldt to the north-west the discovery of diamonds had begun to turn Mzilikazi's old raiding grounds into the richest mining area in the world. Both these territories represented an entirely different way of life from that prevailing in Zululand. Cetshwayo's young warriors – increasingly denied the opportunity to gain wealth and status by war and cattle raiding – were certainly aware of the contrast between the limited opportunities available in their own society and the jobs, money and personal freedom offered by the booming economies outside it. Furthermore, those who earned Cetshwayo's displeasure no longer had to choose between death and flight to the remote north as they had in Shaka's day, for dissident Zulus in the Natal colony were only too willing to receive them. No traditional society could have survived these pressures for long, but the manner in which they resisted them has earned the Zulus a place among the world's best known and most respected fighting nations.

The course of the subsequent campaign has been examined in detail in numerous books and scholarly articles, and some excellent modern research has dispelled many of the myths which have surrounded it. An in-depth study is beyond the scope of this book, but the war clearly deserves attention as the largest, bloodiest and best known of the nineteenth-century clashes between European and sub-Saharan African armies. The British commander-in-chief, Lord Chelmsford, had good reason to believe that a properly deployed force of British regulars could defeat opponents relying mainly on spears, almost regardless of their relative numbers. The 600 or so Boer trekkers at Blood River, though armed only with old-fashioned muzzle-loaders, had routed almost twenty times as many Zulus almost without loss to themselves, and the defenders of Rorke's Drift were soon to show how it was possible to prevail despite an even greater numerical disparity. So Chelmsford's strategy, which involved advancing into Zululand in three separate columns, was not necessarily flawed, especially as mounted scouts should have given the British ample warning of the approach of the enemy. But in practice things were very different, and the fate of the three columns illustrates in classic fashion the folly of underestimating an opponent. Colenso and

Durnford, whose 1881 book on the conflict is bitterly critical of both the war itself and Chelmsford's conduct of it, quote the warning given to him by a Boer veteran, J J Uys: 'The Zulus are more dangerous than you think. I lost my father and my brother through them, because we held them too cheaply. Afterwards we went with Andries Pretorius, but then we were careful, and have always closed our wagons well up, sent our spies far out, and we have beaten the Zulus.'

The British commander ignored this sound advice. On 22 January 1879 a Zulu impi under Ntshingwayo kaMahole, composed of more than a dozen regiments and numbering about 20,000 men, attacked the camp of the centre column beneath the hill of Isandlwana. Chelmsford had further dispersed his command, leaving most of a battalion of the 24th Foot, two 7-pounder guns and some irregulars to guard the camp, while he led the rest of the regulars to support a party of mounted scouts. What was more, he had forbidden the construction of a defensive wagon laager on the grounds that the wagons were needed to bring up supplies (disregarding the instructions in his own 1878 'Regulations for Field Forces in South Africa'), and when the Zulus struck, most of the British infantry were deployed in the open in extended skirmish lines. The finger of blame has been pointed in many directions since, but rather than trying to explain away the British defeat it might be more constructive to acknowledge the success of the Zulu 'chest and horns' tactics (though it has been argued that in this case the deployment was accidental, as the regiments were camped in an extended line and went straight into action in the positions in which they found themselves). The firepower of the British infantry and artillery repeatedly forced the warriors in the centre to go to ground, but they kept up the pressure until the 'horns' had enveloped the position from both flanks. Then, as the redcoats tried to regroup into a more solid defensive formation around the camp, the Zulus followed up and swamped them with superior numbers.

The result was the worst disaster suffered by Queen Victoria's armies since the retreat from Kabul in 1842, with over 700 regulars and probably a similar number of colonial and native auxiliary troops killed. Ian Knight has pointed out that in comparison to other famous disasters of the period, like Maiwand in Afghanistan, Majuba Hill in the First Boer War and Spion Kop in the second, not only were total losses at Isandlwana greater, but the proportion of dead to wounded was far higher, reflecting the hand-to-hand nature of the combat and the Zulu reluctance to take prisoners. The Beja 'Fuzzy-Wuzzies' of the Sudan, whom Kipling immortalized as 'the finest of the lot', did break into a British square at Tamai in 1884, but although they pushed it back nearly half a mile they did not manage to kill more than ninety or so of the regulars. The almost instantaneous destruction of an entire battalion at Isandlwana was unprecedented, but the damage inflicted by the Zulus on the imperial war machine did not end there.

In March 1879 a smaller force under Colonel Redvers Buller was routed when it ran into a previously undetected impi at Hlobane, and more British casualties were incurred when a supply train was surprised at Intombe Drift. Then in June the French Prince Imperial, who was serving as an observer on Chelmsford's staff, was killed in a Zulu ambush, causing acute embarrassment for Queen Victoria and her government. But the rest of the campaign went less well for Cetshwayo. After the victory at Isandlwana a Zulu force tried to storm the nearby British outpost at Rorke's Drift, but the outnumbered garrison had the advantage of a good defensive position, and repulsed the attackers with heavy casualties. At Khambula and Gingindlovu the British commanders learned from the mistakes of Isandlwana and fortified their positions with wagons, earthworks and palisades. Against these the warriors charged bravely but fruitlessly, incurring terrible losses, just as their fathers had done against the Boers forty years earlier. Then, strengthened by reinforcements from home, including the regular cavalry of the 1st Dragoon Guards and 17th Lancers, Chelmsford regrouped his scattered columns and marched on the royal kraal at Ulundi.

The decisive battle was fought near Ulundi on 4 July 1879. The British force formed into a single giant square, made up of forty companies from six infantry regiments, plus twelve field guns and two Gatling machine guns. Irregular cavalry advanced ahead of the square to goad the Zulus into attacking. Overall British strength was about 5,100. Opposing them were contingents from every available regiment in Cetshwayo's army, totalling about 20,000 men. They drove in the cavalry and charged the square, making use of a depression which provided some cover on the British right, and concentrating on the most vulnerable points at the corners. But now the regulars were fighting on their own terms, and their formation was never seriously threatened. At one point the infantrymen on the left face were ordered to fix bayonets, but the Zulus never got close enough to pit their assegais against them. Some warriors on the right came within 10 yards before being shot down, but elsewhere they were stopped between 70 and 300 yards short of their objective. Some regiments took cover in the grass, but the British artillery sought them out and drove them from their positions. Then, as the Zulus started to fall back, Chelmsford ordered the cavalry to pursue, led by the 17th Lancers. Even then many of the warriors did not flee, but rallied in small groups and tried to stab the horses with their assegais, forcing the lancers to sling their lances and resort to sabres. But eventually Cetshwayo's men were forced to admit defeat and flee into the hills, leaving the king's kraal to be burnt by the victorious British.

An interesting analysis of the Ulundi campaign by J J Guy sees it not as the British triumph proclaimed at the time, but as 'a token victory, following a half-hearted Zulu attack', which allowed Chelmsford to save face after his humiliation at Isandlwana, while at the same time allowing for a compromise peace which kept the Zulu state in being. In this view the Zulu armies were not beaten in battle so much as allowed to disperse as they always did after a campaign, successful or otherwise; the real fatal damage to the kingdom was done later, by the civil wars which followed the removal of Cetshwayo. There is evidence from some eyewitness accounts that the Zulus at Ulundi were less reckless in their charges than they had been previously. Colonel Evelyn Wood, for example, referred to a 'half-hearted' attack. But in view of the casualties which they had already suffered, even in victorious engagements such as Isandlwana, it is not surprising that the regiments were modifying their tactics by this stage of the war. The 'half-open order' described by Ashe was as likely to be a deliberate ploy to minimize casualties as it was to be a result of lack of enthusiasm or discipline. The strongest evidence that the Zulus were mounting much more than a token resistance must be the estimated 1,500 dead which they left on the field, some of them only nine paces from the British square. (Guy quotes Sir Garnet Wolseley, who arrived to take over command from Chelmsford eleven days later, as estimating that the Zulu dead numbered no more than 400, but Wolseley was not present at the battle and may well have succumbed to the temptation to play down his predecessor's victory.)

Obviously the war was a victory for modern firepower, but it is worth remarking that the rifle and bayonet had also proved a match for the assegai in close combat. With its 18 inch bayonet the British Army's Martini-Henry rifle had a total length of about 5½ feet, giving it far greater reach than the short-handled *iklwa*. Also, being a two-handed weapon it could be wielded with greater force, while the butt could be employed as an effective club. Possession of a shield might seem to have given the spearman an advantage, but the cowhide shields were too light to push the heavier British weapons aside, and were easily penetrated by a bayonet thrust. Several eyewitnesses confirm that man for man the Zulus were outclassed in hand-to-hand combat by the British regulars, in sharp contrast to their usual experience against African opponents. According to Private Hitch at Rorke's Drift, 'they seemed to have a great dread of the bayonet' (Boucher), and a Zulu veteran of Isandlwana recalled that 'any man who went to stab a soldier was fixed through the throat or stomach' by a bayonet thrust (Norris-Newman). The Zulus' shock at the losses inflicted by bullets is easily understood, but it must have been scarcely less demoralizing to realize that they were outclassed even in the close combat at which they had traditionally excelled.

Guy is certainly correct in emphasizing the post-war years as the ones which saw the final collapse of Zulu power. Cetshwayo was captured and sent into exile, while his country was partitioned among thirteen chiefs, each of whom signed treaties agreeing – among other things – to disband their regiments and allow their young men to seek work in British territory. This arrangement might not have been deliberately designed to provoke civil war, but that was the inevitable result. For the next seventeen years Zululand suffered from famine, smallpox and bloody internal strife: the Zulus are said to have lost more men at the Battle of Msebe (fought in March 1883 between the uSuthu faction, loyal to Cetshwayo, and the followers of a rival for power, Zibhebhu kaMaphitha) than in any other battle in their history. Boers from the Transvaal, invited in to support one of the warring factions, seized land and cattle from their old enemies. In 1897 the country was incorporated into the self-governing colony of Natal, and huge areas of land were appropriated for white settlement. In 1906 the Zulus rose in revolt under Chief Bambatha, only to be cornered by superior numbers in two battles in the Mome and Izinsimba gorges and massacred by rifle and artillery fire. Like the other native peoples of South Africa who had once lived in fear of them, the

Zulus came under the domination of the whites for the next eight decades.

The Defeat of the Matabele

Only the remoteness of their country enabled the Matabele to survive for a while longer. After Mzilikazi's death his favourite son, Lobengula, succeeded to the throne, despite the opposition of a group of nobles led by Mbigo Masuku, the commander of the Zwangendaba regiment. The dissidents apparently believed that as Lobengula's mother was a foreigner he was not a true Zansi, and therefore was ineligible to succeed. In June 1870 the dispute was settled when Lobengula attacked Mbigo, who had barricaded himself inside the regimental kraal, and stormed it after a hard fight lasting several hours. The Zwangendaba was disbanded and the survivors incorporated into other regiments, as part of a major re-organization implemented by the new king. It seems that the main incentive for this move was the low birth rate among the Zansi; this was a perennial problem with military aristocracies, shared for example by the ancient Spartans, but it was made worse by the custom of not allowing the men of a regiment to marry until the king was prepared to stand them down. The habit of late marriage was useful for maintaining a large standing army, but inevitably limited the number of children each man could have. Hence Mzilikazi had left several Zansi regiments which were too small to be viable units, while the less reliable Enhla and Holi now dominated the army. Therefore Lobengula decided to concentrate the Zansi into two crack units. One was based on a regiment recently raised by his predecessor and reinforced with those young Zansi who had come of age since, and became Lobengula's bodyguard. It was named Ingubo. The other, Imbizo, was formed by amalgamating four other regiments and keeping them up to strength with Zansi recruits as they became available. It became a socially as well as militarily elite unit, in a similar manner to the Guards in the British Army. Its first commander, however, was not a Zansi nobleman but an otherwise unknown officer called Halimani Mtimkulu, which seems to be a Zulu name. It would be interesting to know whether Lobengula had hired an expert from Zululand to bring his new regiment up to scratch, but this can only be speculation.

Once securely in power Lobengula reverted to raising regiments in the traditional way, and for the next twenty years, until the arrival of the

British in Mashonaland in 1890, he ruled over a stable and fairly prosperous kingdom. His impis continued to campaign in all directions, consolidating Matabele rule over the neighbouring tribes and in some areas extending it beyond the boundaries established by Mzilikazi. However, Lobengula was careful to avoid conflict with the whites. He encouraged hunters and traders to visit his country, and raised no objection when in 1885 Britain established a protectorate over Bechuanaland to the west (now Botswana), and closed it off to Matabele raids. But by this time there were those in South Africa who saw Matabeleland as an obstacle to their own ambitions. In 1887 the businessman and imperialist Cecil Rhodes founded the British South Africa Company, and in October 1888 his agents tricked Lobengula into signing away the mineral rights in his kingdom. The king soon repudiated this agreement, but was persuaded to allow prospectors to enter the country in search of gold and diamonds. Then in May 1890 Rhodes showed his hand, organizing a heavily armed 'Pioneer Column' which set out from Bechuanaland with about 200 civilians and an escort of 400 British South Africa Company and Bechuanaland Police. Avoiding a direct confrontation with Lobengula, the column skirted round Matabeleland proper and marched into the Shona country further north. There the pioneers established a fortified post at Fort Salisbury.

Lobengula protested and threatened to attack the column, but the order was never given. It is not clear whether he still hoped for a peaceful accommodation with the whites or whether, as Summers and Pagden suggest, he was still uncertain of the loyalty of some of his regiments even two decades after the revolt of the Zwangendaba. But by allowing an expansionist colony to establish itself in close proximity to his own seat of power, he may have missed his best chance to preserve Matabele independence. Just as in Zululand, it proved impossible for a traditionally organized African monarchy to exist side by side with European settlement. Soon white colonists were building more forts, setting up farms and mining operations among the Shona, and luring young Matabele men across the border to seek employment in the booming new industries. In 1891 Mashonaland formally became a British protectorate. The Shona were traditionally vassals of the Matabele, who referred to them contemptuously as their 'dogs' and were accustomed to extort cattle and other tribute from them. Naturally the victims welcomed Rhodes's colonists as protectors, and took the opportunity to defy their former masters. In June 1893 a Shona chief living near Fort Victoria stole some Matabele cattle and was pursued across the border by an impi. The warriors had instructions not to harm whites, but many Shona were killed in the vicinity of the settlement, and had their kraals burnt and their cattle stolen.

War was now inevitable, and Lobengula hurriedly mobilized his regiments while the colonists prepared to attack him from two directions. One column advanced from the south, but this was intended as a diversion and played only a minor part in the fighting. The main thrust came from the north-east, where two columns, from Forts Salisbury and Victoria, rendezvoused at Iron Mine Hill and marched on Lobengula's kraal at Bulawayo. Their combined force numbered 690 mounted men with Martini-Henry rifles, about 400 Shona tribesmen, two 7-pounder field guns, and eight machine guns, of which five were state-of-the-art Maxims. There was also a steam-powered searchlight for protection against night attacks. This formidable force was accompanied by transport wagons which could be formed in Boer style into a defensive laager. It was believed at the time that Lobengula had around 30,000 warriors under arms, but Summers and Pagden calculate that the true figure was not much more than half that, and that – allowing for an impi which was away raiding across the Zambezi – only about 12,500 men could be mustered to oppose the two columns. The first serious clash occurred at Bonko on the Shangani River on 25 October 1893, when about 3,500 Matabele attacked the two laagers of the eastern column in the early hours of the morning. Confused fighting lasted until about 8 am, but although the warriors pressed the attack with considerable courage in the face of machine-gun fire, they did not succeed in reaching the wagons, and eventually retired after suffering about 500 casualties.

No Matabele army had attacked a laager since 1836, and Lobengula's commanders probably had little idea of the difficulty of doing so. But the king himself showed a shrewd appreciation of the situation. When the result of the battle at Bonko was reported to him, he issued orders that no more attacks were to be launched against laagered wagons, but that the impis should wait until the marching columns were crossing the only practicable ford across the Umguza River on their way to Bulawayo. Then they should charge while the wagons were halfway across, so that the enemy would be unable to circle them into a laager. These orders were designed to minimize the advantages of the white men's firepower, and might have given the Matabele at least a chance of overrunning them. It may not be coincidence that the Zulu victory at Intombe Drift in 1879 had occurred in similar circumstances, when a British column was forced to camp in two detachments on either side of a flooded river and was defeated in detail. The Matabele also attempted to use this tactic at Manyala against the Bechuanaland force, whose march discipline was poor, and actually succeeded in cutting the column. However, in this case the attackers were too few in numbers and were driven off.

Unfortunately for Lobengula, his instructions were not obeyed where it mattered. Just before noon on 1 November the eastern column reached the top of a low hill in open country not far from the Bembesi River, and believing themselves safe from ambush the colonists halted for lunch. They formed their wagons into two laagers, one on either side of a small deserted kraal, but rashly sent their horses and cattle to graze on lower ground about a mile away. Some of the men put down their rifles and began to mend their tattered clothes. Unknown to them they were being shadowed by a large Matabele army, about 6,000 strong, which was moving parallel to them a few hundred yards distant under cover of dense bush. Not only did this impi include the two elite Ingubo and Imbizo regiments, but it was well supplied with guns. In fact, as Summers and Pagden point out, the Matabele possessed more breech-loading rifles in this battle than their enemies did, but they were not trained to use them and as usual their marksmanship was poor. Nevertheless it must have seemed to the *indunas* that their force was overwhelmingly superior, and that this justified disobeying the king's orders and launching an immediate attack on the unsuspecting whites.

The bulk of the Matabele army was still strung out in a long column of march when Ingubo and Imbizo burst out of the bush and advanced towards the nearest laager, that of the Salisbury contingent, across 500 yards of open ground. They fired their rifles on the move, which caused few casualties, but slowed them down and gave the colonists time to get their machine guns into action. These were not just improved versions of the Gatlings employed at Ulundi, but represented a qualitative advance in weapons technology. Powered not by a hand crank like the Gatling, but by chemical energy from the explosions of the cartridges it fired, the Maxim had a theoretical rate of fire of 600 rounds a minute and a range of well over 2,000 yards. It was also far less prone to misfires than earlier machine guns. This was essentially the same weapon as the British Vickers and German Maxim 08 which mowed down whole battalions in the First World War. Summers and Pagden believed, probably rightly, that this was the first occasion in history when an army charged, in the open and in daylight, against Maxim guns, and with hindsight the outcome was inevitable. A survivor from Imbizo recalled that when the 'sigwagwa', as they called the Maxims, opened fire 'they killed such a lot of us that we were taken by surprise. The wounded and the dead lay in heaps.' Nevertheless the two regiments rallied, and over the next forty minutes they returned to the charge three times, advancing to within 110 yards of the laager, and finally retiring only when more than half their number were casualties. Sir John Willoughby, a military adviser with the column, later paid tribute to their courage with these words: 'I cannot speak too highly of the pluck of these two regiments. I believe that no civilised army could have withstood the terrific fire they did for at most half as long' (Boucher).

But their bravery was in vain, because the rest of the Matabele army failed to support them. Whether the effectiveness of the defenders' fire had shaken their commanders, or some of the units on the right flank were less enthusiastic, no attack was mounted from that direction. Another opportunity was missed when the column's horses, which were being driven back to the wagons, took fright at the sound of gunfire and stampeded towards the Matabele right. But instead of attempting to capture them the warriors shot at them, turning them back towards the laager where they were safely corralled. We can only guess at what might have happened if the whole force of 6,000 had been thrown from ambush at a marching column, but it would certainly have given the Matabele a better chance of putting their close-quarter fighting skills into effect.

After the defeat at Bembesi, Lobengula fled northwards, apparently in an attempt to seek refuge among Mpezeni's Ngoni across the Zambezi, but either died of smallpox or committed suicide on the way. There remained to be fought one last battle, which has passed into legend despite its irrelevance to the course of the campaign. Lobengula had sent envoys to Major Patrick Forbes, commanding the force sent in pursuit of him, with a bag of gold sovereigns and an offer of peace. But the messengers handed over the gold to two white stragglers from the column, who failed to pass on the message and instead absconded with the money. This theft led to tragedy, when Forbes dispatched a patrol under Major Allan Wilson across the Shangani River on 3 December 1893 to locate the king. In darkness Wilson rode right through the remnants of Ingubo and Imbizo without spotting them, while the Matabele, believing that a cease-fire had been agreed, let them pass. In the morning the patrol found itself in the middle of the enemy army, and a firefight broke out in the course of which about 300 Matabele and thirty-three whites – Wilson's entire force, except for a handful of messengers sent back earlier – were killed. Later myth-makers have reconstructed the fight as an epic last stand, with Wilson's men standing defiantly round a large anthill and singing 'God Save the Queen' as they were shot down. The actual details remain uncertain (though a Matabele witness did state that they sang a song in praise of the queen before they died), but the heroism of the 'Shangani Patrol' was long remembered by both sides. The Matabele, 'connoisseurs of bravery' as Summers and Pagden remark, buried the bodies with the same honours as their own dead.

Apart from a few skirmishes, the war was over. The British South Africa Company appropriated large tracts of land for sale to white farmers, and confiscated most of the Matabele cattle. But the people survived, and in 1896 they launched a desperate rebellion in which twice as many whites were killed as in 1893. By this time the regimental system had broken down, and the warriors abandoned their traditional tactics and fought mainly in skirmishing fashion with rifles. Eventually, after six months of fighting in the rugged Matopos Hills, they were beaten more by starvation than by military force. It is tempting to wonder whether Lobengula might have survived if his men had used these tactics three years earlier, but no army would willingly abandon a tried and tested system until it had been proved to be obsolete. Instead the Matabele of 1893, like the Zulus of 1879, had attempted to integrate the new tactics required to fight the well-armed Europeans with the doctrine of the age-based regiment and the assegai, essentially unchanged since the days of Shaka.

The End of Ngoni Independence

By contrast the resistance of the Ngoni in the north to the march of European imperialism was hesitant and largely ineffective, belying the ferocious reputation which they had acquired among the local tribes. The Ngoni of Tanganyika came under German control in piecemeal fashion during the 1890s. Many of them were recruited to fight along-side the Germans in the Hehe War of 1891–98 (see Chapter 8), but others resented efforts to curtail their traditional raiding. The Tuta were nominally subjugated by a German column led by Emin Pasha in 1890, but in fact they avoided contact with the expedition and Emin was unable to inflict significant damage on them. They continued their customary raiding for several more years, but perhaps because of their notorious dread of firearms they never attempted to confront a German-led force in open battle. Eventually a column led by Captain Langheld caught up with them and forced them to settle south of Lake Victoria. In 1897 another expedition under Captains Engelhardt and Fuleborn was sent to subdue the Gwangwara of Songea in the south of the country, who had continued to subject the hinterland of Kilwa to destructive raids. After several bloody clashes the Germans resorted to deceit, and a number of Ngoni chiefs were lured into their camp under a flag of truce and arrested. The Gwangwara and other Ngoni groups took up arms again as part of the Maji Maji Rebellion of 1905, only to be suppressed with such heavy losses that much of their territory remains depopulated to this day.

The 'Partition of Africa' in the late 1880s brought the Lake Nyasa Ngoni within the British sphere of influence, in territory which was to become known as British Central Africa (subsequently Nyasaland, now Malawi). During the 1890s they too gradually lost their independence. The northernmost of the little Lake Nyasa kingdoms was friendly to the British, mainly thanks to the influence of the commissioner, a Dr Laws. They welcomed missionaries and voluntarily gave up raiding. Laws even proposed to enlist their warriors into the British forces, although in the event local Tonga and Yao recruits were preferred, as they were thought to be more amenable to military discipline than the 'wild' Ngoni. In the central kingdom the *Nkosi* Chikusi accepted British protection in 1890, but during the reign of his successor, Gomani, a group of anti-British headmen gradually gained influence. In 1896 the warriors attacked a mission station, and in response a punitive expedition was dispatched which defeated a Ngoni impi and sacked Gomani's village. The chief was captured, but was shot when he refused to co-operate. The central Ngoni lost most of their cattle, and were brought under the control of the British administration.

Further west, on the plateau between Lake Nyasa and the Luangwa River in what is now north-eastern Zambia, was the smaller kingdom ruled by Mpezeni. This chief had maintained fairly good relations with the Portuguese who were advancing westwards along the Zambezi, but in 1895 his territory came within the area of operations of the newly formed British North Charterland Exploration Company, an offshoot of the British South Africa Company. The company was more concerned with exploiting the mineral wealth of the country than with administering the Ngoni, but Mpezeni found it increasingly difficult to control his people's resentment of the intruders' presence. Bands of young men began to appear at the company's headquarters, extorting tribute and challenging the white men to fight. In 1897 Carl Wiese, who at the time was based in British Central Africa but travelled widely throughout the region, reported to the authorities that the warriors were mobilizing for a full-scale attack. It is unlikely that this was actually the case, and it has been plausibly suggested that they were simply gathering at the chief's village for an annual festival. Nevertheless the authorities took no chances. In January 1898 an expedition left Fort Jameson in the Central Africa Protectorate and marched to Mpezeni's village to suppress what had become known as the 'Angoni Rebellion'. It consisted of five companies of the British Central Africa Rifles, each around a hundred strong, supported by field artillery and Maxim guns. Mpezeni mobilized about 5,000 warriors, but although they attacked the British column on several occasions they never got closer than 50 yards before being broken up by rifle and machine-gun fire. By the end of the month Mpezeni had fled and his son Singu, alleged to be the leader of the 'revolt', was captured and shot. The area was brought under the control of the British South Africa Company and eventually incorporated into Northern Rhodesia. With the fall of Mpezeni the last free representatives of the great Nguni dispersal had lost their independence.

Sources

The volume of material published in English on the Zulu armies, and in particular the Anglo–Zulu War of 1879, is so huge that only a very brief survey is possible. Colenso and Durnford, and Ashe and Edgell, are both readable contemporary accounts. Many readers will be familiar with the contributions of Ian Knight, but the works of Laband, Greaves and Snook are also highly recommended. The last-named is a recent work which benefits from the author's own military background. Spring has a useful discussion of the evolution of traditional Zulu weaponry. Dodds is a more wide-ranging study which treats the Matabele as well as the Zulus. On the Matabele Wars of 1893 and 1896, the recollections of Selous, an experienced hunter who had known the land and the people for twenty years, are of particular interest. Summers and Pagden had access to a large amount of Matabele oral testimony, and their detailed reconstructions of the battles of the 1893 campaign, as well as of Matabele weapons and equipment, are invaluable. The Ngoni are much less well documented, but Cibambo and Read preserve many of their own oral traditions. Burton, Thomson, Wiese, Lugard and Johnston also have useful accounts. A brief survey of the British operations against the Ngoni in Northern Rhodesia is given by Brelsford.

Chapter Three

'The Most Horrible War':
The British and the Ashanti

On the opposite side of the continent, Britain was involved in a long-standing conflict with a power whose reputation at one time rivalled that of the Zulus – the kingdom of Ashanti. By the beginning of the nineteenth century this was one of the most populous and powerful states on the continent. Situated in the hinterland of what was then the Gold Coast of West Africa (modern Ghana), it had arisen during the mid-seventeenth century from a coalition of small chiefdoms dominated by the Akan people. Thanks to their strategic location between the trans-Saharan trade routes, the gold mines of the interior and the European trading stations on the coast, they prospered and were able to purchase foreign goods, including large numbers of guns. In the 1740s they conquered the savannah states of Dagomba and Gonja, whose cavalry had no defence against firearms, and established an empire stretching from the coast far inland towards the valley of the great River Niger. The growing power of Ashanti first came to the notice of the European traders on the coast with the conquest of Denkera, a trading partner of the Dutch, in 1719. But the first clash with the people who were to become their main rivals in the region, the British, did not occur until 1806, when refugees from Ashanti-controlled Assin took refuge in the British headquarters at Cape Coast Castle. At that time the government in London was not interested in political control of the region, so the governor handed over the fugitives and agreed to recognize Ashanti authority over the coastal Fante tribes. He even agreed to pay rent to the Ashanti king for the coastal forts which the British occupied.

Again in 1816 the Ashanti attacked the Fante, and were bought off with British money. Peace treaties followed in 1817 and 1820. In the latter the Ashanti king agreed to accept British protection in exchange for formal recognition of his rights on the coast, but Parliament refused to ratify the agreement, and war broke out again in 1824. This time the governor, Sir

Charles Macarthy, decided to take the initiative. A British expedition was being assembled under a Major Chisholm, but Macarthy was unwilling to wait for it, and mustered a force of local allies which he personally led north to the Adoomansu River. He was one of the first of a long line of European officers in Africa who made the mistake of underestimating his enemy. On 21 January 1824 the Ashanti attacked, using the enveloping tactics favoured by many African armies. Macarthy ran out of ammunition, his allies fled, and the white officers found themselves surrounded. None of them escaped alive, and Macarthy's skull was taken as a trophy to the Ashanti capital at Kumasi. When he learned of the disaster Major Chisholm retreated to Cape Coast, allowing the victorious Ashanti to plunder the Fante at will.

Then, in an engagement at Dodowah in September 1826, the 'Royal African Corps', made up of locally recruited troops under British officers, together with a contingent of Akim allies, inflicted the first serious defeat on the Ashanti. This was due to the courage of the Akim, who captured the enemy camp, and also to the appearance of a weapon new to this theatre of war, a battery of Congreve rockets. These were believed to have had a great moral effect on the Ashanti, and it became standard procedure in future campaigns to deploy rockets whenever possible. They were notoriously inaccurate and the lethality of their small warheads was limited, but these disadvantages were outweighed by their psychological impact and by their manoeuvrability in terrain where conventional artillery could not go: because rockets produced no recoil they did not require a heavy barrel or a wheeled carriage, but could be fired from a light trough-shaped launcher carried by a handful of men.

The British victory at Dodowah persuaded the Ashanti of the advantages of peace, and in 1831 King Osei Yaw Okoto signed a new treaty renouncing his rule over the Fante. The peace endured for thirty years, threatened only by an incident in 1852 when the British arrested an Assin chief for allegedly accepting bribes to take his people over to the Ashanti. Seven thousand Ashanti soldiers marched south, but were persuaded to retire peacefully north of the Prah River, which now marked the boundary between Ashanti territory and that occupied by Britain's Fante allies. Nevertheless from this time the conviction grew among the British authorities that their forbearance had only encouraged the arrogance of this powerful neighbour, which was just waiting for the right moment to bring the Fante back under its control.

The British governor on the Gold Coast began to argue in his reports home that it would eventually be necessary to take the offensive, citing the advantages of opening up the interior to trade, and the desirability of putting a stop to the 'revolting' Ashanti practice of human sacrifice, which he claimed led to the deaths of 3,000 innocent people each year (*British Parliamentary Papers*, vol. 57). He even planned to build a military road as far as the River Prah so that future operations could be properly supplied. This scheme was not pursued at the time, but would later be revived by Sir Garnet Wolseley for his 1874 campaign. In December 1862 another crisis arose over an Ashanti demand for the return of some fugitives. An army once again crossed the Prah, and Governor Pine wrote to London requesting 2,000 British regulars to strike 'a final blow' at King Kwaku Dua, whom he described as 'an arbitrary, cruel, and sanguinary monarch' who had insulted the British flag. Denied these reinforcements, he sent the only troops he had available, six companies of West Indians, to the Prah to deter any further incursions. But it was now the rainy season, and the men were decimated by disease and forced to withdraw. Humiliatingly, their artillery and ammunition had to be destroyed to prevent their being captured, as there were too few able-bodied men left to bring them back.

The Ashanti Kingdom and Its Army

The Ashanti king, known as the 'Asantehene', was not an absolute monarch but presided over a large number of subordinate kings, chiefs and appointed officials, many of whom had their own private armies and pursued their own political objectives. This resulted in an apparently capricious foreign policy, in which peace overtures alternated with threats of invasion. This naturally exasperated the British, but reflected a serious political debate among the Ashanti. Many of their merchants were growing rich on trade in commodities such as kola nuts, palm oil and gold, and genuinely desired peace with their European trading partners. Unfortunately this growth in trade had not made allies of the British companies on the coast. As believers in the prevailing free-trade dogma, they maintained that the Ashanti kings' attempts to keep their economy under centralized control was cheating them of their rightful profits, and they added their voices to the political and humanitarian arguments for putting the Ashanti in their place. On the other hand the old Ashanti nobility felt themselves sidelined. They still controlled the army, but since the abolition of the slave trade by Britain in 1807 they could not employ their warriors to enrich themselves by slave-raiding as had once been the custom. And as the economy prospered and opportunities to get rich through trade increased, their followers became less willing to serve in the armies. The chiefs therefore formed an influential war party, eager to put their military power to use before it withered away.

In the eighteenth century the Ashanti kings had maintained a sizeable cavalry corps, but this had disappeared by the time they encountered the British, probably because they had by then lost control of the grasslands north of the rainforest zone where horses could be successfully bred. By the middle of the nineteenth century their armies were remarkably homogeneous. Chiefs maintained small bands of professional soldiers, but the bulk of the Ashanti armies in time of war was provided by a mass levy of all eligible men. The swords and shields which they had traditionally wielded were by now retained only in ceremonial roles, and the entire fighting strength was armed with long-barrelled smoothbore muskets – or 'Dane guns' as they were known, from the nationality of the traders who first introduced them. The troops were well disciplined, with a sophisticated system of command. There was also a well-organized medical corps.

In the field, armies marched in separate columns which kept in touch by means of messengers. Each column comprised a main body, advance guard, rearguard and two flank detachments, usually provided by allied tribes, which could form the wings when line of battle was formed. When one column encountered opposition the others would converge on it, and attempt to envelop the enemy on both flanks with the aim of encircling him. This is very reminiscent of the system used by Napoleon, but although we have no information on when it was first used in Africa there is no reason to doubt that it was developed independently. The Ashanti themselves believed that it had been inspired by watching the activities of soldier ants – a claim often made about other African armies, including the Azande, and which may well have a basis in truth. All observers agreed that the Ashanti army was one of the largest in Africa, though they disagreed on the exact numbers of men available. Thomas Bowdich, who visited the country in 1817, mentions a figure of 204,000, though most assessments were about half that number. In fact it is unlikely that such numbers could have been supplied even if they had been mobilized; the largest army mentioned in the 1873 campaign was estimated at 40,000, and even this could not be kept assembled for long because of the difficulty of providing it with food. More typical numbers quoted for the battles of this campaign are in the order of 3,000–4,000.

As was usual among African armies, ritual and magic were often considered to be just as important as material considerations. A notable feature of Ashanti war gear was the war shirt, or *batakari*. These garments, usually short sleeved and of varying length, were covered with small sewn-on packets containing magic charms which were believed to give protection against an enemy's weapons. Many of these charms were purchased from the Islamic states to the north, and included slips of paper with quotations from the Koran and other religious symbols, although the Ashanti themselves were not Muslims. More readily available were seashells, large numbers of which were attached to the equipment of the ordinary soldiers. These were supposed to ward off lightning and perhaps, by analogy, bullets. Belief in these charms was not restricted to the wearers, as is shown by an anecdote related by Captain Armitage from the Battle of Obassa in 1900. A Sierra Leonean soldier, reproved by his officer for bad shooting, explained that it was impossible to kill the Ashanti chief he had been ordered to target because of the 'war medicine' on his shirt. This suggests that the *batakari* may have had genuine protective value, especially in inter-tribal warfare, because of the effect on the morale of enemy marksmen. War shirts were most commonly seen among senior officers, though it is unclear whether they were part of a formal system of indicating rank. It has been suggested that in any case the cost of the charms would have put them beyond the reach of the ordinary soldier. An illustration by Thomas Bowdich dating from 1819 shows a chief in a very elaborate outfit, complete with *batakari*, plumed headdress, and feather or animal-tail adornments on his arms. Bowdich also describes chiefs accompanied by huge scarlet or yellow umbrellas and other insignia of rank, but by the 1870s little of this finery was still in evidence in the field. Some very ornate *batakari* from the 1874 campaign still survive, decorated with charms of precious metal and strips of brightly coloured cloth, but most soldiers were dressed more plainly. Photographs show them wearing no more than ankle-length kilts, small caps or turbans, powder horns and bandoliers, and an assortment of small knives. Even this might be too cumbersome for fighting in dense jungle, where equipment could catch on thorns and branches, and several eye-witness descriptions imply that they fought entirely naked.

The Road to War

For a decade after the crisis of 1862 there were intermittent hostilities along the frontier, but the British government continued to withhold the troops who might have settled the issue. The anticipated clash was finally precipitated in 1870, when the British bought out the remaining Dutch forts along the coast. The local people had not been consulted, and some of them objected to their new masters. Fighting broke out between the pro-British Fante and the people of Elmina, who had been loyal allies of the Dutch. King Kofi Karikari, who had succeeded to the Ashanti throne in 1868, chose this moment to assert his power. He informed the authorities at Cape Coast that the Dutch had had no right to cede Elmina, as it had actually belonged to his father, who had received an annual rent for it. Meanwhile an Ashanti chief named Adoo Boffoo had captured a group of missionaries and other European civilians and taken them to Kumasi, where they were held as hostages. Kofi eventually agreed to renounce his claim to Elmina, but he was suspected of secretly supporting the people in their resistance to the British takeover, and ominously the hostages remained in his custody.

Kofi's intentions became clear on 22 January 1873, when 12,000 Ashanti under the king's brother Prince Mensu crossed the Prah at Prahsu and advanced southwards in three columns. Apart from a few companies of Hausa askaris recruited from Nigeria, the only troops available to stop them were the Fante, who were believed to number as many as 70,000 fighting men, but were poorly armed and reluctant to face the Ashanti. They were hastily issued with 300 Snider rifles and 700 older rifled muzzle-loaders, but otherwise they were armed only with old-fashioned smoothbore muskets like those used by their enemies. At Yancoomassie on 10 March a force of 4,000 Ashanti defeated 25,000 Fante, despite the presence of a company of Hausas under a Lieutenant Hopkins. In the recriminations which followed, the Fante accused Hopkins of inactivity, while he blamed them for wasting their limited ammunition, and for making wild claims about their own achievements. According to Captain Brackenbury, the official chronicler of the war, the Fante had claimed to have attacked the enemy from the rear and taken

2,000 prisoners, 'but on investigation this number had to be divided by a thousand, only two prisoners having been taken' – surely one of the wildest exaggerations in military history. British complaints about the Fante's lack of aggression were widespread. They repeatedly refused to mount flank attacks or follow up a retirement, but withdrew to their original position after every fight and allowed their enemies to do the same. On the other hand they were nervous about being encircled by the Ashanti, and would retire as soon as they detected enemy behind their flanks. Unaccustomed to night attacks, they were useless as sentries as they invariably fell asleep.

No doubt to some extent the Fante were overawed by the reputation of the Ashanti, but their behaviour also reflects the different perception of warfare among many African peoples, especially those in the western and central forest zone. In the semi-ritualized conflicts which took place between neighbouring tribes the aim was usually not to inflict heavy casualties, but to satisfy honour by making a display of strength, and perhaps to acquire an enemy corpse or two so that the skull could be put on show as evidence of success. Outflanking moves, or any manoeuvre which might corner an opponent and force him to fight to the death, were deliberately avoided. The missionary J H Weeks was perhaps in a better position to understand what was going on than the officers actually involved in a campaign, who were too liable to judge their allies by their own professional standards. Weeks describes a battle which he witnessed on the Congo in 1882, which seems very reminiscent of the half-hearted clashes between Fante and Ashanti which so incensed the British. The opposing forces formed two lines in full view of each other:

> we could see a man loading his gun, then he walked forward, pointed his gun in the direction of the enemy, and fired, after which he hurried back to cover; then another went and repeated the former's action, and so on up and down the line. The lines were more than two hundred yards apart, and no fighter went in close enough to the other side for his gun to send a bullet among the enemy. The grass hid them from one another, and the only chance of damage was for two men to meet accidentally in the space between the lines, when they had gone forward to fire; but apparently they listened too carefully for every rustle in the grass.

On the other hand the Fante complained, with some justification, that the British had themselves hindered their attempts to raise an effective army. One of their kings, Quasi Kaye, when ordered to muster his troops, promised to cut off the head of any man who refused to serve, but was told that this was no longer permitted. According to Brackenbury, 'months afterwards, when his men deserted, and he was severely spoken to, he complained that he could only make his men turn out like the Ashantis if the same power were allowed to him as to the Ashanti chiefs – the power of life and death over his people.'

In fact the Ashanti were almost equally cautious. By 11 February 1873 they were only a day's march away from Cape Coast Castle, but they never attempted to exploit their advantage. Instead they plundered the Fante in the time-honoured way, inflicting occasional defeats on their enemies and moving their camps from time to time so that they could forage in untouched country, but left the coastal settlements alone. This was a missed opportunity, because the British forts were in a poor state of repair, their weapons badly maintained and the volunteers recruited to man them often under strength. Many of the difficulties were due to the prevalence of malaria and other fevers among Europeans on the coast, and to the humid tropical climate. For example, Lieutenant Colonel Festing of the Royal Marines reported after his inspection tour during the summer of 1873 that 'at Connor's Hill, the first cartridge he put his hand on in one of the gun limbers was so sodden, that water could be squeezed out of it like a sponge . . . one limber contained a well-organised ants' nest' (Brackenbury).

However, the Ashanti were unaware of these problems, and according to prisoners they were suffering from smallpox which they had picked up from the coastal tribes. Their commanders were also worried about hostile armies getting into their rear, not realizing that most of the Fante had dispersed after the recent series of defeats. Meanwhile British reinforcements were arriving piecemeal. On 13 June about 3,000 Ashanti fought a battle near Elmina against a force consisting of a detachment of 100 Royal Marines, the 2nd West India Regiment, and a company of fifty Hausas: 'the only time,' says Brackenbury, 'on which the Ashantis were ever encountered on open ground.' The Ashanti tried to use their standard outflanking tactics, but away from the cover of the forest they were too exposed to the long-range fire of the Snider rifles, so were forced to retreat into the bush before the manoeuvre was completed. Standing orders prohibited the regulars from following up into the dense forest, but the victory boosted British morale at this critical moment and helped to buy time for a counteroffensive to be organized.

The government in London had at last decided to take action, and early in September the officer chosen to solve the Ashanti problem was on his way to Africa. This was Colonel Sir Garnet Wolseley, currently assistant adjutant general under Gladstone's reforming secretary for war, Edward Cardwell. Wolseley was very junior in rank for such a mission, but he had served with distinction in Canada and was earning a reputation as an expert on colonial warfare. He was placed in command of all Her Majesty's land forces in West Africa with the local rank of major general, and was permitted to select his own staff – the genesis of the 'Ashanti Ring' which followed him throughout his career. Many of these men were officers with whom he had previously served in Canada, including Evelyn Wood, Redvers Buller and George Pomeroy-Colley. For several of them this was the start of a long but not always happy association with Africa. Buller survived his defeat by the Zulus at Hlobane in 1879, and he and Wood received knighthoods for their performance in the Zulu War. Buller was also awarded the Victoria Cross. Colley was defeated and killed by the Boers at Majuba Hill in 1881. Wolseley himself gained further glory in Zululand, in Egypt in 1882 and in the Sudan in 1885, and rose to command the entire British Army, only to be forced into retirement as a result of the disasters of 'Black Week' in the Second Boer War.

Henry Stanley, already famous as the discoverer of Livingstone, also arrived to cover the campaign as a war correspondent for the *New York Herald*. Himself a veteran of the American Civil War, Stanley had a fair grasp of military matters and had covered previous conflicts in Abyssinia, Spain and the American West. He was immediately impressed by Wolseley and considered that 'the British government could have found no worthier man' (Stanley, 1874), though the general may not have appreciated being likened to 'a first-class special correspondent' as he was known to despise journalists, 'those newly invented curses to armies, who eat the rations of fighting men and do no work at all'. Eventually, however, he came to admire Stanley, who did not see his role as a non-combatant one, and proved himself to be both cool under fire and an excellent shot.

Wolseley Takes Command

Wolseley began this, his best-known campaign, without any regular British infantry battalions under his command. The reputation of West Africa as a disease-ridden 'white man's grave' was such that the government was reluctant to deploy them unless it was absolutely unavoidable, and unless it could be guaranteed that they would not be exposed to the risk of fever for any longer than necessary. So the commander-in-chief was expected to visit the theatre of war and report back on whether he considered that they were needed. It did not take him long to make up his mind. In an engagement in the forest near Elmina in October 1873 the Ashanti were driven off, but Wolseley was not impressed by the wild firing of the Hausa troops and the quantity of ammunition which they wasted. During another encounter later in the same month he had to watch an Ashanti force march past his position unmolested, because he had too few regulars with him, and his Fante allies refused to attack. His report concluded that 'this war can never be brought to an end, except by disciplined European troops' (Brackenbury). In November the government responded by dispatching three of the best battalions in the Army: the 2nd Battalion of the Rifle Brigade, the 23rd Foot (Royal Welch Fusiliers) and the 42nd Highlanders, the Black Watch. None of these troops had any experience of West African warfare, but Wolseley already had plans for turning them into jungle-fighters.

At Elmina Wolseley had noted that although all the inexperienced troops – Royal Marines as well as Hausas – tended to fire wildly at first, the Marines eventually settled down once their officers established control. His solution was to allocate a very high proportion of officers – as many as one to every twenty men – to counteract the difficulties of command and communication in close country. This involved dividing each infantry company – which had hitherto been the smallest tactical unit – into four sections, with an officer or senior NCO in command of each. The Hausas consistently fired too high, so for them and the local levies a simplified drill was introduced, with the emphasis on aiming low and conserving ammunition. Wolseley also considered that the traditional uniform of the British redcoats was unsuitable for bush warfare, so he arranged for the issue of lighter and more comfortable grey homespun clothing, with the cork helmets which were widely believed to be essential for protection against the tropical sun. Stanley was disappointed to see that even the Black Watch had abandoned their kilts and were dressed like the rest of the infantry, in 'unpicturesque Norfolk grey' (Stanley, 1874).

Because of the risk of disease and heat exhaustion, great care was taken to ensure that rations were adequate, and orders were issued that white soldiers were not to be used for labouring duties. Another serious problem to be overcome was the shortage of men to carry supplies. As pack or draught animals could not survive in the jungle, the only means of transporting goods was on the heads of civilian carriers, but most of the local recruits had deserted through fear of the Ashanti. Some of the British regulars volunteered to take their places, but Wolseley put a stop to this, fearing that their health would be undermined before they could be committed to battle. So Colonel Colley was put in charge of transport, and imposed a system of military discipline on the carriers. In practice this meant adopting methods which would no longer have been considered acceptable in Europe. Men were conscripted at gunpoint, and sometimes the adult populations of whole villages were taken by naval landing parties acting as press gangs. But Wolseley justified this on the grounds of military necessity, and Colley's methods worked.

Artillery support was provided mainly by light 7-pounder field guns, and more modern versions of the rocket launchers which had proved their worth nearly fifty years earlier. Wolseley also had a single Gatling gun brought up as far as the River Prah, but its size and weight (it came complete with an artillery carriage and caisson, which altogether weighed 400lb) prevented it accompanying the expedition any further, and it did not see action. It was, however, demonstrated for the benefit of some visiting Ashanti envoys. The gun was still something of a novelty even to many British officers, and when it at first failed to fire there were mutterings to the effect that the crew would be more use if given rifles. But when a second ammunition drum was fitted the Gatling fired off all its ammunition in a single burst, so impressing the Ashanti that one of them later committed suicide rather than report this ominous experience to King Kofi.

But the most important of Wolseley's secret weapons was quinine. Although the cause of malaria was still unknown, the value of this extract of a South American bark in treating the fever was well established, and the Portuguese had been growing it on the offshore island of São Tomé for centuries. But its use to prevent rather than cure illness was still the subject of debate. Ignorant of the role of the mosquito, early investigators found that the risk of fever fluctuated in unpredictable ways, and this made it difficult to establish the correct dosage. In fact explorers such as David Livingstone adulterated their quinine with all sorts of other substances which later turned out to be useless, and suffered unnecessarily as a result. Dr William Baikie's 1854 expedition up the Niger River was the first in the region on which none of the Europeans died of malaria, and he reported that this success was due to the liberal use of quinine not only to cure fever but to reduce the risk of catching it. Building on this growing body of knowledge, Wolseley was able to order the first large-scale issue of quinine to British troops as a preventive measure. This was not a perfect solution to the problem; there were still some cases of malaria, and other men suffered deafness from an overdose of the drug, but this was the first time that troops from outside Africa had been able to operate at all for long periods in the rainforest, and the relatively small number of losses from disease was one of the outstanding successes of the campaign.

By the end of 1873 the Ashanti armies had withdrawn north of the Prah, the long-awaited road from the coast was under construction, and preparations were being made to concentrate the troops at Prahsu on the south bank of the river, ready to advance on Kumasi. The country ahead of them was virtually unknown to Europeans, and the scanty information available was daunting. Captain Brackenbury was scathing about the so-called local knowledge of the traders and garrison commanders stationed on the coast. When Wolseley consulted them about conditions inland he received a variety of advice. 'It was almost universally represented that the first thirty miles inland were a dead level – a belt of swampy jungle,' reported Brackenbury. But in fact almost from the shoreline the country consisted of countless small rounded hills, intersected by deep gullies. It transpired that few of these advisers had ever been inland, and the maps available were fifty years out of date. A minority agreed that an advance on Kumasi was feasible, but 'a very large majority displayed the gloomiest prospects, and pronounced the bush so deadly, that Europeans could not march through it and live . . . . Our men would march into ambushes, whence there would be no escape. Surrounded on all sides, they would be shot down in the narrow paths upon which alone they could advance.'

One of the best descriptions of the nature of the terrain encountered during the campaign comes from Stanley's dispatches. Near the coast the bush (Stanley preferred the term 'jungle') was mostly secondary growth, having once been cleared for farming. There were few large trees, but the undergrowth was so dense and tangled as to be virtually impassable. 'Fancy an untrimmed English hedge, if you can,' says Stanley, 'fifteen and twenty feet high, scores of miles in depth, where you see only an innumerable variety of brushwood and plants trying to overgrow one another' (Stanley, 1874). A few miles inland, where the soil was sandier and less fertile, the bush was slightly less thick and a greater variety of trees began to appear. Eventually, by the time the River Prah was reached, big trees dominated and their shade inhibited the undergrowth in the interior of the forest, making it possible to cut a way through it. Where roads and clearings allowed light to penetrate, however, the vegetation formed a solid green wall just as impassable as the coastal bush, and even the Ashanti were sometimes forced to keep to the highways. In other places the edges of the jungle were just passable to a half-naked musketeer with minimal equipment, enabling him to shoot from cover while being completely invisible even from a few feet away.

The Battle of Amoaful and the March on Kumasi

It was the next phase of the campaign that attracted most of the public attention at home, and has continued to do so ever since. This is understandable, as until then the well-known British infantry regiments had not been engaged, but Brackenbury – who served throughout the war – felt that, compared with the earlier fighting south of the Prah, the march on Kumasi was 'a pleasant picnic'. By early 1874 the country was better known, better equipment was available and there were more regular officers to share the work. Furthermore the climate was now cooler and drier than in the wet season between October and December. Wolseley, however, continued with his methodical policy, resting the troops as much as possible, stockpiling rations and ensuring that the roads were adequate for the supply caravans before moving on. Stanley's dispatches at this time reveal his growing disillusionment with what he saw as Wolseley's dilatory approach. 'There is no fighting spirit left in the King of Ashantee,' he informed his readers, 'and [the campaign] is destined to end in a peaceful parade at Coomassie' (Stanley, 1874). He thought that the general was waiting too long to allow supplies to catch up, and exposing the white soldiers to unnecessary risks from disease. He sympathized with officers who were 'pining and fretting at delays', but concluded that their frustration might ultimately be a good thing, as when the order to move did come they would 'drive their men forward with astonishing vigour'. Actually this criticism tells us as much about Stanley as it does about Wolseley. The explorer's own expeditions invariably suffered enormous wastage from sickness and desertion, mainly due to his 'astonishing vigour' in driving the men on forced marches, and to his carelessness about supply arrangements.

In any case, this time Stanley's military assessment was wrong. When the army did make its move, on 5 January 1874, there was no peaceful parade to Kumasi. King Kofi's strategy was well thought out. A screen of skirmishers retired slowly in front of Wolseley's force, luring it onto a strong defensive position at the village of Amoaful, 20 miles from the capital. Here an Ashanti army of around 20,000 men was assembled under Kofi's best general, Amanquatia. Once the British were fully engaged trying to break through, the plan was for the wings of the Ashanti army to employ their traditional envelopment tactics, surrounding Wolseley in the jungle while a detachment captured the bridge at Prahsu and cut his lines of communication. Wolseley, however, was aware of the danger, and on 31 January he approached the position in a formation resembling a large square, with the Rifle Brigade in the rear tasked specifically with preventing encirclement. The front face of the square consisted of the Black Watch, which advanced with two companies in front and six in support, with two 7-pounder guns in the centre and rocket launchers on each flank.

As they approached the village of Egginassie, less than a mile from Amoaful, the Highlanders came under ineffective long-range fire, so their commander, Brigadier General Alison, deployed the two leading companies into line and attacked. When they got to close quarters with the enemy hidden in the bush, casualties mounted and the attack stalled, so two more companies were sent out to the left to outflank the village. This party got lost in the jungle and had to return, but the concentrated battalion, supported by a Hausa company and some local levies, pressed on and eventually cleared Egginassie, though casualties were so high that a request had to be sent back for more surgeons. Alison recalled that:

The peculiarities of Ashanti warfare were now strongly developed. We were in the midst of a semi-circle of hostile fire, and we hardly ever caught sight of a man. As company after company of the 42nd descended with their pipes playing into the ravine, they were almost immediately lost sight of in the bush, and their position could only be judged from the sharp crack of their rifles, in contrast to the loud, dull boom of the Ashanti musketry. (Brackenbury)

Soon the battle became a series of disconnected skirmishes as small parties on both sides, unable to communicate with their comrades in the thick jungle, fired blindly at each other's smoke. But the small unit tactics introduced by Wolseley worked well, and slowly the advance continued. The Royal Welch Fusiliers were sent up to maintain contact with the Highlanders, while 200 yards behind them the Rifle Brigade still guarded the rear. Both these units were soon engaged with enemy detachments attempting to encircle them. Meanwhile the Black Watch fought their way through a swamp and found a clear space on the other side where the artillery could be deployed, so a 7-pounder was brought up and fired canister into the bush at a range of 50 yards. The Ashanti could not stand against this and fell back to another position immediately in front of Amoaful, but the gun was moved forward again, and this time they broke. Although most of their firing was more or less blind, the 7-pounders were capable of extraordinary accuracy when a target did present itself. Stanley saw an escaping Ashanti chief and his escort picked off by a gun commanded by a Lieutenant Saunders, which exploded a shell 'a few inches above their heads'. Fighting continued for a while on both flanks, but when the Ashanti flanking parties learned of the defeat of the main body they gradually fell back. Their losses were estimated at 2,000–3,000, including Amanquatia himself and the subordinate King of Mampon. The Black Watch had suffered 25 per cent casualties, but astonishingly only two were actually killed in action (though some died later of wounds), and one of those had been beheaded after being wounded while advancing ahead of his comrades.

At Ordahsu, 5 miles from Kumasi, the Ashanti tried another envelopment manoeuvre. It succeeded as planned: the road back to the Prah was cut and the abandoned British camp occupied, but Wolseley's square was now facing outwards in all directions, with the supply train inside it, and it continued to press on slowly towards its objective. This must have bewildered the Ashanti commanders, because in traditional warfare an encircled army invariably accepted defeat. Instead the Black Watch charged forward with the bayonet, brushing aside a series of ambushes in what General Alison called 'one of the finest spectacles I have ever seen in war' (Brackenbury). Soon the road was littered with discarded equipment as the defenders fled towards their capital, followed by the Highlanders. The scene in Kumasi as Alison's men marched in must have been extraordinary. Although the town was still occupied, neither side fired a shot. Instead the Ashanti were collecting their weapons and ammunition before pulling out, and Alison was not strong enough to risk provoking another fight.

At the same time as Wolseley prepared to march on Kumasi an entirely separate expedition – though nominally under his command – had been mounted under Captain Glover, a Royal Navy officer who had a great deal of experience with the local tribes. His mission was to recruit a cadre of Hausa soldiers from Nigeria, supplement them with Yoruba levies, and sail up the River Volta to attack Kumasi from the east. (In another reversion to old-fashioned methods which would hardly have been approved of at home, Glover actually bought many of his Hausas in the local slave markets.) Although mainly intended as a diversion, the expedition made an important contribution to Wolseley's victory by occupying a large Ashanti army under the King of Juabin. When battle was joined at Amoaful this army was only 30 miles away on Wolseley's right flank, and its intervention could well have turned the tide, but it dared not move with the Nigerians threatening its front, and eventually surrendered to Glover when King Kofi evacuated Kumasi. This brought the campaign to an end, and Wolseley was relieved to be able to withdraw his army before the rainy season brought increased risk of fever and turned the roads into swamps.

Although celebrated by the war correspondents and the British government as a great victory, with hindsight the war appears less of a triumph. King Kofi had temporarily lost his capital and agreed to the terms offered by the British, but in practice his country's independence had been preserved. Wolseley admitted that he would not have dared to risk another battle because of his mounting casualties. Of the 2,500 regular troops deployed, 68 had been killed, nearly 400 had been wounded and over 1,000 were sick. Officer losses were even higher: of the 36 on the commander's staff, only one – the indestructible Brackenbury – was still fit when the march back to the coast began. No wonder Wolseley later described it as 'the most horrible war I ever took part in'.

Muskets versus Rifles

It is impossible to understand the course of this campaign without attempting to assess the effectiveness of Ashanti musketry. The Ashanti consistently outnumbered their regular opponents, and on many occasions they managed to approach close enough under cover of the jungle to open fire at point-blank range. Several eyewitness reports confirm that they knew how to fire from the shoulder and take proper aim, and to fire volleys on a word of command. And yet they failed to inflict the casualties which might have been expected. Many British accounts describe leaves and twigs falling from the trees during a firefight, 'as thick as flakes in a snowstorm' (Stanley, 1874), which implies that despite their attempts at drill their opponents were still firing too high. Wounds were nevertheless common, but were often too slight to put the victim out of action. Stanley describes men with black eyes, or chunks cut out of their beards by Ashanti slugs, who still remained on their feet. Brackenbury refers to 'such slight touches by slugs as the officers took no notice of'. Evelyn Wood was hit near the heart by a nail at Amoaful, but quickly recovered. Later Wolseley himself was struck on the head, but the slug did not penetrate his cork helmet. This requires explanation, as even obsolete Dane guns could be deadly if the range was close enough. During the retreat from Kumasi in the campaign of 1900, an attempt was made to armour the hammocks in which the sick and wounded were carried with sheets of corrugated iron. According to one witness this experiment was abandoned because not only were the sheets too heavy to carry, but when they were tested by 'friendly native levies' firing at various ranges, the slugs went through them 'as if they were paper' (Hodgson).

The poor quality of the weapons and powder supplied to African armies has already been discussed. The Ashanti tried to counteract this by loading with as much powder as possible, then placing whatever improvised ammunition was available loose on the top. This meant that their muskets were effectively used as shotguns, discharging a hail of assorted projectiles which would quickly spread out on leaving the muzzle, each one propelled by only a fraction of the energy of the charge. The use of pieces of scrap metal instead of lead shot was not necessarily due to a lack of proper ammunition. In June 1873 an interpreter reported that two dead Ashanti left behind after a skirmish had been carrying oddly shaped pieces of iron – apparently taken from doors and shutters in captured villages – instead of conventional shot for their muskets (*British Parliamentary Papers*, vol. 58). He had at first assumed that this indicated that the enemy was already suffering from shortages, but was told by the local people that they were well supplied with lead shot. Instead these improvised projectiles were deliberately issued to men 'in the hottest part of the fight', 'as the most destructive and hurtful'. No doubt the Ashanti soldiers were expected to open fire at such short range that the damage done to those struck by these jagged chunks of metal would outweigh their inferior ballistic properties.

On the other hand, although the Snider rifle used by the British was sighted to much longer ranges than the Ashanti muskets could achieve, this was not its only advantage. Being a breech-loader it could be reloaded and fired much more rapidly, and its high-velocity rounds were less easily deflected by vegetation, so that even firing blind into the bush they could inflict casualties 200–300 yards away. The Ashanti always tried to carry away their dead and wounded after a fight, so it was never possible to establish exactly what their losses had been, but there can have been few minor wounds from a .577in. Snider bullet. In a pamphlet distributed to the troops, Wolseley claimed that one soldier with a Snider was equal to twenty 'wretchedly armed' Ashanti musketeers (Vandervort). This was admittedly intended to boost the men's morale, but after the campaign Stanley and others also praised the rifle's 'terrible force and penetration' (Stanley, 1874), as proved by the wounds inflicted on those Ashanti dead who were found after the battles.

Another war correspondent, Winwood Reade, admitted to taking cover in front of a tree at Amoaful, believing that the danger from stray rounds fired from the British rear positions was greater than that from the close-range volleys of the enemy. Reade also has some interesting comments on the contemporary controversy over the merits of shotguns for bush fighting, as recommended by Samuel Baker after his experiences in Bunyoro (see Chapter 4). Reade agrees that as a lone traveller he would have preferred to take a shotgun for self-defence against ambushes, but says that having seen the Snider in action he believed that rifles were far more effective when used en masse. Wolseley is said to have admitted that if the enemy had had Sniders he would never have taken Kumasi, and Richard Burton (1876) dismissed the whole campaign as 'a poor scuffle between the breechloader and the Birmingham trade musket'. (Although still known on the coast as 'Dane guns', by the late nineteenth century most of the muskets were indeed made in Birmingham.)

Nevertheless the British had learned some hard lessons. According to Stanley the infantry officers realized that they had sustained unnecessary casualties at Amoaful by following the standard British Army doctrine, first identifying their targets and then engaging them with deliberate, aimed shots. 'Fire slow, fire low' was an order frequently given. At Ordahsu they changed their tactics in favour of what would nowadays be called 'suppressive fire'. As soon as they came under fire the men would now lie down and shoot as rapidly as possible into the bush, not waiting to see their targets, but aiming about a foot above the ground. Wolseley approved this method on the grounds that the expenditure of ammunition was more than compensated for by the lives saved, as the enemy were quickly driven from their positions by the sheer weight of fire.

It may seem surprising that the Ashanti made no attempt to upgrade their arsenal with more modern weapons. One reason was that by the time better guns came onto the market in the 1860s and 1870s, their British and Fante enemies controlled the coastal trade, cutting the kingdom off from the most direct source of supply. It is also unlikely that the Ashanti commanders were aware of their disadvantage until it was too late. They understood that they could not defeat rifle-armed regulars in the open, but before 1874 the regulars had never followed them up into dense jungle, and they probably still believed that their own soldiers could meet them on equal terms in such close country. King Kofi's predecessor, Kwaku Dua, had once dismissed the threat of the British artillery with the remark that 'the white man brings his cannons to the forest, but the bush is stronger than the cannons' (Ellis). It has often been noted that the Ashanti had a long history of encounters with Europeans, and that unlike many more isolated African peoples they were not overawed by the shock of encountering the white men and their weapons. However, this may have worked against them, as most of the whites they had encountered so far had been merchants or officers in command of native troops. That

British soldiers could actually fight in African conditions was not necessarily obvious to either side before Wolseley's demonstration.
Furthermore, Ashanti commanders seem not to have realized that a
British army of the 1870s was a very different proposition from its predecessor fifty years earlier. Not only had its weapons improved, but its
supply arrangements were more efficient, and medical advances could
now keep white troops in the field even in areas notorious for fever. It may
be significant that before the 1873 invasion, when King Kofi approached
the neighbouring state of Dahomey to suggest an alliance against the
British, he was rebuffed. The Dahomeans were renowned warriors, and
being in closer contact with coastal traders they had modernized their
weaponry to a much greater extent, but they had seen enough of
Europeans to know that even fighting together the Africans could not win.

The War of 1900

Ashanti power never fully recovered from the blow which Wolseley had
dealt it. Internal political divisions further weakened the kingdom, and in
1896 the British again invaded, this time not so much because the Ashanti
were still a threat as for fear that the French might take over the region.
They met with no resistance, and King Prempeh I, who had refused them
permission to build a fort at Kumasi, was arrested and sent into exile,
ostensibly for failing to pay the reparations which Kofi had promised in
1874. The fort was built and garrisoned by Hausas led by British officers,
and an official British resident was installed. The king's stone palace was
demolished to provide the materials for the fort, which was square in
shape, with a rounded bastion at each corner incorporating a platform for
a Maxim gun or light field gun. The only entrance, on the south side, was
via a pair of bullet-proof iron gates. The surrounding buildings had been
cleared to provide a good field of fire, and, with the demolition of the
palace and the old place of human sacrifice, very little of the once-
impressive town was left standing.

Naturally many Ashanti resented the occupation and the destruction
of their ancient capital, but it was not until March 1900 that they rose in
revolt, apparently provoked by a bizarre diplomatic gaffe, in what became
known as the War of the Golden Stool. Sir Frederick Hodgson, the
governor of the Gold Coast, visited Kumasi in person to insist on payment
of the reparations, and added for good measure the demand that the

Golden Stool of Ashanti should be produced for him, as the Queen's representative, to sit on. (Lady Hodgson, who was present, denied that he had ever suggested sitting on it, but notes for his speech published later in a government blue book do include this demand.) To the Ashanti this was not just insulting, but blasphemous. The stool was an important symbol of the power of the Ashanti monarch, and Hodgson presumably supposed that it had the same function as a throne would have in Europe. This was a grave mistake, because the Golden Stool was believed to have been sent directly from heaven and was sacred to the Ashanti's ancestors. Even the king had never dared to sit on it. Hodgson's audience trickled away quietly, and it was still not realized how much offence had been given. It had also been supposed that in the absence of King Prempeh the chiefs would not take action, but the Queen Mother, Nana Yaa Asantewa, was still in Kumasi, and she urged her people to fight rather than allow the stool to be taken.

The relic had been hidden somewhere in the bush, and Hodgson dispatched a party under Captain Armitage, the chief commissioner of Ashanti, to find it. Armitage was ambushed and lost twenty men, but he escaped back to Kumasi under cover of a rainstorm. There he found Hodgson besieged in the fort with his wife, four subordinate Ashanti kings who had remained loyal, and a group of white missionaries, traders and civil servants. The garrison consisted of only 300 Hausa askaris, but they were supported by the firepower of six 7-pounder field guns and four Maxim machine guns. On 29 April the Ashanti launched an all-out assault, but were repulsed with heavy losses and settled down to blockade the fort. The recently constructed telegraph line to the coast had been cut and Ashanti patrols intercepted many of the messengers who tried to get through to the coast, but a request for help did somehow arrive at Cape Coast, and a column of 250 men was sent to relieve the defenders. Unfortunately their carriers deserted en masse, so they were unable to bring up food or ammunition, both of which were running short. In fact they only just got through themselves, with half of their number sick or wounded by Ashanti snipers.

The only contribution of this relief force to the defence was to eat up the rations even faster, and Lady Hodgson described graphically how they were now forced to live on tinned meat which had been stored for four years in the West African climate, and biscuits 'that even at this distance of time make one shudder to think of'. However, despite the undoubted sufferings of the besieged, there were indications that the Ashanti were reluctant to destroy them altogether. Lady Hodgson noted that, although the fort's main water supply came from a well 50 yards outside the walls, the rebels never attempted to poison the water or to interfere with parties sent out to collect it. Later, during the Hodgsons' retreat to the coast, they expected the blockading forces to converge on their column as soon as its escape was detected, but this never happened. Probably the Ashanti leadership was aware that if they wiped out the garrison and killed the governor they would be inviting severe retaliation, but hoped that if they merely drove them out of the country the British government might accept the fait accompli.

In June another relief force reached Kumasi, this time numbering 700 men, but like its predecessor it had been dispatched in haste, and now had to march through the rainy season, which made paths impassable and brought outbreaks of malaria. Far from being able to resupply the defenders, it had barely enough food to sustain itself on the march. On 23 June, Hodgson and Armitage broke out with most of the fit troops, leaving Captain Bishop behind, with rations for three weeks and about 100 of the less fit who were still able to fight, to look after the civilians and the sick. The Ashanti had built wooden stockades to block the escape routes, but the British force broke through the barrier on the road leading to the south and began a 140-mile retreat. Luckily for them the rains were less heavy than usual and the Ashanti pursuit was slow, but local villagers set up more barricades along the road, and small parties of rebels sniped at them from the cover of the dense forest. The porters became so weak from starvation that all the baggage had to be abandoned. After sixteen days the column finally reached safety with a loss of around 120 dead, wounded or missing.

Meanwhile a proper relief column had at last been organized, led by Major James Willcocks, the commanding officer of the West Africa Frontier Force (WAFF), which was recruited mainly among the Yorubas of Nigeria. Altogether 1,000 askaris had been assembled from throughout West Africa, including detachments from the 1st and 2nd West India Regiments, the WAFF and the Sierra Leone Frontier Police. Six field guns and the same number of Maxims provided unprecedented firepower. Wolseley had always argued that even African troops could not operate in the bush outside the dry season without risking heavy losses from fever, but Willcocks did not have the option of waiting. Hodgson had reported that the garrison at Kumasi would have consumed all its rations by 15 July. It was noted by several observers that in this war the Ashanti no longer manoeuvred in large armies, but fought in smaller bands using mostly defensive tactics. The stockades which they erected across the roads were another new feature of this campaign. They had long been a feature of warfare in Sierra Leone and surrounding areas, but had not been encountered in the war of 1873–74, and it was widely believed that the Ashanti had learned to make these stockades from deserters among the Sierra Leonean contingents brought to the Gold Coast by the British in 1896.

The British Army was also learning from experience and developing new tactics. In an appendix to their 1901 book on the war of 1900, Captain Armitage and Lieutenant Colonel Montanaro – both veterans of the campaign – set out some rules for operations in West Africa which encapsulate the lessons learned from fighting the Ashanti and similar opponents. Supplies were always a problem, because little food was available locally even if the people were friendly, so the native carriers were just as important to the success of an expedition as the fighting troops. They should therefore be organized along military lines, into 'battalions' of about 1,000 men, commanded by British officers and NCOs. A battalion was divided into ten companies, each under a native 'captain', each of which in turn consisted of five 'gangs' of twenty men each. The writers recommend the use of 75mm field guns in preference to the much lighter 7-pounders, as the former could damage wooden stockades which were invulnerable to the latter's shells, but admit that this made the logistic problem much worse. A 7-pounder gun required twelve carriers for the gun, carriage and limber, plus another ten for ammunition, but the 75mm and its ammunition required sixty-two men altogether. By contrast, a Maxim and its ammunition could be carried by only eight porters.

A marching column should always be prepared to encounter an ambush, and the authors distinguish between a purely defensive ambush, which consisted simply of a concealed defensive position blocking a road or track, and an 'offensive defensive ambush', in which most of the enemy force would be waiting parallel to the road to attack the column as soon as it was halted by the blocking detachment in front. A British column would usually have to proceed in single file along the narrow jungle paths, so it was particularly important for all units to stay within sight of each other and maintain communication at all times. In 1900 this had often been done by bugle calls, but these gave away the column's position to the enemy, so it was eventually found best to post men in between each unit, with the task of preventing their losing contact and carrying messages between them if necessary. It had also been discovered that a commanding officer marching in the middle of a column was often unable to get to the front if it ran into opposition because of congestion on the track, so he should instead station himself immediately behind the advance guard. Field guns or Maxims should be well to the front, and should open suppressive fire – using case shot or shrapnel in the case of field guns – as soon as shooting started, without waiting to identify targets visually.

The best counter to ambush tactics, however, was to deploy flanking parties, who would cut a path into the bush for about 30 yards at right angles to the line of march, then move parallel to the main column. This would place them on the flanks of any enemy lying along the edge of the path, and enable them to get behind any stockades which might have been constructed parallel to it as cover for the ambushers. These stockades were exceptionally well camouflaged, but were usually situated close to villages to ensure a water supply, so scouts should be especially vigilant near a village or cultivated fields. Enemy positions were also sometimes given away by 'Jujus' or fetishes placed on the path nearby. These were intended to invoke magic against an attacker, and might consist of a sacrificed chicken, puppy or even a human being, though by 1900 the Ashanti appear to have abandoned the human sacrifice for which they had once been notorious.

It is often alleged that the Ashanti of 1900 were better armed than they had been in 1874, but although witnesses occasionally mention breech-loading rifles, it is clear that the vast majority still used the old-fashioned smoothbores. Certainly they could not seriously hope to stop a force with the firepower of Willcocks's column. The Maxim gun especially had revolutionized colonial warfare since its baptism of fire in the Gambia in 1888, as it was more portable than Wolseley's Gatling and had both a longer range and a higher rate of fire. But the dense bush provided few fields of fire for long-range weapons, and the Ashanti refused to oblige

Willcocks by attacking him en masse. In any case he could not afford the time for a cautious approach, and on several occasions he was forced to order his infantry to attack enemy stockades without artillery support. At the town of Kokofu he was repulsed with heavy casualties, but bypassed it and continued the advance on Kumasi, collecting some loyal Ashanti allies on the way. He found the besiegers waiting for him behind four huge stockades perfectly placed to block his advance, on high ground covered with thick jungle which concealed them from his artillery. With only two days to go before Bishop's garrison was due to run out of food, Willcocks ordered his Yorubas to fix bayonets and charge. Although perhaps born more of desperation than of careful military planning, this tactic proved entirely successful. As the major concluded in his report, although they were well prepared for a firefight, 'Ashantis will not await arrival of bayonet charge' (Hernan). One by one the stockades were cleared, and on 15 July the defenders of Kumasi, many now too weak to stand, were finally relieved.

The final battle was fought on 30 September 1900, at the town of Obassa. The rebels had surrounded their encampment with the usual wooden stockades, but were taken by surprise by the arrival of a column commanded by Lieutenant Colonel Morland, comprising 800 African and Sikh troops and three guns. The enemy rushed to occupy their defences, but a company of Hausas led by Major C J Melliss of the Indian Staff Corps got there first and shot the Ashanti down from the cover of their own stockade. Morland's men then followed them up as they retreated into the town and routed them with no loss to themselves. Thirty Ashanti were killed, and large stocks of guns and ammunition were captured. Major Melliss was awarded the Victoria Cross for this action. The citation is preserved in The National Archives in London, and sheds some interesting light on what actually happened at the sharp end in this sort of bush fighting. It also hints that the battle did not go quite as smoothly as Willcocks's report suggests. According to this document, Melliss gathered a scratch force of stragglers and charged at their head, with drawn sword, into an area of dense bush where the enemy were making a stand. He became involved in a hand-to-hand fight with an Ashanti soldier, stabbing him with his sword and struggling with him on the ground, until a second Ashanti shot the major through the foot. He was only saved when a party of Sikhs charged and routed the enemy, who were already shaken by his wild rush. It may seem strange to a modern reader that a senior officer should be decorated for his involvement in a brawl of this nature, but this is another example of the different rules which had to be applied to bush fighting. British officers of all ranks were expected to lead by example, and where visibility was so limited this could mean coming to very close quarters with the enemy.

This was the last major engagement of the Ashanti wars. By the end of 1900 the last of the hostile chiefs, including Nana Yaa Asantewa, had surrendered. The Ashanti kingdom was incorporated into the Gold Coast colony, and now forms part of the independent state of Ghana, but the people still retain their ancient monarchy and a measure of self-government. The British never did find the Golden Stool.

Sources
The most comprehensive and authoritative source for the 1873–74 campaign is Brackenbury. The author was a participant in most of the events he describes, and also had access to the relevant official documents. The British Parliamentary Papers series also contains some interesting material on everything from political deliberations to small unit tactics. Stanley (*Coomassie and Magdala*) and Winwood Reade supply some interesting local colour and tactical snippets. Unfortunately Stanley is at his most pompous in this book on the campaign, and some of his criticisms of Wolseley all too obviously stem from his own impatience. Maxwell's study of Wolseley's 'Ashanti Ring' includes a good modern narrative. Armitage and Montanaro attempt with some success to do for the 1900 campaign what Brackenbury did for the earlier war. Lady Hodgson's account of the siege of Kumasi is very readable and contains numerous useful tactical snippets, although she accepts no criticism of her husband's role in the conflict.

Chapter Four

'That Inhuman Fiend':
Kabarega's Twenty-Seven-Year War

It is perhaps inevitable that the attention of the public at home in Europe – then as now – should focus on short and spectacular campaigns such as the Zulu and Ashanti Wars. But few African peoples had the manpower or the type of military discipline needed to stand up to a European army on a conventional battlefield. Native resistance more often took the form of protracted guerrilla warfare, exploiting inhospitable terrain to delay and frustrate an invader, and presenting him with a diffuse target which could not be crushed simply by the occupation of territory or the capture of a capital. Using such methods, the people of Bunyoro under their king Kabarega had been defying would-be conquerors long before the Zulus took up arms, and were still doing so almost twenty years afterwards. The kingdom of Bunyoro (known to most nineteenth-century Europeans by the Swahili version of the name, Unyoro) was located on the Upper Nile, north of Lake Victoria and east of Lake Albert, in what is now northern Uganda. This was a transitional zone between the pastoral tribes of the southern Sudan and the sophisticated kingdoms of the Central African lakes region, of which the most important was Bunyoro's southern neighbour Buganda, situated on the shore of Lake Victoria.

The existence of these kingdoms, with their strict social hierarchies and complex systems of government in a region so remote from the outside world, was a puzzle to early explorers. Europeans were reluctant to believe that the local Africans were capable of developing such things on their own, and claimed to detect the legacy of immigrants from the ancient centres of civilization in Egypt or Ethiopia. Neither local tradition nor modern anthropological studies provide any support for these theories, but there was a grain of truth in the idea of outside influence in the region. Like several of the neighbouring kingdoms, Bunyoro was a so-called 'Bahima' state, in which the population (collectively referred to as

'Banyoro') was divided between a farming caste of local origin, the Bairu, and an aristocracy of Bahima cattle-herders who had migrated from the north at some unknown date. The country had once been at the heart of a larger empire, known as Bunyoro-Kitara, and its ancient monarchy still possessed immense prestige: the Banyoro historian J W Nyakatura gives details of elaborate coronation rituals and the strictly prescribed routines of the king's daily life, which bear comparison with Louis XIV's court at Versailles. Since its peak in the seventeenth century, however, Bunyoro's military power had gradually been eclipsed by that of Buganda. Another setback was the secession of the rich and populous province of Toro, which had gained independence in the 1820s, and whose recovery was to be an overriding aim of Banyoro foreign policy for the rest of the century.

In September 1862, during the reign of the *omukama*, or king, Kyebambe IV Kamrasi, the country's isolation was broken by the arrival of the first Europeans. These were the explorers John Speke and James Grant, who arrived from the south via Lake Victoria and Buganda. They were followed by Samuel and Florence Baker, travelling via the Sudan, in February 1864. These explorers were inevitably ignorant of local politics, and they unwittingly intruded on a civil war between Kamrasi and his brother Rionga. Both sides had allied themselves with parties of Turkish slavers from the Sudan, and put pressure on Speke and Baker to join in the conflict as well. In their published accounts the harassed explorers complained bitterly of the delays and hardships which Kamrasi inflicted on them in pursuit of this policy, leaving the British public with an impression of the king as devious and untrustworthy. Baker particularly had bad memories of Bunyoro. Kamrasi, apparently suspecting that the presence of his wife meant that he intended to settle in the country, was reluctant to supply him with either food or porters, so Samuel and Florence had been forced to remain under virtual house arrest for nearly a year, and eventually had to requisition supplies by the threat of force in order to avoid starvation. The result was a legacy of mutual suspicion which was eventually to have disastrous consequences.

The Succession of Kabarega

Kamrasi died in 1869, and in accordance with tradition his surviving brothers met to decide who should perform the ritual of burying his jawbone, and so succeed him. Kamrasi's own nominee, his son Kabarega (otherwise referred to as Kabba Rega or Kabalega), was supported by Prince Nyaika and most of the common people, while a party headed by Prince Omudaya backed a rival claimant, Kabigumire. For the ensuing campaigns we are dependent on oral tradition, which provides no tactical details, but Kabarega quickly proved to be an able commander. He annihilated two armies sent against him in quick succession, then counter-attacked and routed Omudaya. Unfortunately the latter escaped with Kamrasi's body, and the war dragged on for six more months. Slave traders from the Sudan were again invited to supply troops to both sides. Eventually Kabarega defeated Kabigumire at the Battle of Buziba, recovered the corpse, and had himself crowned as Omukama Chwa II Kabarega. There then followed brief campaigns against the slavers, who demanded half the kingdom as a reward for their support and had to be driven out, and then against an army from neighbouring Ankole which invaded in an attempt to restore Kabigumire. The invaders were defeated with such heavy losses that the Ankole king refused to provide his protege with any more troops, but Kabigumire did not give up, and fighting continued for another year until he was finally defeated and killed. This left Kabarega in un-disputed control of the Banyoro heartland, though his father's old rival Rionga remained effectively independent in the north.

Kabarega's Army

The population of Bunyoro in the nineteenth century was probably not much more than 100,000 – about a tenth of that of its neighbour Buganda. Inevitably, therefore, military organization played a large role in the life of the kingdom. The total numbers of troops available were, according to Baker (1873), 'impossible to guess', but certainly a high proportion of the total manpower could be mobilized, and mercenaries were often hired from elsewhere to supplement the local levies. An equally important factor in Bunyoro's protracted resistance to its enemies was its geographical remoteness. Until the British established a secure base in Uganda in the 1890s, any approach from the south had to traverse hundreds of miles of poverty-stricken bush country, a journey which could take many months if not years. A few explorers did get through, but they did so either with small parties, relying on the co-operation of the local rulers as

Speke did, or at the cost of enormous losses to disease, starvation and exhaustion.

The northern approach, up the Nile from the Sudan, seemed an easier proposition on the map, and this was the route taken by Baker. It was much shorter, and river transport should in theory have been able to solve the supply problem, but navigating the Nile had its own special difficulties. North (downstream) of Bunyoro the river enters a huge swamp known as the Sudd, where the channel is frequently clogged with masses of floating vegetation thick enough to bring even a modern steamer to a halt. Flotillas of boats were sometimes stuck there for months in stifling heat, at the mercy of swarms of malarial mosquitoes. Baker (1866), in his account of his 1864 expedition, gives a vivid picture of the hardships endured in crossing the Sudd: 'malaria, marshes, mosquitoes, misery; far as the eye can reach, vast treeless marshes perfectly lifeless. At times progressing slowly by towing, the men struggling through the water with the rope . . . it is a heartbreaking river without a single redeeming point; I do not wonder at the failure of all expeditions in this wretched country.' Not until about 1900 did the British authorities in the Sudan manage to clear a permanent channel for river traffic, and until then lines of communication through the Sudd remained precarious.

Another of Bunyoro's strengths was its lack of a physical focus whose occupation might force the people into submission. There were no paved roads, no bridges or other infrastructure, and even the royal capital was only a large village which could be quickly relocated if threatened. The pre-eminence of cattle in the economy further reduced its vulnerability, as in the event of invasion the herds could be driven to safety with relative ease. And yet in other respects the country had the characteristics of a centralized state, organized around the almost sacred person of the king. Legally the whole country was the king's personal property, though in practice it operated as a loose confederation of provinces or *saza*, ruled by chiefs known as 'the king's spears'. The army was a mass levy drawn from both the Bahima and Bairu populations – in contrast to most other Bahima states, where the Bairu were not permitted to bear arms. Most of the troops served as provincial levies, the *obwesengeze*, who were called up when required through their *saza* chiefs. Promotion, even up to the level of army commander, seems to have been by merit, based on military ability rather than tribal origin or social class. By the late 1860s the levies were supplemented by a small standing army, recruited in part from mercenaries, which Baker calls the 'bonosoora' (referred to elsewhere as 'barasura' or 'wara sura'). According to Baker (1874) this unit was 1,000 strong in 1872, but it grew rapidly in strength after that. In 1885 the Egyptian governor Emin Pasha mentioned 3,000 bonosoora, and by the 1890s they numbered 20,000, organized into ten divisions or *ebitongole* of varying size. The founding of this standing army is generally attributed to Kabarega, but Baker had encountered a bodyguard of 500 men in Kamrasi's service in 1864. This may have been the precursor of the bonosoora, though Baker says that Kamrasi's guards were used mainly as an internal police force, to suppress dissension and intimidate potential rebels.

In fact in Kamrasi's day the army had a poor reputation. Speke (1863) describes the 'Wanyoro', as he calls them, as 'a wild set of ragamuffins', and his African informants supported this impression. One, he says, 'informed us they had been twice sent with an army of Wanyoro to attack the king's brothers . . . but each time it ended in nothing. You fancy yourself, they said, in a magnificent army, but the enemy no sooner turn out than the cowardly Wanyoro fly, and sacrifice their ally as soon as not into the hands of the opponents.' Speke also records a chief's remark that Kamrasi never retaliated when raiders from Buganda stole his cattle, and draws the conclusion that this was because his troops could not be relied upon to fight. Whether justly or not, Kamrasi himself is depicted in most European accounts as a coward. Baker described his reaction to an invasion by 'Turks' from the Sudan in 1864 in humorous terms:

> I was much amused at his trepidation, and observing the curious change in his costume, I complimented him upon the practical cut of his dress, that was better adapted for fighting than the long and cumbrous mantle. 'Fighting!' he exclaimed . . . 'I am not going to fight! I have dressed lightly to be able to run quickly. I mean to run away! Who can fight against guns?' (Baker, 1866)

During the reign of Kabarega, however, the kingdom regained its reputation as a military power and began to re-establish its former moral advantage over its neighbours. In 1876 the explorer Henry Stanley recorded his exasperation at the conduct of his Baganda escort. They had been ordered to accompany him to Lake Albert, but refused to continue when they learned that there were Banyoro in the vicinity, admitting that they were terrified of Kabarega's men. Baker, writing about the situation in 1872, compares the Banyoro with another of his opponents, the Bari tribe of the Sudan:

> Although the natives of Unyoro are inferior to the Baris as warriors, they are far more dangerous, as that extensive country is thoroughly organised . . . in case of war, every Chief of a district arrives at the head-quarters with an army, an army called suddenly by the war-drum, and it is most extraordinary to see the celerity with which these people collect. (Baker, 1873)

Two decades later Colonel Colville paid tribute to the speed and efficiency with which an army of 15,000 was collected to oppose him, even though the different contingents came from areas up to 200 miles apart. Flags and drums were used in the field to maintain cohesion, and probably to transmit orders. In 1889 a group of Emin Pasha's men encountered a column of bonosoora marching 'in a pretty disciplined manner' with two flags at their head, and at the Battle of Fort Hoima in August 1894 the two commanding generals were each accompanied by a standard, which was carried along the line to encourage the troops.

Equipment and Tactics
Until late in the nineteenth century the only armament carried by Banyoro warriors – apart from a small knife – was a pair of spears, one of which was intended for throwing and the other for close combat. According to Grant, these spears were weak and badly made, but another witness claimed that they could be thrown accurately up to 50 yards. Clearly they could inflict lethal wounds: one early king was said to have been derided as a poor fighter because he speared an opponent twice without killing him. Light oval shields made of wicker were also carried. As might be expected from the lightness of their equipment, the Banyoro traditionally specialized in surprise attacks and ambushes. Frederick Lugard, who fought them in the 1890s, claimed that they favoured night attacks, but these are seldom mentioned in battle accounts. During Baker's retreat from Masindi in 1872, in fact, they made no attempt to

attack his column at night, although they could probably have overrun it fairly easily had they done so. Speke (1863) described the Banyoro rank and file as 'squalid-looking . . . and anything but prepossessing to our eyes', but their dress was in fact ideal for concealment. It was made from a single piece of reddish-brown bark-cloth, wrapped round the waist and usually tied over one shoulder, and it is probable that most soldiers wore no other clothing than this. In the 1860s Baker encountered what were probably guardsmen in a striking outfit made of leopard or monkey skins, cow tails and antelope horns, 'perfect illustrations of my childish ideas of devils – horns, tails, and all' (Baker, 1866). By the following decade the chiefs had begun to adopt white Arab-style robes, and at least some of the bonosoora followed their example, though even in the 1890s most of the Banyoro could still be distinguished at a distance from the white-uniformed Baganda by their brown bark-cloth or skin garments.

Firearms began to appear in the country early in the 1860s and were soon in demand among the wealthier Banyoro, though they were at first in short supply. In 1862 Rionga sent ten slaves and ten elephant tusks to buy a single gun from the trader John Petherick, but he refused to supply the weapon, fearing that it might be used against Speke's expedition (Speke, 1863). Speke and Grant mention no arms other than spears and shields, and the former describes how a crowd of more than 1,000 people gathered to see a rifle demonstrated, and 'shouted in amazement' when Kamrasi shot a cow. Baker was told that Kamrasi fielded a small number of musketeers against a Baganda invasion in 1864, but neither side had any bullets, so they had to content themselves with a bloodless exchange of blank charges. When he returned in 1872 Baker found Kabarega accompanied by a bodyguard of fifty musketeers, and he claimed that 'many' of the bonosoora possessed guns. Nevertheless, according to his own account of the fight at Masindi in the same year, only about fifty out of 8,000 Banyoro were musketeers.

The supply of muskets steadily increased throughout the 1870s, and by the end of the decade the bonosoora seem to have been completely re-equipped with them. By this time more modern firearms were also being imported by Swahili or Arab merchants or acquired from Egyptian deserters. These included double-barrelled shotguns as well as military breech-loaders such as Sniders and Remingtons. In 1889 Stanley reported that Kabarega's central arsenal contained 1,500 guns, including

Jocelyn and Starr, Sharps, Snider and Martini-Henry rifles, the latter being more up to date than anything which the British forces in Central Africa possessed at the time. Kabarega himself owned a seventeen-shot repeater – probably a Winchester – with which he personally killed the Baganda commander at the Battle of Rwengabi in 1886. The new weapons were easily adapted to the traditional skirmishing tactics, and in the wars against the British we hear of their being used mainly for ambushes from cover, though against African opponents whose own firepower was limited they seem to have been employed more aggressively. At Rwengabi, for example, the bonosoora knelt in a loose line in the open and fired volleys at Kabarega's command, driving off the outgunned Baganda with heavy losses.

Baker's 1872 Campaign

In 1871 Khedive Ismail of Egypt sent Samuel Baker back to the scene of his earlier travels on the Upper Nile with a contingent of troops and the title of Pasha in the Egyptian army. Baker's mission was to annex the southern Sudan and eradicate the slave trade – an ambitious objective which had been only partially achieved when he decided on his own initiative to press on south into Bunyoro. The explorer took with him only 212 Egyptian soldiers, leaving the rest of his troops in fortified camps in Bari territory. He detached 100 men from this small force to form a base camp at Fatiko, just north of the border with Bunyoro, and in May 1872 he arrived at Kabarega's capital at Masindi. Just as in 1864 he was accompanied – unofficially – by his intrepid wife, Florence. As the first white man to meet the new monarch, Baker was in a unique position to influence foreign opinion. No doubt prejudiced by his previous experiences, he was unimpressed: 'a gauche, undignified lout of twenty years of age,' he wrote, 'who thought himself a great monarch. He was cowardly, cruel, cunning and treacherous to the last degree' (Baker, 1874). Emin Pasha, the German-born governor of Equatoria province, who visited the king five years later, gained a much more favourable impression of Kabarega, which may be closer to the unbiased truth. He writes of the king's generosity and kindness, his lack of the capriciousness so common among African rulers, and the cleanliness and attractiveness of his appearance. But although he remembered him as a friend, Emin was aware of the menace which could lie beneath the suave exterior. 'One thing must be admitted,' he added ominously, 'his face was frightening.'

Samuel Baker himself was a physically powerful and somewhat over-bearing character who had gained the respect of the warrior tribes of the southern Sudan by his courage and marksmanship. Modern writers, using selective quotations from his own books, like to portray him as a virulent racist, a sort of caricature of all that was wrong with Victorian attitudes towards Africans, but this is unfair. He does complain of the 'ignorance' of the 'savages' of the Sudan, but he attributes this to their geographical isolation rather than to innate inferiority, and although he believed that it would take centuries to raise them to a European level of civilization, he clearly thought the task was worth undertaking. His rough and ready attitude was not confined to Africans: in later life he once thrashed the future King George V for damaging one of the trees in his garden. But he failed to appreciate that the ruler of a powerful and self-confident kingdom such as Bunyoro could not be overawed by the usual methods, and his actions at Masindi were tactless in the extreme.

Without waiting for permission, Baker built a wooden fort outside the town, raised the Egyptian flag and announced that he was annexing Bunyoro in the name of the Khedive. Kabarega pretended to acquiesce, while secretly sending out messengers to assemble the army. He supplied 300 men as porters to bring up supplies from Fatiko, but gave them secret orders to massacre the garrison there and occupy the place in order to cut off Baker's retreat. (For reasons which are unclear this order was not carried out, and Baker found the camp still intact when he returned.) Baker claimed that the king also tried to kill his men with poisoned plantain cider, but the Banyoro always denied this, saying that the men had simply got drunk. Then at dawn on 7 June 1872 Kabarega launched a surprise attack on the still unfinished fort. Baker and his men were already standing to outside the fort, and as soon as Baker heard shooting he ordered the bugler who accompanied him to sound the alarm. The well-drilled Egyptians immediately formed square, just in time to meet a charge by a force which Baker estimated at 8,000 Banyoro. The majority of these were spearmen, but the few who had muskets fired a volley from the cover of tall grass and bushes growing near the fort. Two men were killed at Baker's side, but the attack on the square was a failure. The Egyptians were armed with a mixture of muzzle-loading rifles and Snider

A contemporary map of Africa, *c.*1880, showing territory claimed by the European powers and some of the most important of the native kingdoms. (Anon., *Life and Discoveries of David Livingstone*, London, [*c.*1880])

Victoria Falls on the Zambezi. Almost any attempt to penetrate the interior of Africa by river would eventually be thwarted by impassable rapids: this is the best known and most spectacular of these obstacles.
(Copyright Kate Peers)

'The white man's burden.' Especially in West and Central Africa, it was often believed that the climate made physical exertion dangerous for Europeans and obliged them to have themselves transported in hammocks or litters on the shoulders of African bearers.
(From Anon., *Stanley and Africa*, Newcastle-under-Lyme and London, no date [before 1890])

Baker's Egyptian askaris skirmish with Sudanese tribesmen, 1861. (Baker, 1866)

Map showing the migration routes of the Matabele (dashed line) and the Ngoni (solid line) north from Zululand in the nineteenth century.

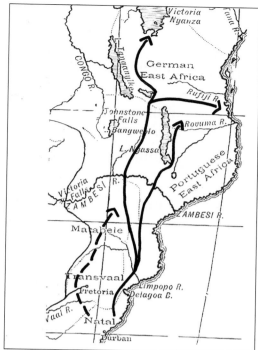

A 'Cape wagon', one of the versatile ox-drawn vehicles which served the Boers as transport, accommodation and portable fortification.
(W Burchell, *Travels in the Interior of Southern Africa*, London, 1822)

Rocky escarpments and belts of thorn bush make the bushveldt of the Transvaal (now Limpopo province, South Africa) difficult country for military operations. In the 1820s Mzilikazi's Matabele took refuge here from their Zulu enemies. (Author's photograph)

A Matabele warrior of the 1830s. (Harris)

Portrait of Mzilikazi,
founder of the
Matabele nation.
(Harris)

A group of
Nyasaland Ngoni
photographed in the
1890s. (Elmslie)

Cock's-feather headdress of a Tuta warrior from the shores of Lake Victoria. (Stanley, 1879)

Zulu warriors of the 1840s in full dress uniforms. The different regiments were distinguished by their headdresses and shield patterns. By the time of the Anglo-Zulu War of 1879 these elaborate outfits were no longer worn on the battlefield, if in fact they ever had been. (G F Angas, *The Kafirs Illustrated*, London, 1849)

A Ngoni warrior from Lake Nyasa, armed with Zulu-style shield and throwing assegai. (Johnston, 1897)

The posts built by the colonial powers were usually substantial and well designed, even in the remotest parts of the continent. This is the north-west bastion of the British fort at Karonga, Lake Nyasa, in the early 1890s. (R Brown)

A Matabele attack on a British wagon laager, Matabeleland, 1893. In reality it is unlikely that any Matabele got as close to the wagons as represented here. (R Brown)

A typically dramatic illustration of the destruction of the Shangani Patrol, 1893. (R Brown)

Memorial in the Matopos Hills to the 'brave men' who died in the wars for Matabeleland. (Copyright Kate Peers)

A high-ranking Ashanti officer of the early nineteenth century. (Bowdich)

A typical scene in the West African bush. (Author's photograph)

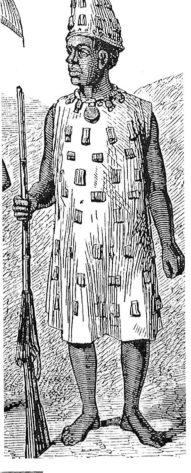

An Ashanti warrior of the 1874 campaign. (Stanley, 1874)

Ashanti envoys cross the River Prah, escorted by British officers. (Stanley, 1874)

Banyoro officials greet Baker on his first visit to the country. (Baker, 1866)

A 'satanic escort' of Banyoro warriors in traditional horned headdresses and animal skin costumes. (Baker, 1866)

An early model of the Maxim gun, taken to the Congo on H M Stanley's Emin Pasha relief expedition, 1887. (Stanley, 1890)

Sudanese askaris in British service with a tripod-mounted Maxim gun. Uganda, late 1890s. (Vandeleur)

A Lango warrior, one of Kabarega's staunchest supporters. (R Brown)

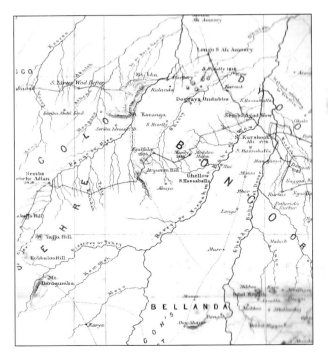

A section of Schweinfurth's map of his travels in Azandeland, showing the theatre of war between the Azande and the Khartoum slavers. (Schweinfurth)

Two Azande warriors in traditional attire, drawn by Georg Schweinfurth in the 1870s. (Schweinfurth)

'Sultan' Djabbir, an Azande chief of the 1890s. He is wearing what appears to be a virtually complete Egyptian infantryman's uniform, complete with Remington rifle. (Burrows)

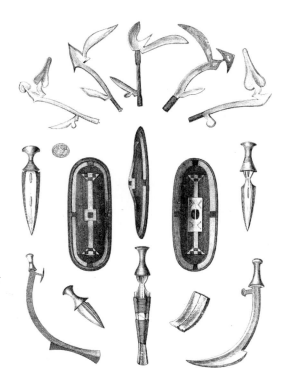

Traditional Azande shields and weapons. Several variants of the famous *kpinga* or throwing knife are shown. (Schweinfurth)

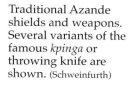

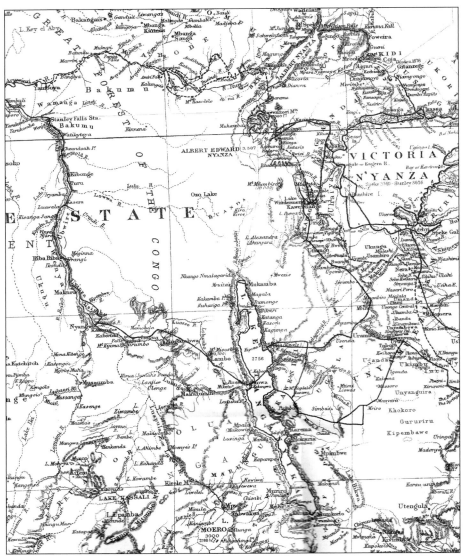

The eastern Congo and surrounding areas, as known to Europeans on the eve of the Congo Arab War. (Stanley, 1879)

Portrait of the notorious slaver Tippu Tib. (Stanley, 1890)

A 'Congo Arab' drummer, probably a local Manyema tribesman in Arab service, during the war against the Congo Free State. (Ward)

Sketch map drawn by Commandant Dhanis and presented to the missionary George Grenfell, showing Force Publique operations against the Congo Arabs, 1892. (Johnston, 1908)

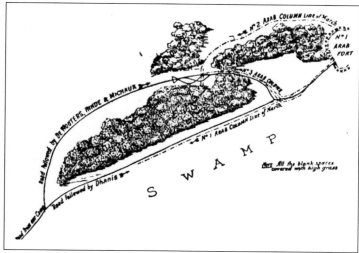

Sketch map drawn by Sidney Hinde of his and de Wouters's battle in the forest against Sefu's Arabs. (Hinde)

A Masai spearhead. This broad-bladed weapon was typical of the nineteenth-century Masai, and was not replaced by the more familiar long, narrow design until around 1900. (Copyright Mark Copplestone)

'On the war path in Masailand': a Masai *moran* in full regalia. (Thomson, 1885)

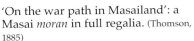

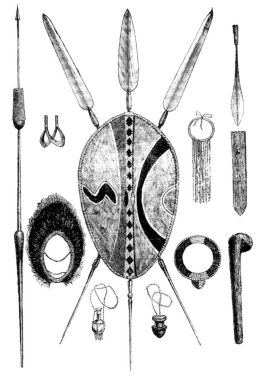

Masai war equipment of the 1880s. (Thomson, 1885)

An artist's impression of the Masai charge at the Battle of Elbejet, 1889. (Peters)

The charge of the Nandi against Lieutenant Vandeleur's column at the Kimonde River, 1895. Unlike many Victorian battle pictures this is probably a reasonably accurate representation, as the Nandi got to within 30 yards of their objective before being stopped by rifle and machine-gun fire. (Vandeleur)

A Congo pygmy. (Stanley, 1890)

A Hehe warrior. The white face and single black eye were typical of the war-paint styles of southern Tanganyika. (After M G Revoil, *L'Illustration*, January 1887)

ES STARBEN DEN HELDENTOD
AM 17. VIII. 91
BEIM WAHEHE-ÜBERFALL
DIE ANGEHÖRIGEN
DER KAISERLICHEN SCHUTZTRUPPE

KOMMANDEUR EMIL von ZELEWSKI
LIEUTENANT WILHELM von ZITZEWITZ
LIEUTENANT EGON von PIRCH
ARZT DR. RICHARD BUSCHOW
SERGEANT RICHARD von TIEDEWITZ
SERGEANT FRIEDRICH TIEDEMANN
UNT. OFFZ. PAUL HENRICH
UNT. OFFZ. AUGUST SCHMIDT
LAZ. GEH. PAUL HEMPRICH
UNT. BÜCHSENM. ALEXANDER HENGELHAUPT

ZU EHRENDEM GEDENKEN
GEWIDMET VON DEN KAMERADEN
1898.

The memorial erected by the Germans to their dead at the Battle of Lugalo, Tanganyika, in 1891. (Right) Close-up of the plaque on the Lugalo memorial, listing the names of the fallen German 'heroes'. (Copyright David Le Breton. Previously published in *Rhino Link: The Journal of the King's African Rifles and East African Forces Association*, vol. 2, no. 8, April 2008. Reprinted by kind permission)

A Somali warrior of the 1880s with shield, throwing spears and a magical charm round his neck, probably containing quotations from the Koran.
(P Paulitschke, *Harar*, Leipzig, 1888)

A Turkana warrior. Note the circular wrist-knife, characteristic hairstyle and neck rings, and the extensive tattooing.
(Von Hohnel)

breech-loaders, and according to Baker the Banyoro 'were cut down in the high grass in all directions'. 'It was extraordinary,' he continued, 'to see how impossible it appeared for natives in masses to produce any effect against Snider rifles.' The soldiers fought their way out through the town, setting fire to the huts as they went, and escaped under cover of the smoke. So effective was their shooting that subsequent Banyoro oral tradition claimed that Baker had used a machine gun against them. This is obviously incorrect. Apart from the fact that Baker's report makes no mention of such a weapon, there was no machine gun in service in 1872 which was portable enough to have been taken along the narrow trails to Masindi. Probably veterans who saw British Maxims in action in the 1890s rationalized their memories in retrospect, supposing that only automatic weapons could have inflicted the damage which they had suffered.

Kabarega was shaken by his losses and proposed negotiations, but Baker realized that his own position was untenable. His lines of communication were in danger, and supplies were running short. At this point Florence Baker revealed a secret store of flour which she had hidden away in sealed boxes in case of emergency. (This was not the only occasion on which her foresight and clear thinking saved her husband's expeditions from disaster, as he admits in his account.) Kabarega had by now assembled most of his army and deployed it around Masindi, ready for another battle, but after two days of waiting his scouts reported that the invaders had gone. Baker was retreating towards Fatiko, a distance of over 100 miles through country covered with tall grass. On the floodplain of the Nile huge areas were overgrown with this dense 'elephant grass', which in the rainy season could grow to 12 feet high or more, with stalks an inch thick, and was penetrable only along narrow tracks made by elephants or other large animals. This characteristic vegetation had an important influence on warfare in the region. It was a serious obstacle to both visibility and movement, but it provided no physical protection against bullets at close range. It could conceal an ambush very effectively, but it was necessary to stand upright in order to make any progress through it, and the waving stalks would betray the position of anyone attempting to do so. When dry the grass burnt easily, and this was frequently done to clear the dense growth and provide a field of fire, or by native warriors to create a diversion and cause confusion in a marching caravan.

Baker describes in detail the tactics he employed during the retreat.

The column was headed by an advance guard of sixteen soldiers armed with Sniders, led by an Egyptian officer and a bugler. Behind them came the Bakers, with another bugler, the reserve ammunition, and a body-guard of ten more men with Sniders. They were followed by the main body, carrying muzzle-loaders, then a rearguard of sixteen Snider-armed men under a captain with another bugler. The column was kept together by means of bugle calls. Without the buglers, says Baker, 'our line would have been cut, and if so, there would have been an end to everything'. The Banyoro harassed the march all the way. They made false trails to lead the column astray, threw spears from the cover of the grass, and constructed elaborate ambushes at river crossings and other points. A screen of tall grass or reeds was left along the trail for concealment, and a large open space was cleared behind it. Spearmen could then get a good run up and throw their weapons over the grass when they heard the enemy passing, while themselves remaining invisible. Meanwhile other warriors would follow behind the column to cut off any stragglers. According to Baker the Banyoro always initiated an ambush by imitating the call of a certain bird, and his men quickly learned to recognize this sound, thus giving them a brief warning of an attack. Standing orders in the event of an ambush were for the men to face alternately right and left and immediately open fire into the grass, even if they could not see the enemy. Baker loaded his own large-calibre elephant gun with explosive shells, which not only made 'a hideous noise', but 'would leave very little of a man' if they hit him. These shells always produced a noticeable moral effect on the Banyoro, even if it was impossible to see if they had actually struck their target.

The lessons which Baker derived from this campaign were presented to the Royal United Services Institution in December 1873 in a lecture entitled 'Experience in Savage Warfare'. He concluded (rather contradicting his own observations at Masindi, quoted above) that breech-loading rifles lacked the rate of fire and stopping power for fighting in dense bush country, where attacks could be delivered from very close range. His solution was for one company per regiment or battalion to retain their Sniders, while the others would be issued with 'single barrelled breech-loader smooth bores of No. 10 calibre', in other words shotguns, firing prepared cartridges each containing a bullet and twenty-four small shot. This suggestion was never acted upon in the

British Army, but Baker did issue smoothbore muskets loaded with buckshot to his Egyptian soldiers when on sentry duty at night.

After seven days of continuous fighting the Bakers arrived in territory held by Rionga, and then marched on to Fatiko. Baker declared Kabarega deposed and proclaimed Rionga king of Bunyoro under the Egyptian Khedive – a gesture which of course had no effect on the reality on the ground. Rionga, however, accepted Egyptian overlordship in return for a promise of protection against Kabarega, and the Egyptians built and garrisoned a string of forts in the territory which he controlled. Baker eventually returned home and claimed victory, but the reality was that the first armed conflict between the Banyoro and an imperial power had ended in the ignominious retreat of the invaders.

After the explorer's departure the post of governor of Egypt's new Equatoria province was taken over by Charles 'Chinese' Gordon, later to become famous as the hero of Khartoum, who had made his reputation during the Taiping Rebellion in China. Gordon sent out several expeditions, which established a total of seven forts inside Bunyoro. This time Kabarega abandoned Masindi on the approach of an Egyptian column, allowing Gordon to repair Baker's fort there, but the king remained firmly in control of the rest of his territory. When Gordon's envoy Colonel Chaille-Long journeyed up the Nile on his way to Buganda in August 1874, he and his escort were attacked by 400 Banyoro warriors in canoes. Chaille-Long was wounded but beat the attackers off, 'after a fight lasting from midday until sunset', by shooting holes in their canoes with his elephant gun.

In June 1876 Gordon reported to the British Foreign Office that Bunyoro had been annexed to Egypt and Kabarega finally deposed, and that he proposed to divide up the country between Rionga and another claimant to the throne, Aufina. But this decree was no more enforceable than Baker's had been. It proved impossible to supply the garrison at Masindi, and it had to be evacuated after less than a year. Gordon brought in field artillery and rocket tubes to protect the other forts, which he surrounded with earthworks and moats. He also launched two steamers on the Nile. But promised reinforcements from Egypt did not arrive, and gradually Kabarega regained the upper hand. In 1877 a column of 200 Egyptian troops operating out of a fort at Mruli was ambushed and annihilated by Lango tribesmen in the king's employ. When the missionary R W Felkin arrived in 1878 he found the forts permanently under siege, and his own escort was attacked on his way home. Before his departure from the Sudan in the same year, a disillusioned Gordon ordered all the remaining forts in Bunyoro to be abandoned.

Like so many militarized states throughout history, Bunyoro could not afford to remain at peace for long, and during the following decade Kabarega went onto the offensive against his neighbours. Henry Stanley describes the dread which Banyoro attacks inspired among the people of Ankole and Toro, and the bonosoora became notorious for the ferocity of their raids for cattle and other plunder. Whether these raids were directly ordered by Kabarega is uncertain, but he would in any case have been unable to forbid them, as he had no other way to pay his troops. Stanley marched through the area in 1888 at the head of an expedition to relieve Emin Pasha, who had succeeded Gordon as commander of the Egyptian garrisons in Equatoria province, and now found himself cut off from home by the Mahdist conquest of the rest of the Sudan. Kabarega had at first been on friendly terms with Emin, but when Stanley's column appeared he became suspicious that the two white men were planning to join forces to attack him. He therefore expelled Emin's agent Captain Casati – leaving him and his servants tied naked to trees in the jungle in an obvious act of defiance – and launched several hit-and-run attacks on Stanley as he passed through the region. The king also continued to raid into Buganda, which was by this time coming under strong European influence, and so confirmed his reputation in the eyes of the British as an irreconcilable enemy of imperial interests.

Lugard's Campaign, 1891

In 1891 a force under Captain Frederick Lugard established a British presence in Buganda which, despite the vacillations of politicians at home, seemed to be permanent. Kabarega had by now taken advantage of the civil wars which had afflicted Buganda to reoccupy Toro, which had gradually come under Baganda influence. Despite Toro's history as a province of Bunyoro, Lugard chose to see this as an act of aggression. He also suspected the Banyoro of harbouring dissident Baganda fighters, and furthermore he wished to open up a route in the north to the remaining Egyptian garrisons, which he hoped to recruit into his own forces. In August 1891, therefore, Lugard led a column of Swahili askaris into Toro, accompanied by a large force of Baganda allies armed with muskets and spears. The expedition soon ran into a 5,000-strong force of Kabarega's *obwesengeze* levies on the Mokia (or Mohokya) River. Lugard's column had become strung out during a long march, and its commander was well ahead of his main body with a patrol of only forty men. He quickly deployed these into a defensive line, sending back messengers with orders to the rest of his force – the exact strength of which he does not state – to catch up as quickly as possible. Ahead of him lay a dense wood, and beyond that a line of low hills, 'black with men' (Lugard, 1893). The Banyoro advanced to occupy the wood and began firing, but the range was too great for their muskets to do much damage, and despite their numerical superiority they did not press home the attack. After an anxious hour of waiting, the rest of the column – which included a Maxim gun weighing 87lb, carried by a single porter – arrived on the field. Lugard then ordered his Baganda allies to advance into the wood, instructing them not to shoot, in order to conserve ammunition, but to rely on their spears. Meanwhile the Maxim gave covering fire, opening up on the hills in front at a range of about 950 yards. This caused panic among the Banyoro, who were unable to reply to the machine-gun fire, and they fled as soon as the Baganda came to close quarters.

In a second encounter a Banyoro army stiffened by a contingent of bonosoora regulars was no more successful; their shooting was so inaccurate that they were driven off by a Swahili bayonet charge, with no casualties on either side. Three more attempts were made to stop Lugard, and each time Kabarega's men were forced to retreat by the firepower of the Maxim gun. The ineffectiveness of Banyoro musketry was very marked. On one occasion an estimated 1,000 rounds were fired at Lugard's caravan from the far side of the Semliki River, a distance of about 100 yards, but there were no casualties. Lugard forced Kabarega to evacuate Toro, then marched on to Lake Albert. There he persuaded the Egyptian garrisons to join him, and returned with them to Buganda. But – perhaps influenced by Baker's prejudices and the views of his Baganda allies – he had adopted an intransigent attitude towards Kabarega. 'When I have time,' he wrote, 'there is nothing I would like better than to turn out the inhuman fiend' (Lugard, 1893). Such language with regard to someone whom Lugard had never met may seem surprising, but by now the Banyoro monarch had become a sort of bogeyman, a symbol of all that was savage and terrifying about 'Darkest Africa'. Tales of mass human sacrifice circulated widely, and books such as Alfred Swann's *Fighting the Slave Hunters in Central Africa* featured photographs of people whose fingers or noses had been cut off at the king's orders. Mutilation was undoubtedly a routine punishment in all the Lake kingdoms, and sacrificial victims were buried – sometimes alive – with a dead king, but these were aspects of many African societies, and there is no evidence that Kabarega especially favoured such practices. In fact Nyakatura relates a tradition that he disapproved of the killings associated with the sacred *Omukewo* tree, and put an end to them after his accession.

War with the British, 1893–1895

In any case, by this time the confrontation between Britain and Kabarega had transcended the personal animosities that had sustained it so far. The situation was bluntly stated by one officer stationed in Buganda, Major J R L Macdonald. Buganda was a nightmare to defend: to station British or Indian troops there would be prohibitively expensive, but the ex-Egyptian garrisons which Lugard had recruited, and which now held the frontier with Bunyoro, could not remain indefinitely. These men originated mainly from the former Egyptian territories in the Sudan, and although in British service they were officially designated the Uganda Rifles, they were usually referred to as Sudanese. They were veteran soldiers but their discipline had deteriorated badly, as had the serviceability of their weapons – an assortment of old and dilapidated Snider and Remington breech-loaders, supplemented with obsolete elephant guns. Their loyalty to the British was also doubtful (they were to mutiny in 1897), and the atrocities which they committed against the local population were causing a scandal.

But Buganda could not be evacuated, because public opinion at home would not allow the missionaries working there to be abandoned. A presence was also necessary to keep the Germans away from Lake Victoria. So a defensive posture was impossible, and, as Macdonald concluded, 'the only other solution is to get rid of Kabarega'. So in December 1893 Britain and Buganda formally declared war on the king, following reports that he had launched another attack on Toro. A force of 200 Sudanese askaris under Major Owen, who had been dispatched to defend Toro, had clashed with a Banyoro army under a local chief called

Kikukuri. The size of the latter's army is not known, but it included about 2,000 men armed with muskets. As usual the battle took place in tall grass, which prevented men from seeing their targets and made both sides' shooting ineffective. Owen had a Maxim gun, but this jammed after firing about a dozen rounds. He therefore ordered a series of bayonet charges, which took several enemy positions in succession and finally drove Kikukuri's troops from the field.

On 15 December an expedition under Colonel Colville of the Grenadier Guards left Buganda and invaded Bunyoro itself. Colville was accompanied by three British officers, 200 Sudanese askaris, 400 porters, half of whom were armed with muskets, and two Maxim guns, as well as a steel boat which could be dismantled and carried overland in sections. (One Maxim did not work, but it performed good service as a dummy, mounted in the bow of the boat to deter potential attackers.) In addition there were 15,000 Baganda allies, of whom about a fifth had firearms, and a contingent of porters also provided by the king of Buganda. Kabarega was believed to have 20,000 men under arms, 8,000 of whom were musketeers, but most of the bonosoora units were still campaigning in Toro, and though they were hurriedly recalled they were too late to meet the invaders on the frontier.

Colville reported that enemy detachments kept his column under continuous observation. They were seldom seen, but frequently killed stragglers within 100 yards of the main body. The ubiquitous elephant grass made long-range shooting very difficult, and helps to explain why casualties on both sides in this campaign were relatively low. Colville took with him a bamboo tripod designed to enable an observer to see over the vegetation, but it was of little use: even though the officer's head was 12 feet above the ground, he was still unable to see over the grass stems. Paradoxically the Banyoro musketeers had adopted Baker's tactic of firing blindly into the grass, and wasted enormous amounts of gunpowder and ammunition, but the British-trained askaris were instructed to hold their fire and attack with the bayonet instead. This tactic was almost always successful, as the Banyoro were neither trained nor equipped to fight at close quarters. Unlike their Baganda enemies, who generally retained their spears even when they acquired guns, Kabarega's musketeers seem to have abandoned their traditional weapons and now relied entirely on firepower.

Colville's column brushed aside the Banyoro levies, bridged the Kafo River and reached Kabarega's new capital at Mparo, only to find it abandoned and burnt. Soon afterwards a patrol of fifty Sudanese askaris was ambushed by about 200 Banyoro, who opened fire from a patch of grass at a range of only 10 yards. Once again the Banyoro musketry was hopelessly inaccurate, and the ambushers were driven off with the bayonet. In January 1894 Colville's scouts located what they believed was the main Banyoro defensive position, on the edge of the Budonga forest. The British force deployed for a frontal attack with the askaris and the Maxims in the centre, Baganda musketeers echeloned back on their flanks, an advanced guard of 1,000 spear-armed Baganda, and the rest of the spearmen further back on both wings. However, the enemy force turned out to be only a rearguard, which disengaged and retired without serious fighting.

Soon afterwards the Baganda, now operating independently, managed to surprise Kabarega's camp on the edge of the Budonga forest and disperse its defenders, though the king himself escaped. From now on the Banyoro increasingly resorted to guerrilla tactics and avoided contact with the invaders' main forces as much as possible, although there were a few more skirmishes with the Sudanese. The Baganda army was soon forced to return home suffering from an outbreak of smallpox, but Colville marched unopposed as far as the shore of Lake Albert and built two new forts, at Hoima and Kibiro. Fort Hoima was designated as the headquarters of a permanent garrison in Bunyoro, consisting of three and a half companies of Sudanese under the command of Captain Thruston. Colville returned to Buganda in March 1894 and followed the precedent set by Baker and Gordon by claiming a victory, even though he had never brought Kabarega's main force to battle.

Kabarega was certainly not yet beaten. He had withdrawn temporarily across the Nile, but returned as soon as Colville departed. Another expedition was sent back under Captain Gibb to confiscate his store of ivory at Mruli, but the king again avoided a pitched battle and succeeded in escaping with his ivory intact. Meanwhile the Banyoro continued to harass Thruston with guerrilla tactics, blockading the garrison at Hoima and striking at isolated patrols and supply caravans. One of Kabarega's generals, Babachwezi, occupied a steep hill at a place called Masaja Mkuro, from which he began to launch attacks on British supply caravans as they passed along the trail below. In May 1894 Thruston stormed the hill – ordering his Sudanese to use their rifle butts, as they had no bayonets – and took it without any serious casualties. (Colville says that the Banyoro, who were poor marksmen at the best of times, found it very difficult to shoot downhill and eventually resorted to throwing stones.) Another supply convoy was ambushed in October by 220 Banyoro armed with rifles, but escaped with only three men killed and three wounded. Witnesses said that all the casualties appeared to have been inflicted by a single Banyoro rifleman, all the others having been completely ineffective.

A more serious battle was fought in August, when an army under the Banyoro generals Rwabudongo and Ireyta launched a direct attack on Fort Hoima. They deployed several thousand spearmen, but all the actual fighting was done by 750 riflemen. These, however, were outclassed in a preliminary firefight by the Sudanese garrison, and a flank attack delivered by fifty askaris rolled up their line and put them to flight. Again the Banyoro shooting was very bad; British losses amounted to only eight wounded, while about 200 Banyoro were allegedly killed. (However, Colville also says that only 3,000 rounds of ammunition were expended in the battle. This gives a ratio of one casualty for every fifteen rounds fired, which seems improbably high.) Then, in November, Thruston received a report that Kabarega was at Machudi, 78 miles from Fort Hoima. He led 237 Sudanese on a forced march which reached the objective in three days. The king was aware of Thruston's approach but had not believed that a military column could move so fast, and delayed his departure so long that he was nearly captured. The alarm was raised by the lowing of a cow and Kabarega escaped at the last moment, but Thruston captured the drum, copper spear, and brass and iron sceptre which were the insignia of Banyoro royalty. To a state so dependent on the prestige of its monarchy, this was a severe psychological blow.

The Final Campaigns, 1895–1899

Tired and demoralized, Kabarega sent an envoy to Buganda to sue for peace, but a group of his own generals, including Ireyta, Kikukuri and Babachwezi, refused to surrender. Another chief, Rwabudongo, carried out a daring operation on his own initiative. He invaded Buganda and defeated the local forces sent to intercept him, then went on to make contact with an Arab caravan smuggling in fresh supplies of guns from the south. The British retaliated in March 1895 by attacking a defensive position established by Kabarega on Kajumbera Island in the Nile, north of Mruli. This expedition was led by Major Cunningham, and consisted of four and a half companies of Sudanese, 2,000 allied Baganda and two Maxim guns. At least some of the Sudanese had been re-equipped with Martini-Henry rifles brought up by a caravan under Lieutenant S Vandeleur of the Scots Guards, who also brought another six Maxim guns.

The island was held by a force of bonosoora, entrenched in fortified positions protected by wooden stockades which guarded all the possible landing places. Cunningham had no choice but to attack frontally, so he led the Sudanese across the Nile in a fleet of small canoes, while the Maxims under Lieutenant Vandeleur were placed on a platform on the shore to give covering fire. However, there was a dense mist along the river, and Vandeleur was unable to see clearly enough to engage targets on the island. The bonosoora opened fire on the canoes at close range, and on this occasion their shooting was accurate. Cunningham was badly wounded, and another British officer and several Sudanese were killed. The column retreated to Fort Hoima, where it was besieged by the triumphant Banyoro, but another British force was soon collected and advanced to Mruli. Here Kabarega tried to repeat his success in preventing a crossing of the Nile, but the invaders were now in much greater strength. They deployed six companies of Sudanese, 20,000 Baganda, three Maxim guns and two small Hotchkiss field guns, which Vandeleur describes as 'wonderfully accurate and of great value'.

On the far bank of the river, which was about 900 yards wide at this point, Kabarega's men extended their trench system and erected more barricades, working at night to avoid harassing fire from the Maxims. On 22 April the Sudanese and the Baganda crossed together, under the cover of the artillery. This time, despite the amount of enemy fire, they succeeded in getting ashore and stormed the stockades. About forty Banyoro died defending them, but the rest escaped through a swamp. Vandeleur pays tribute to the courage and discipline of the Baganda, who made a vital contribution to the victory. He also records that the pursuit was hampered by crocodiles, which devoured several Sudanese soldiers while crossing the swamp. (Wild animals were another of the unusual hazards of campaigning in this region. During the same campaign six Baganda soldiers were bitten by crocodiles, two of them fatally, while on patrol in another swamp. Major Macdonald's casualty returns from his 1898 expedition included ten men killed by enemy action, plus another eaten by a lion.)

Kabarega himself got away yet again, taking refuge across the Nile in the land of the friendly Lango, but most of his cattle and several members of his family were rounded up by the Sudanese and Baganda patrols. Among the captives was the king's mother, who defected to the British and issued messages urging her countrymen to abandon the struggle. For the moment, though, the Lango at least remained loyal, and in May their spearmen succeeded in surprising and annihilating a party of 150 Baganda. Some of the most important Banyoro chiefs, however – including Babachwezi, Rwabudongo and Kikukuri – now began to surrender to the British. New forts were built on the sites of the former Egyptian bases at Mruli and Masindi in an attempt to prevent Kabarega reoccupying the territory he had abandoned, and patrols were sent out to intensify the blockade against the Arab traders who were still bringing supplies into the country. In June this policy paid off when Lieutenant Vandeleur intercepted two caravans laden with guns and ammunition for the Banyoro army.

After 1895 Kabarega lost control of the Banyoro heartland, and was reduced to raiding into British-occupied territory from across the Nile. Eventually even the Lango turned against him. Desperate, the king even tried to approach the Mahdists in the Sudan with an offer of alliance, but his emissaries were killed by tribesmen and the survivors were forced to turn back. Nevertheless the king's son Jasi and his general Ireyta, who remained loyal, took over command of the Banyoro forces and continued to dominate the Nile with a fleet of canoes. They gained a breathing space in 1897 when three companies of Sudanese askaris mutinied against their British officers over arrears of pay. Then in May 1898 the Banyoro received unexpected reinforcements with the arrival of King Mwanga from Buganda, fleeing after a failed revolt against the British. Kabarega and Mwanga had been long-standing enemies, but now they found them-selves briefly on the same side. At about the same time a group of Sudanese survivors of the previous year's mutiny also went over to Kabarega. Meanwhile his opponents had also received reinforcements, with the arrival of a contingent of Sikhs from the 27th Bombay Light Infantry, and another of Swahilis from the British East African Rifles.

Major J R L Macdonald now led a column incorporating some of these reinforcements into unexplored country north of Bunyoro, in pursuit of fleeing mutineers and Banyoro guerrillas. There was little serious fighting, but the major's report on this expedition includes some interesting notes on the characteristics of the troops and the problems encountered in these campaigns. The Sudanese had long been acclimatized to conditions in Uganda, and were 'very hardy'. They were usually accompanied on campaign by their wives or concubines, whose assistance with cooking, building shelters and other domestic tasks helped to keep the men in good condition. Colville added that the Sudanese, having learned through experience the dangers of being surprised, never allowed themselves to be separated from their rifles and wore their cartridge belts at all times – a habit that he wished English troops would adopt as enthusiastically. The Sikhs were at least as professional as soldiers, but were susceptible to malaria, though with the provision of enough antimalarial drugs they could usually be kept in action. The Swahilis were less affected by this disease, but suffered badly from ulcers and other leg and foot problems. Macdonald blamed this on the soldiers' 'carelessness', for example by discarding their issue sandals and puttees and marching barefoot. It is likely, though, that the real cause was unfamiliarity with a local parasite, the 'jigger', which could burrow into men's feet and leave them lame. Ironically the jigger was no more native to Uganda than it was to the Swahilis' homeland on the east coast, but had been accidentally introduced from the west by white explorers. To judge from the frequency with which it is mentioned in the later campaigns against Kabarega it was clearly a major nuisance, and could sometimes bring an entire expedition to a halt. Unfortunately we have no record of its effects on the Banyoro themselves, though in view of their habit of going barefoot it must have been significant.

Kabarega's forces won their last victory in September 1898, when Kikukuri, who had changed sides again, attacked Fort Hoima. The Sudanese garrison had been withdrawn, and the fort was held by supposedly pro-British Banyoro. Whether out of fear or from sympathy with the enemy, this garrison evacuated the stronghold and allowed Kikukuri to burn it. A few days later a British column reoccupied the fort, but it was now recognized that the only way to defeat Kabarega once and for all was to take the war to him in his refuge across the river. By now the king was losing the initiative, and the only strategy open to him was to try to avoid the British columns which marched at will across his country, while sending out small forces to ambush them and slow them down. In April 1899 a column under Colonel Evatt, accompanied by a party of Baganda who had remained loyal to the British, was conducted by a Lango defector to the king's camp. The remnants of the Banyoro army had been sent away south to intercept another British column which was rumoured to be approaching, and only Kabarega, Mwanga and a few of their chiefs and followers remained in the camp. Nevertheless they resisted when the askaris broke in, and in the ensuing gunfight Jasi was killed, while Kabarega was wounded in both arms and forced to surrender when he could no longer hold a gun. Several British accounts describe his arrogant defiance, even in captivity. The Banyoro had fought for so long mainly because of their loyalty to the monarchy, and the capture of the king effectively ended the struggle. A month later Ireyta and Kikukuri surrendered, and the longest war of resistance in nineteenth-century East Africa was finally over.

It was twenty-seven years since Baker had first marched into Masindi. For a pre-industrial state to maintain its independence for long in the face of repeated invasions by well-equipped imperial armies was a remarkable achievement, and should earn Kabarega recognition as one of the most outstanding African commanders of the age. The 'inhuman fiend' was sent into exile in the Seychelles, and remained there for twenty-four years, until the British authorities yielded to the pleas of his subjects and allowed him to return home. He died en route on 6 April 1923, but his body continued its journey back to Bunyoro for burial. The prestige of the dynasty was undiminished by his captivity, and three of his numerous sons in turn became kings of a pacified Bunyoro under British rule. Even the British had finally come to admire Kabarega's courage, energy and resolve. As one of his former enemies, Frederick Jackson, put it, 'he always kept his end up (in spite of his treacheries and cruelties) and was at least a man'. To his own people, he was and remains a national hero.

Sources

Baker, Chaille-Long, Colville and Lugard (1893) all provide detailed narratives of their military operations in Bunyoro. Modern accounts which make use of Banyoro testimony to give a more balanced view can be found in Beattie, Kiwanuka and Nyakatura.

Chapter Five
'The Zulus of the Congo': The Azande

A few hundred miles to the north-west of Bunyoro, another proud and independent people were simultaneously coming to terms with the encroachment of the modern world. At some time in the seventeenth or early eighteenth century a group known as the Avongara had migrated southwards from the Sudan into the fertile country which forms the watershed between the region's two great rivers, the Nile and the Congo. They dominated and gradually assimilated the local tribes, including the Ngbandi, Bombeh, Bongo and Banda, while themselves coming under the influence of their powerful neighbours to the south, the Mangbetu. Out of this melting pot emerged the Azande, who still dominate this region, straddling the borders of Sudan, the Democratic Republic of Congo and the Central African Republic. Culturally they were always remarkably cohesive, but they never achieved political unity, and by the nineteenth century they were divided into a number of kingdoms and principalities of varying size, whose rivalries often flared into internal conflict.

The Azande country lies just to the north of the great Congo rain-forest, and in many ways the terrain resembles that of Bunyoro. The gently rolling hills are covered with tall grass, dotted with rocky outcrops and broken by steep valleys along which streams run towards one or other of the great river systems. In the valleys grows what the nineteenth-century explorers called 'gallery forest', miniature outliers of the rainforest, characterized by tall trees and thick undergrowth. Also like Bunyoro, the region was insulated against most of the encroachments of the outside world. Situated in the very heart of the continent, remote from any coastline or navigable waterway, it was cut off on the east by the Nile swamps and on the south by hundreds of miles of unexplored jungle. One major river system, the Ubangui and its tributary the Uele,

107

flowed out to the west, but the Ubangui then turned south into the Congo, and was inaccessible until the Congo itself was opened to navigation in the 1880s.

Early European visitors often referred to the Azande as 'Niam Niam', an epithet which they probably copied from the Arabs and which was believed to carry implications of cannibalism. It is in fact a variant on the word for 'meat' in the languages of the local Niger-Congo family, and Stanley (1879) records it (in the form 'Nyama! Nyama!') in use as a war cry among the Congo tribes. The earliest written notice of a people who may have been related to the Azande was in 1799. In a letter written from Tripoli to his sponsor Joseph Banks, the German explorer Frederick Hornemann referred to a report of 'tailed men' called 'Yem Yem', who lived 'ten days south of Kano' and were said to be cannibals (*Proceedings of the African Association*, 1802, quoted in Wellard). Hornemann was sceptical, but intended to follow up the report after his planned crossing of the Sahara. Azandeland is much further than ten days' travel from Kano (in northern Nigeria), but the resemblance of the names 'Yem Yem' and 'Niam Niam' is suggestive, and the 'tails' may have been a misinterpretation of the animal skins which the Azande traditionally wore around their waists. Unfortunately Hornemann disappeared somewhere in the desert, and was never heard of again.

The Azande and the Arabs

The first outsider known to have actually visited the country was the Cornish ivory trader John Petherick, who arrived from the north via Khartoum in 1858. He found that the Azande had no trading relations with the outside world and hence no idea of the market value of ivory, which could be obtained very cheaply. On his return to the Sudan, Petherick's discovery soon became known to the trading companies based in Khartoum, which set up bases in the region of the Bahr al-Ghazal River from which they mounted regular expeditions towards Azandeland. At first the Khartoum Arabs (or 'Turks' as they were often called, being nominally subjects of the Ottoman Empire) followed their usual practice in the southern Sudan, which was described in detail by Samuel Baker (1866). A company registered in the town (of which several were owned by unscrupulous Europeans, though run by local managers) would borrow money for a trading expedition in return for a promise to repay the loan in ivory. The merchants hired men and boats locally, and spent the rest of the money not on trade goods but on guns and ammunition. (The justification generally offered for this was that as the tribes of the southern Sudan did not wear clothes, they would be unwilling to take cloth in exchange for the products of the country.)

On arrival in their area of operations the Arabs would select a compliant chief and offer to use their guns against his enemies, who might be a neighbouring tribe or simply the supporters of a political rival. With the benefit of local knowledge they would then locate a suitable village, and launch a surprise attack. Their victims were likely to be unfamiliar with firearms and could seldom mount an effective defence. The men would be killed and the women and children captured, along with the cattle. Returning to the base provided by their host, the invaders would then trade the cattle, and any of the hostages who could be ransomed, for ivory: 'a profitable business,' observes Baker, 'as the cows have cost nothing.' The rest of the prisoners were given to the men in lieu of wages, and were usually sold in the Khartoum slave markets. By this process one tribe after another lost the cattle which were its only wealth, and was reduced either to beggary or to joining forces with the slavers as the only way to deflect their attacks. The whole business was well established and given an appearance of respectability by the connivance in the Sudan of the Egyptian authorities, who could easily be bribed to draw up false documents giving the impression that the ivory had been obtained by legitimate trade. The largest firm, Agad and Company, employed about 2,500 armed men and controlled an 'ivory concession' 90,000 square miles in extent. Nor were the troops simply an armed rabble: they included a high proportion of deserters from the Egyptian army, and were organized into companies, trained in drill and marksmanship, and controlled by drums, fifes and flags.

In Azandeland, however, these methods were less successful. At first the political fragmentation of the country enabled the Arabs to ingratiate themselves with certain local rulers, but others refused to be intimidated and quickly adapted their tactics to counter the invaders' guns. Prominent among these were two rival kings, Ndoruma and Gbudwe (whose name means 'the disemboweller'). These men gradually expanded their spheres of influence to cover most of the other principalities, and in May 1870 the leading trader in the country, Muhammad Abu Sammat, led an expedition against Gbudwe. Our main source for this campaign is the German explorer Georg Schweinfurth, whose own caravan marched with the Arabs on this stage of his journey to the Mangbetu country further south. Schweinfurth gives few details of the fighting, but Muhammad soon found himself forced onto the defensive. He built a barricade of straw bales, from behind which the Arabs kept the Azande at bay with musket fire, but was eventually obliged to retreat. Meanwhile another column, led by one of Muhammad's officers, had fared even worse. Attacked by the forces of three Azande chiefs, he had been besieged in his camp for six days, thirty-five of his ninety-five armed men had been killed or wounded, and he had only escaped by abandoning all his ivory.

Later in the same year Ndoruma, who had at first welcomed the Arabs, fell out with them and captured a trading post which they had set up in his territory, along with a supply of muskets and ammunition. Some of Ndoruma's followers had once been slaves of the traders and had learned to handle firearms, so these prizes were hurriedly issued and the recipients instructed in their use. Then in December the combined contingents of three Arab traders, totalling at least 300 musket-armed soldiers, invaded Ndoruma's territory. The Azande attacked with guns and spears and routed them, killing half of them and capturing all their baggage, including further supplies of ammunition. Perhaps because they were easily adaptable to their traditional skirmishing tactics, the Azande seem to have taken readily to guns and to have used them effectively. Also, according to Schweinfurth, the Arab soldiers – who regarded the wars primarily as business undertakings and were reluctant to take undue risks – were demoralized by the realization that their enemies now possessed weapons as good as their own.

By the early 1870s the Egyptian government was beginning to take an interest in Azandeland, and established a series of garrisons on the northern fringes of the country. But far from imposing order, this simply exacerbated the endemic warfare. The Khartoum traders resented the government troops, who tried to impose taxes on them while at the same time engaging in slaving and ivory trading on their own account. Ndoruma and Gbudwe were hostile to each other as well as to the Arabs, and although both made occasional gestures of submission to the

Egyptians, they remained in practice independent. In a report dated 1880 the Egyptian governor, the Italian Romolo Gessi Pasha, stated that 'these two kings have massacred all the Arab expeditions that entered their district' (Evans-Pritchard). He went on to describe how four years earlier Ndoruma, who now possessed 600 guns, had destroyed an invading army of 2,000 musketeers and 3,000 allied spearmen. Gbudwe, meanwhile, had avoided all contact with the Arabs and so still had few if any firearms, though this did not seem to affect his ability to defend himself.

An oral tradition collected in the twentieth century by the anthropologist Sir E E Evans-Pritchard related how, some time after 1875, Gbudwe had attacked a prince called Ngangi, accusing him of sheltering Arab slaving parties. Advancing to meet his enemy on the River Bambu, Gbudwe organized his army into three divisions, the two leading ones commanded by his sons and the third, under his own command, bringing up the rear. Ngangi deployed his elite troops, well equipped with muzzle-loading guns, on his right flank and succeeded in driving back Gbudwe's left, but Gbudwe wheeled his own division into their rear as they pursued, and routed them. At the same time Gbudwe's men were pushing forward on their right, and the whole of Ngangi's line soon collapsed. A few years later, however, Gbudwe's fortunes changed. His rival Ndoruma had been defeated in a campaign against a trader named Rafai, who was acting as an agent of the Egyptian government, and blamed Gbudwe for failing to support him. Therefore he joined Rafai and a contingent of Egyptian regulars in an attack on Gbudwe, who was now the only remaining independent Azande ruler north of the Uele River. After a season of intense fighting in 1881 they failed to overrun him, but Rafai built a fort on the frontier and garrisoned it as a base for further operations. Gbudwe besieged this fort for several months but was unable to take it, while repeated Arab sorties devastated the countryside and began to affect his army's morale. So the king opened negotiations, but was treacherously seized and imprisoned in one of the Egyptian forts. When the German explorer Wilhelm Junker travelled through the region in 1882 it seemed to him that the Azande were doomed to fall completely under Egyptian control, but their enemies were about to be overtaken by an even greater disaster.

In 1883 the followers of the Mahdi in the Sudan destroyed an Egyptian army under Hicks Pasha and cut off the whole of the south of the country. They also captured the fort where Gbudwe was being held and inexplicably released him, despite his record of opposition to the Arabs. On his return home Gbudwe expelled the remaining traders from his territory and spent the next fifteen years consolidating his position among the Azande, establishing himself as overlord of all the remaining independent chiefdoms. Then early in 1898 a Mahdist army under Arabi Dafalla was discovered approaching from the east. At first unsure of its intentions, Gbudwe nevertheless sent his sons to mobilize the warriors of their own districts, and raised three new regular companies, known as Audie, Awili Singu and Awili Manziga, from the territory under his direct control. When the Mahdists ignored the Azande envoys and pressed on across the River Hu, it became obvious that they were hostile. But despite a successful ambush by the Awili Gine company which netted them a few guns, Gbudwe's men were not strong enough to stop the invasion until his sons returned with their forces. So the king was forced to evacuate the village of Birikiwe, where his court was situated, and allow the Mahdists to fortify it. For a month all he could do was blockade the fort, but when reinforcements arrived he launched an all-out assault which lasted for three days.

Few armies so poorly supplied with firearms could have made an impression on musketeers behind prepared defences, and our sources unfortunately do not go into detail about the tactics used by Gbudwe's men. But other accounts tell of Azande spearmen making rushes, often under cover of darkness, to throw their spears over the parapets of an enemy camp, and if the Mahdist 'fort' consisted of no more than a wooden stockade without overhead cover this method might have been fairly effective. The defenders must also have made sorties, in the course of which some of them were killed, because we are told that Gbudwe encouraged his men to eat the enemy dead as a method of psychological warfare. We also know, however, that Azande casualties were severe: Gbudwe later moved his court from Birikiwe because he could not bear to be reminded of all the men he had lost. On the fourth night of the battle the Mahdists broke out undetected and escaped. At dawn, finding the ramparts unoccupied, Gbudwe sent men in pursuit, but they did not catch up with the retreating enemy until nearly nightfall, when they found them encamped behind a barrier of thorn bushes beside the Bodo River.

Rashly the leading Azande warriors ran down to the river to drink and were cut down by a volley of musket fire. Reluctant to risk further losses, Gbudwe called off the pursuit and the invaders retired unmolested. They never returned, and eight months later the Mahdist state was overthrown by Kitchener's Anglo-Egyptian army at the Battle of Omdurman.

Azande Warfare

The reasons for this remarkable record of success against invaders armed with firearms are complex. Despite the lack of any overall political authority, the individual Azande chiefdoms tended to be well organized and tightly controlled. The larger ones at least consisted of a central 'royal domain' under the direct control of a king, plus a variable number of peripheral 'provinces' or clusters of villages, each ruled by a governor appointed by the sovereign. The governors allocated day-to-day responsibility for each section of their frontiers to a local headman, who established his headquarters in a spot along the border chosen for its strategic position. This would often form the nucleus of a fortified village inhabited by the headman's retainers and relatives. Each kingdom was therefore demarcated and protected by a ring of these villages, outside which was an uninhabited buffer zone separating it from neighbouring kingdoms. It was one of the duties of the frontier villagers to patrol this no-man's-land and report any suspicious activity to the king, which was no doubt one reason why foreign armies were never able to surprise the Azande in their own territory. According to Captain Guy Burrows, who campaigned in Azandeland in the 1890s, the villages were very different from the compact, stockaded type common among other tribes, but applied on a smaller scale the same defensive principles as the kingdoms themselves. The chief's house would be on a small hill surrounded by scattered huts, with smaller groups of huts further away, usually situated behind a bend in the path so that they could not be seen from a distance. These outlying habitations served as sentry posts, and it was the responsibility of their occupiers to prevent the main village being taken by surprise.

Most of what is known about traditional fighting methods comes from the work of Evans-Pritchard, who in the 1920s was able to interview several surviving veterans of the great wars of the nineteenth century. He estimated that a large Azande kingdom might deploy up to 20,000 warriors. The professional core of such an army consisted of permanently embodied companies known as 'aparanga', recruited from unmarried youths, and '*abakumba*', or married men. In normal circumstances each company varied in strength from around twenty to over a hundred, but in an emergency all the able-bodied men of the kingdom could be called up and attached to the existing companies, which might therefore be much larger when they actually took the field. Azande warfare was strongly influenced by the topography and vegetation of the country, which impeded the movement of large bodies of troops but provided ideal cover for ambushes. Evans-Pritchard's informants emphasized the difference between raids, 'basapu', and full-scale campaigns, or 'sungusungu vura'. Raids were directed at neighbouring settlements – usually, if not always, those of fellow Azande owing allegiance to a rival king – and followed a formal overall pattern.

Before any campaign was undertaken it was first necessary to consult the poison oracle or 'benge', in which, says Burrows, the Azande had 'absolute and unshaken faith'. The procedure involved administering a certain poison to chickens, accompanied by statements along the lines of 'If this bird lives the war will be successful'. It appears that the poison was highly variable in its effects, so the outcome was unpredictable enough to be taken as an indication of the views of the supernatural powers. Of course the potential for manipulation is obvious – for example by altering the dose or composition of the poison or using a chicken already known to be resistant – but nineteenth-century accounts are unanimous that the Azande genuinely believed in the oracle, so it is impossible to tell how far it was actually manipulated. There were certainly instances where chiefs followed the advice of 'benge' even when it might seem to have been against their interests. In 1870, for example, a slaving party accompanied by Georg Schweinfurth was saved from almost certain annihilation when a prince called Wando declined to support his allies in attacking it because the oracle was unfavourable.

Assuming that the result of this procedure was satisfactory, a war party would approach an enemy village in three or four separate units, two or three of which would be deployed in ambush along the path leading to their own village. The remaining warriors entered the target village quietly, under cover of darkness, and took up positions outside the doors of the huts. As dawn broke they would call out, challenging the men inside to come out and fight. Usually they did so, fearing that otherwise their assailants would set fire to their huts. Inevitably the defenders were at a disadvantage as they emerged into the open, and a few might be fatally speared. Most escaped with minor wounds and were not pursued, as the real aim of the raid was not to kill but to plunder. Internal Azande conflict was not always so innocuous, however, and chiefs were often deliberately murdered by political rivals during these affrays, or captured and later put to death. Discussing one family, the Nunga, Evans-Pritchard observes that during the late nineteenth century 'hardly a prominent person died a natural death'.

The Azande kept no livestock apart from chickens, so the booty consisted mostly of portable goods and the women and children, who were carried off as slaves or for ransom. Non-combatants were never killed deliberately, although there might be casualties if the raiders set fire to the huts and grain stores to cover their retreat. The attackers then fled as rapidly as they could along the trail leading to their own villages, which usually led through the tall, dense grass typical of the country in the rainy season. By this time their victims were rallying and were beginning to beat drums to summon help from friendly villages. As Azande villages were generally situated close together, reinforcements might start to arrive within a few minutes. The defending warriors then went in pursuit, and – being unencumbered by booty and captives – would catch up with the fleeing raiders fairly quickly. But meanwhile the first of the attackers' ambushes was being prepared. Although the pursuers of course knew what to expect, their options were limited. The thick grass made it very difficult to manoeuvre off the established paths, and in any case it was a point of honour to come briefly to blows with at least the first ambush, so that their own ruler could not accuse them of cowardice. In the words of one of Evans-Pritchard's informants:

> The warriors in ambush trod down the grasses a few yards back from the path, parallel to, and at one side of it, so that they might have concealment and also room for movement. They crouched in this clearing with about six yards between man and man. The leader of the company was alone exposed. He stood in the middle of the path to observe the approach of the enemy and give the signal for attack, but on a curve in the path and at the tail of the ambush, so that the

pursuers might be well into the ambush before they saw him . . . .
The retreating raiders arrived at a trot at the point where the leader
of the first ambush stood on the path and they passed under his raised
arms, the last of them maybe running hard with the enemy in close
pursuit. They continued through the second and third ambushes to
where the prince was waiting. Here they were stopped by a man
holding a spear across the path and shouting to them to halt as the
prince was present. No one would retreat past him. Meanwhile when
the first of the enemy, in hot pursuit of the raiders, was well into the
first ambush its commander hurled a spear at him and gave a shout;
and at once the warriors lying in wait began to hurl their spears.

If the ambushers inflicted enough casualties in the ensuing exchange of
missiles, their opponents would turn back and the fighting would end
there. Otherwise the men making up the first ambush would retreat, and
draw the pursuers into the second ambush a little further back. At this
point the pursuers usually contented themselves with a token skirmish
before returning to their village.

A full-scale war between rival Azande kingdoms was conducted very
differently. It involved more troops and was more thoroughly planned,
but no attempt was made to achieve surprise. Schweinfurth witnessed a
formal declaration of a war of this kind in the form of an ear of maize, a
chicken feather and an arrow hung from a branch above a path. This, he
says, was interpreted to mean that 'whoever touched an ear of maize or
laid his grasp upon a single fowl would assuredly be the victim of the
arrow'. In fact the intention of the invading force was to provoke a pitched
battle, which was fought according to traditional rules designed to minimize casualties. A battle always began late in the afternoon, so that the
losing side could take advantage of darkness to slip away. Each side
deployed with a centre and two wings, and the aim was to push back the
enemy wings and threaten to envelop his centre. Burrows refers to a crescent formation like that of the Zulus. However, the victors were careful
not to encircle their enemies completely, but always left a gap in their rear
so that they could escape. The only eyewitness account of internal Azande
combat by a European observer is given by the Italian explorer Carlo
Piaggia, who confirms the impression of ritualized conflict involving little
real bloodshed:

Only the men go to war, with a few women – the most daring, who do not wish to abandon their husbands and lovers. The others go and hide for fear of becoming the prey of their enemies, should they be victorious . . . . It is rare for the battles to last many hours, or for them to cause much carnage, because as soon as five or six men can be seen dead on the field the fighters run away full of trepidation, and their opponents claim victory. The latter, satisfied by their efforts after this skirmish, return calmly to their villages. (Evans-Pritchard)

In contrast, Piaggia continues, wars against 'foreign tribes' were far more ferocious. These, he says, 'foster the thirst for "vendetta" so far as to make [the Azande] eat the flesh of their dead enemies. Piaggia was a witness to one of these wars, from which comes their reputation for being cannibals.' Whether the Azande were really habitual cannibals is uncertain. The whole subject remains controversial in anthropological circles, but there is a great deal of evidence that cannibalism did occur among the rainforest tribes further south. Among the Azande this passage is the nearest we have to a first-hand report. However, Piaggia does not explicitly say here that he witnessed acts of cannibalism, merely that he knows how the accusation arose. A few years later Schweinfurth heard the A-Banga, who were relatives and allies of the Azande, taunting Sudanese invaders with 'the repeated shout, "To the cauldron with the Turks!" rising to the eager climax, "Meat! Meat!"' Perhaps the closest we can get to the truth is to say that the Azande may have eaten human flesh occasionally as an act of revenge, but that cannibalism was not an established part of their culture. They were no doubt happy to foster their reputation as a psychological weapon against their enemies, especially the Arabs, who for religious reasons attached great importance to the burial of their dead intact.

Against Arabs and Europeans the Azande went to war with the same ruthless attitude as Piaggia describes in their conflicts with other outsiders, in combination with the skirmishing skills learned in their internal conflicts. Several commentators describe their desperate courage and their willingness to accept heavy casualties. In the words of Guy Burrows:

Their courage and pluck are admirable; their contempt for death is supreme. They will stand a fire that is dropping them by dozens, charging time after time until absolutely compelled to retire. Coming upon seven or eight men armed with rifles, they will throw away their own arms and rush their opponents, though they may lose twenty or thirty men in the attempt, knowing that ultimately the rifles will be theirs.

The men interviewed by Evans-Pritchard also provided much fascinating detail on exactly how Azande weaponry was used, and the minor tactics which were employed when two hostile forces clashed at close range:

A battle consisted of individual combats between warriors on either side all along the line and at short range, usually only a few yards separating the combatants, for the spear had to pierce a man's shield before it could pierce the man . . . . The Zande shield, however, protected two-thirds of the body, and when a man crouched behind it, as he did if a spear or knife was aimed high, his body was fully covered. If the missile came at him low, he jumped into the air with remarkable agility to let it pass under him . . . men have demonstrated to me with old shields or ones I had made for me, how they moved in fighting, and it was a most impressive display in the art of self-defence, in the movements of the body to give the fullest protection of the shield, and in the manipulation of the shield to take the spear or throwing-knife obliquely.

The skirmishing fights typical of internal Azande wars were always accompanied by the shouting of challenges and the names of the kings and princes commanding the various contingents. According to Schweinfurth the fighting would be interrupted by long intervals during which men would climb to the tops of ant-hills and exchange insults. He describes the large basketwork shields of the Azande as 'so light that they do not in the least impede the combatants in their wild leaps', and goes on to praise the skill and agility of their users in a much-quoted passage:

Nowhere, in any part of Africa, have I ever come across a people that in every attitude and every motion exhibited so thorough a mastery over all circumstances of war or of the chase as these Niam-niam – other nations in comparison seemed to me to fall short in the perfect ease – I might almost say, in the dramatic grace – that characterized their every movement.

The so-called throwing knife was a characteristic weapon of the region north of the Congo rainforest, from the Sudan in the east to northern Nigeria in the west. It took many different forms, not all of which were suitable for use as missiles, and in many places 'throwing knives' seem to have been used for ritual or magical purposes, as status symbols or as currency, rather than as weapons. Among the Azande, however, the multi-bladed knife or *kpinga* was certainly an effective weapon of war. Nineteenth-century explorers were unfamiliar with this type of artefact, and often had difficulty in describing it for a European readership. Hence Petherick, writing in 1858, refers to 'singularly-formed iron projectiles, resembling a boomerang of rather a circular form, bearing on their peripheries several sharp projections' (Petherick, *Egypt*, 1861). In his report to the Royal Geographical Society in 1860 he also mentions an 'iron boomerang' which was designed to return to the thrower's hand, but this rather unlikely story is probably a misinterpretation based on the visual analogy with the well-known Australian weapon. Schweinfurth calls these throwing weapons 'trumbashes', and explains that 'the trumbash of the Niam-niam consists ordinarily of several limbs of iron, with pointed prongs and sharp edges'. Fortunately we also have detailed drawings by Schweinfurth and others, as well as surviving artefacts in museums, which enable us to reconstruct their appearance accurately.

Evans-Pritchard says of the *kpinga* that 'when correctly thrown, one of its several blades was certain to strike the objective squarely, and the sight of the blades circling towards one in the air must have been frightening'. He did not, however, believe that it would have been a particularly effective weapon against a warrior armed with a shield, as the multiple blades would dissipate the impact on the shield and the spinning motion cause it to bounce off. By contrast the early twentieth-century anthropologist Emil Torday speculated, in his account of the Kuba or Bushongo kingdom of southern Congo (which he believed had been founded by an offshoot of the Azande), that throwing knives might have given the newcomers a decisive advantage in battle: 'all of a sudden, some objects, glistening in the sun as if they were thunderbolts, come whirling with a weird hum through the air. The enemy warriors raise their shields; the shining mystery strikes it, rebounds into the air and returns to the attack; it smites the warrior behind his defence with its cruel blades.' Torday's theory of the Azande origin of the Kuba is discounted nowadays, and consequently this passage is usually dismissed as a product of his fertile imagination. But tests carried out with reproduction throwing knives tend to confirm his assessment of their capabilities. In one such test, staged for the *Ancient Discoveries* television series, the missile did indeed bounce off the top edge of a shield attached to a dummy, but its momentum carried it forward to strike the target in the middle of the forehead with enough force to embed it several inches deep. The psychological impact of the 'weird hum', magnified several hundred times as an Azande regiment threw its weapons in unison, may also have been a significant factor.

The amount of metal as well as the skilled craftsmanship required to make a *kpinga* made it a valuable piece of equipment, and these weapons were usually the property of the ruler, stored in royal arsenals and issued only to regular troops for specific campaigns. Evans-Pritchard was told that before a man hurled a throwing knife he would shout a warning that he was going to do so, because men did not want to risk being accused of throwing them away in panic. Spears seem to have been far more common, and receive far more mentions in battle accounts than throwing knives. In fact Burrows, writing of the 1890s, refers exclusively to spears and shields as 'the national Azande weapons'. He adds that a single broad-bladed stabbing spear was the usual weapon of the western principalities, while further east lighter throwing spears were favoured, with each man carrying between four and six. Schweinfurth's symbolic arrow notwithstanding, the Azande did not use bows, which they regarded with contempt as 'Pygmy weapons'.

In 1858 John Petherick had found that the Azande were completely unfamiliar with firearms, and reacted with terror when he demonstrated his gun by shooting a vulture: 'before the bird touched the ground, the crowd was prostrate and grovelling in the dust, as if every man of them had been shot'. But they quickly recovered from the shock, and by the time Schweinfurth arrived in 1870 most of the important rulers had at least a small bodyguard of musketeers. Evans-Pritchard's informants described four different types of gun. The first were muzzle-loading smoothbore flintlocks or 'biada', in widespread use among the Arabs in the 1860s and usually acquired from them by trade or capture. Alongside these were 'orumoturu', also muzzle-loaders, but using percussion caps rather than flints for ignition. In the mid-1870s the Remington breech-loader or 'sipapoi' began to make an appearance. This was the standard infantry weapon of the Egyptian army, and was supplied by the Egyptians to friendly princes such as Zemio. Finally there was the 'abeni' or Albini. This was a variant of the Snider breech-loader used by the Belgian King Leopold's Congo Free State forces from the late 1880s, and was captured in large numbers as well as being supplied by the Belgians to friendly princes.

The Remington was invariably the weapon of choice among the Azande, however, partly no doubt because its unique 'rolling block' action made it difficult for inexperienced users to burst or jam it. By the 1890s some Azande chiefs even maintained regular units of riflemen, dressed, armed and drilled in European style. The Belgian Lieutenant de Ryhove described Rafai's small standing army as wearing 'startling' white uniforms, and carrying brightly polished rifles (Levering Lewis). He expressed his astonishment that 'After having encountered so many naked people with heads dressed with plumes, bodies covered with tattoos and rigged out with bizarre or grotesque accoutrements, I was able to see people clothed, armed, disciplined, and manoeuvring with military correctness in the sunshine – and in the very heart of Africa.' Unfortunately no detailed description of the appearance of such units seems to have survived, but it is likely from the description that the men seen by de Ryhove had been outfitted in surplus Egyptian army equipment.

War with the Congo Free State

With the disappearance of the Arabs and their Mahdist successors, the only remaining threat to Azande independence came from the encroaching European powers – the British from the north, the French from the west, and the Congo Free State from the south. The latter was an anomaly in colonial Africa, because it did not belong to any of the imperial powers. King Leopold's colonial ambitions were not shared by the Belgian government, and he pursued them instead under the name of the International African Association, ostensibly a philanthropic enterprise dedicated to free trade and the abolition of slavery. The king had already spent much of his personal wealth in trying unsuccessfully to establish a presence east of Lake Tanganyika. Thwarted there, he transferred his ambitions to the west, and on H M Stanley's return from his famous trans-Africa expedition in 1877 he hired him to break trails and set up stations on the Lower Congo. By 1884, when the Congress of Berlin met to apportion spheres of interest in Africa, the Congo was becoming a problem which none of the European powers were eager to take on. The Arabs were rapidly overrunning the region from the east, but the rapids at the mouth of the great river made access from the west much more difficult, and despite the prospect of vast wealth (principally in ivory), it seemed that bringing 'civilization' to the region would be an extremely costly undertaking. Leopold's potential rivals were therefore happy to give him a free hand in the region. However, the king had no intention of spending his own money on developing infrastructure or introducing any benefits for the natives of his Free State: behind the facade of the anti-slavery movement was an operation designed simply to enrich him personally, and based on nothing more than violence and extortion.

The armed force of the Congo was the 'Force Publique' – a title just as misleading as that of the 'Free State', as it was in reality King Leopold's private army. Mercenaries had been hired on an ad hoc basis since Leopold began to establish stations on the Congo in 1879, but the force was not officially established by royal decree until October 1885. It was placed under the command of a Captain Roget of the Belgian Carabineers – who arrived in Africa with a staff of only twelve – and the first infantry companies were formally raised in 1888. At first there were eight companies, which rose to sixteen by 1893 and eventually to twenty-two by 1897. The establishment of each company varied widely. Originally each comprised between 100 and 150 men, plus around 50 labourers and porters. By the mid-1890s, however, companies reinforced for specific campaigns or to provide garrisons were often 200 or even 300 strong. There was no permanent organization above company level, but for large-scale campaigns they could be grouped into ad hoc battalions: at Stanleyville in 1896, for example, Commandant Dhanis had three battalions each of three companies, the whole force totalling 3,000 fighting men. Initially the askaris were issued with a mixture of Winchester and

Chassepot breech-loading rifles (the latter having been acquired from French troops interned in Belgium during the Franco-Prussian War). By the 1890s these were being replaced by a more modern breech-loading design, the Albini.

In the late 1880s the authority of the Free State was limited even on the Lower Congo, and it was necessary to rely on mercenaries recruited from elsewhere in Africa. Many of these were Zanzibaris, often veterans of various exploring expeditions, but recruiting officers were also sent to other parts of the continent. Hausas from British West Africa were recruited in large numbers, as they were believed to make particularly good soldiers. A number of Xhosa were also brought from South Africa, having allegedly been mistaken for Zulus. In 1896, however, Leopold's agents were banned from operating in British territory following reports that men had been lured to the Congo under false pretences, and were being subjected to cruel treatment and even summary execution. White officers and NCOs were mostly seconded from the Belgian army, but others were hired directly by Leopold, mainly from Britain, Sweden and Italy.

Soon the expense of hiring mercenaries became prohibitive, and by the 1890s local Congolese – mainly Bangala, and later Tetela and Azande – were providing the bulk of the rank and file. Most of these were conscripts, and the few volunteers joined mainly in order to escape the intolerable forced-labour requirements which were imposed on civilians in order to meet Leopold's demands for ivory and rubber. In fact many so-called volunteers were delivered against their will by their own chiefs, often in chains. Secret instructions set out bonuses to be paid to officers who press-ganged men for military service, under the innocuous heading of 'reduction in recruiting expenses' (Morel). The death rate among these men en route to their posts was high enough to cause officials serious concern, and in 1892 one report claimed that 75 per cent of the recruits died in transit (Hochschild). Inevitably desertion was another problem, and in the same year another officer, apparently without conscious irony, mentioned 'volunteers' who had drowned while trying to escape. At first each company was recruited from a single tribe, but not surprisingly this encouraged the men to conspire against their officers, and after a mutiny at Luluabourg in 1895 companies usually comprised a mixture of ethnic groups. It also became the usual practice to post men to units stationed at a distance from their own homelands. The term of service was normally five years, but in 1887 several thousand slaves 'liberated' from the Arabs were obliged to enlist for seven years in return for their freedom, and the seven-year term was later standardized.

Discipline was a widespread problem in the Force Publique, reflecting the violent and exploitative nature of the State as a whole. In order to keep down costs, pay and rations were both set at inadequate levels. It was reported by several scandalized European observers that some units were allowed or even encouraged to eat their dead enemies in order to solve the supply problem. The officers were very often of bad character, and Europeans were so few in the Congo that they were quickly promoted beyond their abilities. Leon Rom, for example, had been rejected as an officer candidate in the Belgian army, but soon after arriving in Africa he was given the rank of captain and placed in charge of training recruits for the entire Force Publique. He was feted as a hero of the war against the Arabs, but turned out to be a psychopath who gained notoriety for the collection of severed human heads with which he decorated his garden. He is said to have been the inspiration for Mr Kurtz in Joseph Conrad's *Heart of Darkness*.

Other station commanders were placed in remote outposts where they were inadequately supervised, were seldom if ever punished for excessive brutality, and often lived in fear of their own men. Few of them ever learned to speak Bangala, which was the lingua franca of the rank and file, and they gave orders only in French, which few Congolese understood. They were also distracted from their military duties by the pursuit of ivory or rubber – either on their own accounts or on behalf of the State. The result was that normal methods of training and disciplining the troops were neglected, and order was routinely kept by brutal flogging; even Dhanis, another hero of the war against the Congo Arabs (see Chapter 6), and a diplomatic commander by Force Publique standards, was known to his Tetela troops as 'Fimbo Nyingi', or 'many lashes'. Courage in battle was stimulated in medieval style by bounties paid on severed heads or hands, and as early as 1887 one officer, Guillaume van Kerckhoven, admitted to paying his men five brass rods for every enemy head brought in.

The eventual result of this treatment was a series of mutinies which began in 1895 and threw the Congo into confusion for several years.

Nevertheless many of the Force Publique's African troops were not only surprisingly loyal, but performed far better in battle than their masters had any right to expect. This may have been largely due to the fact that most were recruited from traditionally martial tribes such as the Hausa and the Tetela, to whom military service offered social status which outweighed the lack of material rewards. Another factor was that however bad life in the Force Publique may have been, civilian life in the Free State was far worse. Soldiers were at least spared forced labour as porters or rubber collectors, or the hostage taking, shooting and mutilation which they themselves inflicted on those who failed to meet production quotas. The fate of the civilian porters employed by the Force Publique was especially grim. They were conscripted for the work, often at gunpoint, and although they were theoretically paid – in beads or brass wire – corrupt officials or their own chiefs generally kept their wages for themselves. They were driven on long marches with inadequate rations, with discipline enforced, as usual, by flogging. In 1896 a Belgian observer, Edmond Picard, described most of the porters he saw as 'sickly, drooping under a burden increased by tiredness and insufficient food – a handful of rice and some stinking dried fish' (Hochschild). A few years later an Italian officer saw the caravan route between Kasongo and Lake Tanganyika 'strewn with corpses of carriers, exactly as in the time of the Arab slave trade. The carriers, weakened, ill, insufficiently fed, fall literally by hundreds' (Morel). Mortality on some expeditions could be comparable to the worst of the Japanese 'death marches' of the Second World War. In 1891 District Commissioner Paul Lemarinel rounded up 300 porters to carry supplies to a new outpost, a journey of around 600 miles. Not one of these unfortunate men survived the round trip.

In February 1895 this extraordinary army was about to pit itself against the Azande, a people who had so far defeated every invader sent against them. A column of Force Publique troops left N'Yangara on the Upper Uele on an expedition against the small independent Azande principalities along the river. Its fighting strength was ten white officers and 670 African askaris in five companies, armed with Albini rifles. Three of these companies consisted of new recruits from Sierra Leone, one of Hausas from Nigeria and one of local Mobangi tribesmen. One of the officers, the Englishman Guy Burrows, left an account of the ensuing battle. After marching for nine days through uninhabited country the Free State force, which was advancing in three columns in close contact with each other, was attacked without warning by an Azande army. The askaris managed to form into a single square, which soon found itself enveloped on three sides. The two flank faces of the square were apparently occupied with a diversionary attack, while the front face bore the brunt of the main assault by three lines of spearmen, who charged yelling across open ground. Such a reckless attack on riflemen formed in square would normally have been a recipe for disaster, but the raw Sierra Leonean troops broke before contact, and the Azande rushed into the square. One officer and around sixty askaris were killed in the mêlée, and about the same number wounded; the Hausas stood their ground but were overwhelmed, suffering more than 70 per cent casualties in a few minutes. Only the Mobangi company forming the rear face of the square remained intact, and fortunately for its comrades it stood firm, allowing the officers to rally the Sierra Leonean companies around it. The Azande, whose losses are unrecorded, withdrew and allowed the survivors to escape, but the expedition had been decisively defeated. With the Hausa company almost destroyed and the Sierra Leoneans demoralized, the invaders had no choice but to withdraw to their fort at Dongu and abandon the campaign.

The most famous victory which the Azande ever won over a European-led force took place in the same year, also against the Force Publique. In 1894 Leopold, who had long cherished an ambition to conquer the Sudan, persuaded Britain to recognize his claim to the Lado Enclave, a small strip of territory along the Upper Nile including the strategically important river-port of Lado. The following year the first of several expeditions intended to occupy this territory was dispatched under a Lieutenant Franqui. Bafuka, an Azande ruler who had until then been friendly to the Belgians, decided to refuse it permission to pass through his territory. The reason for his change of policy is unclear, but the Force Publique's indiscipline was already notorious, and inadequate supply arrangements usually obliged its expeditionary forces to live off the land. So Bafuka may well have feared with justification that his territory would be plundered or subjected to excessive requisitions. Franqui advanced regardless, and set up a camp inside the borders of Bafuka's country. His force consisted of 700 regular askaris and an unknown number of Azande auxiliaries supplied by a rival king, Zemio. Bafuka refused Franqui's offer to negotiate, and ordered his people to keep watch over the invaders and alert him as soon as they resumed their march. When they finally did so, advancing towards Bafuka's capital in a single long column, the king mustered his army. Its numbers are not known, but according to Evans-Pritchard's informants, when fully deployed it 'stretched to a great distance'. A chief called Tombo commanded the advance guard, Malingindo led the right wing and Kana the left. The reserve was under the command of Bafuka himself and his deputy, Kipa.

The Azande scouts had provided detailed information on the movements of the enemy, so Bafuka was able to prepare an ambush on both sides of the path which they were following. 'A scout hastened to tell Bafuka: "Ai! Be very much on guard today. It will be today. Ai! Bafuka, it will be today"' (Evans-Pritchard). Lieutenant Franqui, on the other hand, seems to have been confident that the Azande would not dare to attack his powerful force. He failed to reconnoitre the route ahead of him, and it was later alleged that the Hausa platoon at the head of the column had not even loaded their rifles. When they reached the spot where Bafuka's senior *abakumba* companies were hidden in the tall grass, the Azande attacked from both sides. 'That began the fight,' an Azande veteran recalled, 'and it went on for a long time. The subjects of Bafuka were killed like grass in number, and the Belgians were killed like grass also.' The Hausa platoon was effectively wiped out, having lost thirty-seven dead, including their officer, and another eighteen men wounded. The rest of the column rallied and fought on until dusk, but then the survivors finally broke and fled back the way they had come, pursued by the victorious Azande.

Franqui was wounded but escaped, though more than fifty dead askaris were left behind. The contrast between this Azande victory and the failure of the Banyoro in very similar tactical situations (see Chapter 4) could scarcely be greater, but the reasons are difficult to quantify. The Force Publique hardly maintained the highest professional standards, but its troops were well armed and had easily defeated Arabs and other opponents in the region. We do not know the proportions of firearms, spears and throwing knives in Bafuka's army, though he certainly did possess guns in significant numbers. Schweinfurth's comment on the Azande's 'thorough mastery' of warfare simply describes the situation without explaining it; clearly they were exceptionally skilled fighters, but why? They may have learned to shoot more accurately with firearms than the majority of African warriors, but they are unlikely to have learned the technique from the Arabs, whose own marksmanship was notoriously poor. Perhaps the likeliest explanation is that generations of internal warfare in their remote homeland had enabled the Azande to develop their skills to a high level, and that the individual skirmishing tactics which their home terrain encouraged were, fortuitously, already suited to the use of guns when these became available.

According to the account given to Evans-Pritchard, Bafuka's men captured a 'great number' of Albini rifles. The news of the engagement quickly spread throughout Azandeland, greatly enhancing Bafuka's reputation. A second Belgian expedition was sent against him a few months later, but this time he avoided contact with it and there was no further fighting. In 1897 Bafuka came to terms with the Free State, and together with other Azande princes he agreed to supply troops for another campaign in the Sudan, then still under Mahdist control. This expedition, led by a Belgian officer named Chaltin, was ostensibly intended to complete Franqui's mission by occupying the Lado Enclave, but in fact its commander had orders to pre-empt the British invasion which was under way from the north, and press on to Khartoum. Leopold had actually informed the British government of his intention to take over the Sudan, and then by way of compensation to lend his troops to the British for a hypothetical campaign in Armenia. This caused Queen Victoria to remark that 'It really seems as if he had taken leave of his senses' (Langer), and there is no doubt that the plan was utterly impractical. Chaltin's army comprised 700 askaris and a single 75mm Krupp mountain gun, reinforced by 580 Azande allies. It was supposed to link up with another force of 3,000 men under Baron Dhanis, but Dhanis's force mutinied before it even reached the rendezvous. Chaltin, after waiting in vain for news, decided to continue the advance unsupported. This was a rash decision which should have led to disaster. That it did not was due mainly to the loyalty and courage of the friendly Azande.

The Battles of Bedden and Rejaf, 17 February 1897

The Force Publique column reached the Nile near Bedden unopposed, but as dawn was breaking on 17 February a Mahdist army under Ali Badi Muhammad could be seen approaching. The strength of the Mahdist force is not known, but it occupied a frontage of about 2 miles along a low ridge, with its left flank resting on the river. As Chaltin began to deploy in front of him, Ali Badi transferred troops from his centre to strengthen his right wing, which he sent on a flank march round the Belgian left. Chaltin immediately attacked the weakened enemy centre, and Ali Badi's force fell back in confusion. The askari companies continued the advance, and four hours later they again made contact with the enemy. This time the Mahdists were supported by two modern quick-firing Krupp guns and deployed in strength around the small town of Rejaf, which was fortified with a thorn-bush fence or 'zeriba'. The Belgians again beat off an outflanking move and attacked in the centre, but after three hours of fighting they had made little progress and the battle was becoming a stalemate. Then the Azande contingent, which had made a long detour round the Mahdists' right flank, appeared in their rear. Thrown into confusion by their sudden attack, the defenders took refuge inside Rejaf and were quickly followed up by the askaris, who gradually fought their way inside the town. Despite this success, however, the loss of Dhanis's column meant that the advance on Khartoum had to be abandoned (though of course even their combined strength would have been utterly inadequate for such a task). The Lado Enclave was occupied, and the approach of Kitchener's army from the north prevented the Mahdists from making any serious attempt to recapture it, but ultimately Chaltin's victory was futile. Lado proved to be too remote to be a useful base, and in 1906 Leopold agreed to return it to Britain.

Gbudwe and the End of Azande Independence
Meanwhile in 1899 the triumphant Gbudwe faced yet another threat, this time from a rival Azande prince called Renzi, who had fought alongside Bafuka against the Franqui column. Renzi had since changed sides, acquired an additional supply of rifles from the Belgians, and was anxious to make a name for himself as a war leader. In their first engagement, on the River Yubo, Renzi's men forced a crossing of the river with the aid of the riflemen, but were repulsed when they ran out of ammunition. They then built a wooden stockade on their own side of the river, apparently inspired by those constructed by the Arabs, and Gbudwe besieged it without success for several days. Then Renzi, who had presumably been resupplied, sent a group of riflemen to occupy a hill on Gbudwe's side of the river, from where they gave covering fire as his spearmen attacked.

Gbudwe's camp was some distance from the river and his companies were committed in succession as the enemy advanced, but after a fight lasting all day Renzi was again driven back to his fort. Gbudwe took two days to concentrate all his strength and then counter-attacked, this time capturing the fort and forcing Renzi to abandon the campaign. Again Gbudwe had been victorious despite his enemy's great superiority in guns, many of which were breech-loading Albini rifles.

In 1904 the hated white men finally began to close in on Gbudwe. A Force Publique column under Capitaine Colin, reinforced by a contingent supplied by Renzi, marched into his territory and built a fort at Mayawa. The king once again mustered his forces to attack, but the Belgian fort was a very different proposition from those built by the Arabs. It was based around a similar wooden stockade, but a deep ditch had been dug around the outside and the earth piled up against the walls to reinforce them. Concealed firing ports were constructed at different heights to allow the defenders to shoot prone, kneeling or standing, and additional wooden poles were attached to the inside of the stockade to provide overhead cover. The exact size of the garrison is uncertain, but it appears to have comprised two companies, or about 250 men altogether, all trained shots armed with Albinis. The resulting battle was a disaster for the Azande. Following their usual practice each contingent advanced in succession to throw their spears over the stockade, only to be shot down by unseen marksmen within. Azande survivors later admitted that as far as they could tell they inflicted no casualties on the askaris, but their own losses mounted until, after three days, Gbudwe ordered his demoralized troops to retreat.

For the next year Gbudwe licked his wounds at his old capital of Birikiwe. The Belgians did not follow up their victory, as Birikiwe was in territory now allocated to the Anglo-Egyptian Sudan, but they did plunder the villages in their own sphere of influence. One day in 1905 a column of Sudanese askaris led by a British officer entered Gbudwe's country. The king believed the British to be friendly and gave orders that they were not to be opposed, but when they arrived at Birikiwe they were found to be leading one of his sons as a prisoner. A disturbance ensued, in the course of which two Azande were shot and the prisoner escaped. Gbudwe no doubt learned of this and realized that the column was hostile. There was no time to organize resistance, but he had no desire to be a prisoner again, so when the soldiers approached him he opened fire with a rifle and a revolver. In the ensuing gunfight Gbudwe shot four of the askaris, but was wounded and captured. A few days later he was dead, either by suicide or poisoned by a rival while in British custody. With his demise the day of the independent Azande kings was over, though sporadic guerrilla warfare continued in some areas until 1915.

Sources

Petherick, Piaggia (whose comments are quoted by Evans-Pritchard), Schweinfurth and Junker all witnessed aspects of traditional Azande warfare during their travels, and their books are our main sources for the pre-colonial period. Burrows is worth reading as the only one of our English-speaking sources who personally fought against the Azande.

The oral traditions collected by Evans-Pritchard are equally important for internal Azande affairs and their wars against the Arabs and Belgians. Wack is useful for the organizational details of the Force Publique and for an official perspective on its campaigns, but he was an unashamed apologist for the Free State. He quotes innumerable official directives on matters such as conditions of service and the humane treatment of civilians without giving any hint of the reality on the ground, but Morel and Hochschild have collected damning evidence about actual conditions in the Congo and its armed forces from a wide variety of late nineteenth- and early twentieth-century sources.

Chapter Six

'An Impossible Rider Haggard Romance':
The Rise and Fall of the Congo Arabs

One of the most powerful arguments which the advocates of European intervention in Africa could muster was the continued existence of the slave trade. Britain, which had once been a prime mover in this ghastly business, abolished the trade in its dominions in 1807, and for the rest of the century devoted considerable resources to suppressing it throughout the world. With the abolition of slavery in the USA after the Civil War, and in Brazil in 1871, the Atlantic trade was greatly reduced. Public attention in Britain – and increasingly in the rest of Europe – now turned to the situation in East Africa, where the activities of Arab slavers and their African allies were causing devastation across a vast region. The Arab version of slavery differed from that practised by Europeans and Americans in several respects, and is sometimes presented as being more benign. The unbridgeable racial gulf between the black slaves and their white masters did not exist in the East, and slaves who adopted Islam could often rise to positions of authority, receive their freedom, and become part of a society which offered them far more opportunities than their former isolated life in the interior. A gang of labourers might be seen working under the supervision of a man with a gun, and a European traveller would be astonished to learn that while the workers were free men, the foreman was a slave.

But if Arab slaves were at least sometimes treated better than their counterparts in the Americas, the methods used to obtain them were horrific. In the course of a slave raid whole villages would be burnt and victims who were unable to march slaughtered out of hand, while the survivors would be driven to the coast on forced marches with minimal food and water, at the end of which only one in ten might still be alive. By the late 1870s the epicentre of this murderous business was a group of Arab settlements deep in the interior of Africa, between Lake Tanganyika and the Lualaba River, which Henry Stanley had recently shown to be the main headwater of the mighty River Congo. From this embryonic Congo Arab 'state', slaving expeditions were spreading their devastation north and west into previously untouched territory. It was from here that before his death in 1873 David Livingstone made a heartfelt plea for Europe to heal this 'open sore' (Coupland, 1947), but it was to be another twenty years before a European-led army arrived on the banks of the Lualaba. And when it came it was no 'civilizing mission' such as Livingstone might have envisaged, but an Old Testament-style instrument of vengeance as cruel and ruthless as the slavers themselves.

The Origins of the State

Arab slave and ivory traders had been active on the east coast of Africa for centuries. When the Portuguese navigators entered the Indian Ocean early in the sixteenth century, during their quest for the Spice Islands, they found Muslim city states dotted along the coast as far south as what is now Mozambique. They quickly subjugated them with the aid of seaborne cannon, and built impressive forts to control their newly won trade routes, like the one which still survives at Fort Jesus, Mombasa. But in the seventeenth century the Muslims launched a counteroffensive under the leadership of the Sultan of Oman, who built up a large navy of seagoing warships with which to challenge the Christians. The Portuguese were driven out of the northern half of the Indian Ocean, and the Omanis took over as the leading trading power. The city states along the African coast were now subject to the Sultans of Oman, but by the dawn of the nineteenth century their inhabitants – mainly Swahilis, the descendants of local Africans who had been converted to Islam – were in practice independent. Then in 1832 Sultan Seyyid Said transferred his capital from Muscat to the island of Zanzibar off the coast of what is now Tanzania, once a remote outpost of the empire but now increasingly the source of its wealth. After Seyyid's death in 1856 the island gained its independence from Oman, and became the centre of a commercial empire in its own right.

Zanzibar was well placed to control the caravan routes which ran inland towards Lakes Victoria, Tanganyika and Nyasa, and during the 1840s slavers and ivory traders had begun to establish permanent settlements along these routes. The slave and ivory trades were in fact part of a single network, since prisoners were often taken in order to be ransomed for tusks, and those who carried the ivory to the coast could themselves be sold on arrival. Harry Johnston describes the Arab methods in terms reminiscent of those used by Baker in his account of the 'Turks' in the Sudan (see Chapter 5): they would befriend a local chief, provide him with guns and assist him against his enemies, and then enslave the defeated victims. In this way they depopulated large areas, especially in the south of Tanganyika, though some peoples – notably the Nyamwezi of central Tanganyika and the Bemba of the Lake Nyasa region – escaped the devastation by going into partnership with the slavers. In the interior, even more than on the coast, the distinction between Arabs and native Africans was often blurred. In fact most so-called 'Arabs' were born in Africa, and although they may have been able to trace their descent from a genuine immigrant from Oman, they differed from the Swahilis mainly by their social position and their ability to speak Arabic. It has been suggested that generations of interbreeding with African populations gave them a degree of immunity to malaria and other tropical diseases, which made it possible for them to thrive in regions where other outsiders became ill or died. According to strict Islamic teaching it was not permissible to enslave fellow believers, and so Africans who had been captured and subsequently converted were often freed. Many of these men went into business as slavers or ivory traders themselves, and by the late nineteenth century some individuals were even commanding large bodies of Arabs. The elephant hunter 'Karamoja' Bell once encountered a former slave named Shundi, originally a native of Kavirondo on the shore of Lake Victoria, who was in command of a caravan composed of Arabs, Swahilis, Persians and even Baluchis from what is now Pakistan.

The most famous and successful of all the Zanzibari pioneers was Hamed ibn Muhammed ibn Juma, who became better known by his native nickname of 'Tippu Tib', variously said to refer to his habit of rapid blinking, or to be an onomatopoeic word representing the sound of gunfire. According to Tippu Tib's own story he was born in the 1840s, of mixed Arab and African descent, and began trading on the African mainland in the employ of his father, who was a wealthy merchant. Stanley (1879) described Hamed in later life as 'a tall, black-bearded man of negroid complexion . . . a picture of energy and strength'. 'A good-looking man,' says the explorer Commander Verney Cameron, 'and the

greatest dandy I had seen amongst the traders.' He was dedicated to physical fitness, always walked on his expeditions instead of riding a donkey,
and once decisively won a foot race against Stanley's companion Frank
Pocock. Strangely, this notorious slave raider impressed most of those
who met him – including men such as Livingstone, who abhorred his
business activities – as humble, courteous and generous. He was said to
have been kind to his own personal slaves, and helped many of the
European explorers who were trying to put him out of business. Several
of these, including Cameron, admitted that without his assistance they
would have perished.

In 1867 Tippu Tib fell out with his father and formed a caravan of his
own, financed by loans from his relatives and the Indian bankers in
Zanzibar. According to his own account and those given to European visitors by his followers, his family were at that time peaceful traders, who
did not take slaves by force but merely bought them when offered for sale
by local chiefs. Circumstances (and no doubt the pressure of his debts)
forced the young Hamed into taking a different direction. He arrived at
Tabora, the main commercial centre in the interior of Tanganyika, to find
that there was little there to buy. He moved on to visit a powerful chief
called Nsama at his village of Ruemba, despite dire warnings from the
local Arabs of the chief's predilection for treachery. As predicted, Nsama
first welcomed his caravan into the village and then attacked him, but
Hamed's twenty guns enabled him to put the spear-armed warriors to
flight. He then rounded up all the women and children he could catch,
ransacked Nsama's storehouses – netting a fortune in ivory – and returned
to Tabora in triumph. Over the next few years several similar incidents
occurred, in which real or alleged treachery gave Tippu Tib a convenient
excuse to plunder the country. 'I learned that day in Nsama's village,' he
is recorded as saying, 'that the gun is the Sultan of Africa' (Brode). It is
likely that among Nsama's people, as elsewhere in Africa, women and
children were never molested in the course of traditional warfare, so the
men were not reluctant to abandon them if they felt themselves outclassed
in battle. Only later would they realize their mistake when they returned
to their empty villages.

Tippu Tib and his followers grew rich on this destructive 'trade', but
in order to sustain it they needed constantly to move on to new territories.
The spoiling of the East African slave-hunting grounds was undoubtedly

a major factor in the Arab expansion beyond Lake Tanganyika towards the Upper Congo. This process seems to have started as early as 1869. The Manyema people who lived west of the lake were notorious cannibals, greatly feared by their neighbours, but their spears and shields proved no match for Arab firepower. At first they suffered heavily at the hands of the slave raiders, but within a few years Manyema warriors were fighting alongside the newcomers, who recognized their value as soldiers and supplied them with guns. When Cameron passed through Manyema in 1874 he found that the Arab settlements at Nyangwe and Kasongo were already sizeable towns, though still at least nominally subject to the Sultan of Zanzibar. The main settlement, Nyangwe, consisted of two villages and a market place on the Lualaba River which flowed northwards into the unexplored rainforest. In nearby Kasongo one Arab alone employed 600 armed Nyamwezi tribesmen, who were permitted to loot the surrounding countryside in lieu of pay.

Livingstone had visited Nyangwe in 1871, and his first-hand account of the Arabs' treatment of the local population scandalized his readers in Britain. Describing a massacre in which the followers of the slaver Dugumbe fired on unarmed people in the marketplace, killing several hundred, he wrote 'It gave me the impression of being in hell' (Waller). In 1873, largely as a result of Livingstone's revelations, the Sultan of Zanzibar was persuaded to prohibit the slave trade in his dominions, but although in theory the Congo Arabs were Zanzibari subjects, they were too remote from the coast for the edict to be enforced, and they continued to expand their activities unmolested. At first, however, they encountered formidable obstacles to the west. The dense forests of the Congo were alien territory to them, inhabited by ferocious cannibal tribes whose lack of firearms, in such difficult terrain, was less of a disadvantage than it had been for the Arabs' earlier victims.

The wars which took place between the Arabs and the jungle tribes are mostly undocumented, but we do have a detailed description of one battle. Unfortunately it is not a first-hand account, having been collected by Stanley (not always himself a reliable witness) from one of Tippu Tib's men named Abed ibn Jumah, who claimed to be a survivor of the encounter. Nevertheless it contains several features of interest, and is worth recounting with due allowance for exaggeration on the part of one or both of the tellers. Some time around 1870 a man named Mtagamoyo mounted an expedition into the forest in search of a land where ivory was said to be available very cheaply, as the local people had no idea of its worth. Mtagamoyo was well known as a successful leader, and soon assembled a following of 310 fighting men, all armed with guns, and a large number of slaves. From the start they met resistance from the cannibal tribes of Uregga and Usongora Meno, who lurked invisible in the undergrowth and shot at them with poisoned arrows. By the time they reached the village of Chief Kima-Kima on the Lomami River after a month's march, they had already lost twenty men, but the information they received from the chief gave them fresh hope. According to Kima-Kima they were not far from the country of the 'little men' or Pygmies, who possessed vast stores of ivory. The Arabs spoke to a few Pygmies in the village, who confirmed that their people were eager to trade. They also gave them directions to their king's village, which turned out to be a large permanent settlement surrounded by banana plantations.

This presents a problem, because although the Pygmies are described as small and bearded, like the Mbuti who inhabit the region today, the Mbuti have traditionally lived by hunting and gathering, in small mobile camps rather than permanent villages, and do not practise agriculture. There are a few other nineteenth-century accounts which suggest that some Pygmy groups were once organized on a larger scale than they have been in recent times, but there is another possible explanation. Some forest peoples like the Lele have intermarried with the Mbuti and are referred to disparagingly as 'Pygmies' by the materially more advanced river tribes, even though they are of normal stature and grow crops as well as hunt. But according to Abed ibn Jumah the people they encountered were so small that they seemed harmless. In fact the Arabs were at first amused rather than alarmed by their acts of aggression. Perhaps in this case the story has shrunk rather than grown in the telling, but it is at least possible that we have here a glimpse of a type of Mbuti society not otherwise known to have existed.

For the first ten days things went well, and the Pygmies produced hundreds of tusks in exchange for beads, copper and cowrie shells, which served as currency in many parts of Central Africa. But when the Arabs announced that they had all the ivory they could carry and were ready to leave, the Pygmy king refused to allow them to do so until they had traded all their cowries. Bearing in mind Mtagamoyo's reputation as a freebooter, and that the only account we have comes from his party, the Arabs may have been guilty of some act of provocation; alternatively Kima-Kima and his allies might have deliberately led their visitors into a trap. But it is equally likely that the affair arose from a misunderstanding about the role of trade. Many non-western societies have tended to see trade in terms of mutual gift-giving which reinforces the social and political status of the participants, with economic prosperity as a secondary goal. In this case it may well have seemed to the Pygmies discourteous or even treacherous for the Arabs to depart without sharing out all the goods they had brought with them. Certainly Mtagamoyo's men seem to have been genuinely surprised by their reaction. The traders held a meeting and decided to attempt to escape, but before the meeting had finished news arrived that the Pygmies had shot one of their slave women. The Arabs seized their guns just in time to meet an attack by hundreds of tribesmen, shooting 'clouds' of poisoned arrows.

Here we confront one of the enduring myths of African warfare. Abed described how 'many of our people fell dead instantly from the poison' (Stanley, 1879), apparently confirming numerous statements in nineteenth-century literature regarding the deadliness of the poisons used by Central African archers, and especially by the Pygmies. Cameron was told that 'a mere scratch' invariably proved fatal in four or five minutes, unless an antidote – known only to the archers themselves – was applied. But reliable first-hand accounts describe much slower-acting and less lethal effects. For example, Paul du Chaillu, who received several wounds from poisoned arrows when attacked in Gabon, describes only a feeling of exhaustion and a raging thirst, which did not prevent him and his followers from making their escape on foot. Stanley's own party suffered numerous arrow wounds in their descent of the Congo, but the wounds were treated with 'a timely application of caustic' (Stanley, 1879), and there were no fatalities definitely attributable to the poison. Significantly, the dogs which accompanied du Chaillu's expedition were all killed, which suggests that the poison was designed for hunting small animals such as monkeys, and that the dose normally applied to an arrowhead would be insufficient to kill a man, unless perhaps it happened to penetrate a major organ or blood vessel.

In Abed's account, despite the alleged fatal effects of the Pygmies' arrow poison, the Arabs somehow rallied and returned fire. Mtagamoyo even charged with his two-handed sword and killed several of the enemy, but being so small ('a yard high' according to the Arab, though this is certainly an exaggeration as modern Pygmies average slightly over 4 feet) they could conceal themselves easily behind bushes or in trees. Therefore the Arabs found themselves at a disadvantage in the firefight, despite their guns. 'Had they been tall men like us,' Abed lamented, 'we might have picked off hundreds of them.' Mtagamoyo therefore ordered his men to cut down the Pygmies' banana trees and demolish their houses, using the wood to build a *boma* or defensive stockade. Somehow this was accomplished under fire, and the Arabs took cover inside their improvised defences. Now that they had the leisure to aim and shoot more deliberately they eventually drove off their attackers, only to find themselves besieged in the middle of a hostile village. After two days of heavy fighting the Arabs were desperate for water, so Mtagamoyo led a sortie to the nearby river. He aimed his charge where the enemy were densest, and there was a brief hand-to-hand fight before the Pygmies let them through to the water. The Arabs took several prisoners here, and when they returned to the boma they saw that one of them was the king. He was released in return for a promise of safe passage, but his people did not honour the promise, and after fighting them off for another day and a night the traders realized that their stocks of gunpowder were running low. So they launched another sortie with the 'broad long swords, bright as glass', which many of them carried in addition to their muskets. The enemy would not face these blades and fled, suffering heavy losses in the pursuit. Taking advantage of the respite, the Arabs packed up what ivory they could carry and started the retreat, but that night the Pygmies caught up with them in the forest and the relentless rain of arrows began again. This time, unable to reply effectively because of shortage of powder, Mtagamoyo's men broke and fled, 'throwing down everything except our guns and swords'. According to Abed, he was one of only thirty who eventually escaped from the forest alive.

Since that time the Congo Arabs had tried twice more to fight their way through the forests downstream of Nyangwe, but had given up after losing nearly 500 men altogether to the cannibals, the rapids of the river and other perils of the jungle. In 1876, however, Stanley arrived from the east on his epic journey which was eventually to cross the continent and make the first descent of the River Congo. He was determined to sail down the Lualaba, rightly suspecting it to be a tributary of the Congo, and persuaded Tippu Tib to join him with an overland column of his own. The Arabs turned back after a few weeks, but once the Lualaba route had been shown to be practical they soon returned in force. Applying their usual methods, they spread the horrors of the slave trade across the eastern half of the Congo. When Stanley returned in 1880, he found the banks of the river – where only three years before he had been repeatedly attacked by large war parties – almost deserted. The surviving people had fled inland into the forest, and in some places had left their great war canoes stuck vertically into the mud, their bottoms hacked open as if in token of surrender.

The Arrival of the Congo Free State

On this later expedition Stanley was employed as an agent of King Leopold II of the Belgians, who was in the process of setting up his own private empire in the Congo Basin. In 1880 his Congo Free State was still in the early stages of formation, and there was as yet no military force to back up its authority. When Stanley finally reached the great series of waterfalls at Stanley Falls (which he had named after himself on his last expedition), he found an advance post belonging to his former ally Tippu Tib. The Arabs were only recently established there, and Stanley's lines of communication were stretched to breaking point, so neither side was in a position to threaten the other. The explorer built a post on an island in the river not far from the Arab settlement, and left without disturbing the status quo. It was not long, however, before inevitable friction between the two sides led to the first armed clash. The brief war which broke out in August 1886 was precipitated by a dispute about a runaway slave woman, whom the Free State commander, an Englishman named Walter Deane, had refused to return to her master. Deane commanded a small garrison which was intended to do no more than 'show the flag'. It consisted of a Belgian officer named Dubois, two modern Krupp artillery pieces, and seventy-two African askaris. Of these, thirty-two were experienced Hausa mercenaries from Nigeria, and the remainder were new recruits drawn from the Bangala people of the Middle Congo. The askaris were armed with a mixture of Snider and Martini-Henry rifles but were very short of ammunition, as the supply steamer had recently arrived without the equipment and reinforcements which Deane had requested.

One morning Deane discovered the Arabs' Manyema soldiers entrenched behind roughly constructed earthworks only 800 yards from his stockade. Over the next two days the two sides exchanged fire, but with little result, as the range was too great for small arms fire to be effective, and Deane hesitated to use up the few rounds available for the Krupps. On the third day the Manyema tried to approach closer to the stockade. Dubois led two sorties which drove them back, but nearly all the rifle ammunition was used up in the fighting, and seven of the Hausas were killed. That night the Bangalas deserted, followed the next night by most of the surviving Hausas. Although the Krupp guns were still in action, it was clear that the remaining garrison – two officers, four Hausa askaris and one local tribesman – could no longer hold the fort. So they spiked the guns, set fire to the buildings, and waded across the river to the north bank. Dubois was swept away and drowned, but Deane reached the shore and spent thirty days in hiding in the forest until a Belgian steamer rescued him. Walter Deane had more than his share of bad luck on the Congo. According to E J Glaive, who had worked for Stanley on the Congo since 1883, he had another narrow escape in 1887 when he and thirty Hausa askaris were attacked by tribesmen while camped at the village of Monongeri. The spear-armed Congolese took advantage of a storm to cover the sound of their approach, and killed half the force before the survivors managed to escape in their steel boat. Deane was seriously wounded, but he survived the Arab wars only to be killed afterwards by an elephant.

The Free State's control of the Upper Congo was still tenuous at this time, and no immediate attempt was made to retake the station. Instead King Leopold, using Stanley as an intermediary, appointed Tippu Tib as his governor in the Eastern Congo. From the Arab's point of view the nominal loss of sovereignty was a minor consideration: he could not have expected Leopold ever to make good his claim in this remote region, and so he was happy enough to draw a salary for governing – with effectively a free hand – a territory which was already under his control. But in 1890 Tippu Tib returned to Zanzibar to pursue a legal dispute with Stanley. He never returned to the Congo, but left his thriving state in the charge of his son Sefu and his nephew Rashid. By then the situation was changing dramatically.

The Congo War, 1891–1894

Conflict began unofficially in 1891, when a Belgian expedition led by Guillaume van Kerckhoven intruded into the Arabs' elephant-hunting preserves in the Uele region. Van Kerckhoven's men acted with complete disregard for their official alliance with the Arabs, and several caravans were robbed of their ivory at gunpoint. The expedition was apparently acting on orders from Leopold, and the next stage of its mission shows how divorced from reality the king had already become: van Kerckhoven was to invade the Sudan, then occupied by the Mahdists, and march on Khartoum from the south with his 600 men, entirely unsupported! In the event he was accidentally shot dead by his own gun-bearer, and the mission collapsed before it could embroil the Free State in an unnecessary and unwinnable war. (Leopold did not give up, however; for his subsequent attempts to overthrow the Mahdist state see Chapter 5.)

By the 1890s the Free State had its own well-equipped armed force, the Force Publique (as discussed in more detail in Chapter 5), and its officers no longer felt obliged to conciliate the Arabs. In May 1892 a Lieutenant Michiels provoked more bad feeling by insisting on raising the Free State flag in an Arab settlement at Riba-Riba. Michiels, and an ivory trader named Hodister who was accompanying him, were killed and allegedly eaten by the people of the village, apparently on the orders of the Arab commander at Nyangwe, Mohara. Tippu Tib's son Sefu, however, was still eager for peace and refused to follow the urging of hawks such as Mohara, who argued that they should strike at once, while the Belgians were apparently still too weak to resist a full-scale invasion. In this Mohara was right, as the only Free State forces in a position to oppose him were at an isolated outpost called Lusambo on the Sankuru River, at the end of a very long supply line. However, the commander at Lusambo, Commandant Dhanis, was informed of the deliberations in the Arab camp, and in the absence of orders from home was obliged to rely on his own initiative. He opened negotiations with the local Tetela tribe, whose musket-armed warriors had been among Sefu's staunchest allies, and persuaded their chief, Gongo Lutete, to change sides with a force estimated at 10,000 strong – though only a minority of these were armed with guns, and their actual performance in battle proved to be disappointing.

The Battle of Chige, November 1892

This diplomatic coup solved Dhanis's immediate manpower problem, but it also precipitated the attack he had feared. Sefu retaliated by joining forces with Mohara to attack Lusambo, and in November 1892 the two commanders crossed the River Lomami at Chige with 10,000 men. Facing them was a screen of Tetela musketeers under Gongo Lutete, who fell back in front of the invaders while sending a warning to the Belgians. The nearest Free State force in the field was a patrol of 150 askaris under a Lieutenant Michaux, who made a twelve-hour forced march through a tropical storm to reinforce the Tetela. When he arrived at the Lomami, Michaux discovered that Sefu had gone over to the defensive and built a wooden stockade on the river bank, apparently in the hope that Gongo would attack him. But when Michaux ordered him to do so the Tetela chief refused, explaining that the rain had soaked his men's powder and temporarily rendered their muskets useless. The young Belgian immediately realized that the Arabs would be in the same situation, whereas his own men, who were equipped with breech-loading rifles firing metal cartridges, were unaffected by the weather. He withdrew the Tetela, and ordered his askaris to assault the stockade at once.

The lieutenant's judgement was proved correct, as the enemy fire was completely ineffective. Sidney Hinde, an Englishman who served as a medical officer in the Force Publique, says that about thirty 'good repeating rifles' were captured after the fight, so not all the Arabs were armed with muzzle-loaders. But these modern weapons were obviously too few to make much difference, and their users were probably quickly demoralized by the collapse of their comrades. Two Force Publique NCOs reached the stockade at the head of their men, and one of them, Corporal Benga, a powerful man described by Hinde as a 'great athlete', physically knocked out the posts to create a gap. The defenders tried to fall back to an inner ring of defences, but the askaris poured through the stockade and shot them down as they ran. The Tetela now followed them, and a massacre ensued. The Arabs tried to swim across the river to safety, but hundreds were shot or drowned as they did so. Hinde estimated that 600 bodies were later found on the battlefield, and as many as 3,000 more died in the river. Michaux's loss was only two men. As soon as he arrived on the scene and took command – and without waiting for orders from Belgium – Dhanis ordered his men to cross the river and advance into

Arab territory. The resulting war took place in a remote, almost unexplored corner of Africa, and pitted those stereotypical Victorian
bogeymen – the Arab slavers – against what seemed at the time like a
heroic band of idealistic adventurers. No wonder Harry Johnston
described it, in a reference to the writer of *King Solomon's Mines* and
similar exotic tales of African adventure, as 'an impossible Rider Haggard
romance' (Johnston, 1908). In reality, however, it was far from romantic.

The Free State Offensive

On 26 November the advance guard of the Free State forces crossed the
Lomami and began the march on Nyangwe. Hinde describes the order of
march of the expedition as it travelled along a single narrow trail through
the dense bush:

> Our formation was generally headed by a strong advance-guard of
> soldiers, who were not allowed to carry anything but their rifles and
> ammunition; after them came the loads with the guard, then the
> women, and lastly a strong rear-guard. The white officers, each with
> a good bodyguard, were distributed along the whole line, which was
> sometimes two or three miles in length . . . . All auxiliary forces and
> camp followers were sent on in front of the caravan, and if overtaken
> had to withdraw from the road, since they were not allowed to
> mingle with or interfere in any way with the main caravan. (Hinde,
> 1897)

In early January 1893 Sefu and Mohara came out to meet the invaders,
and a confused series of engagements ensued in the mosaic of tall grass
and forest which covered the area. Sefu took up a position in front of
Dhanis's camp while Mohara led another column into their rear. While a
Force Publique detachment under the splendidly titled Belgian aristocrat
Captain le Chevalier d'Oplinter de Wouters was searching for Mohara,
the Arab leader ambushed a caravan under an officer named Cassart, who
was bringing up 50,000 rounds of desperately needed ammunition and a
consignment of Chassepot rifles. Hinde graphically describes the
suspense in Dhanis's camp as the men listened to outbreaks of firing in
their rear and realized that they were surrounded, but had no way of
knowing how the fighting was going. Eventually Cassart marched in,

wounded, but bringing his precious cargo of cartridges intact. That morning he had been camped about two and a half hours' march to the west, knowing nothing of Mohara's proximity. His escort consisted of twenty-six askaris and 250 Tetela porters, some of whom had muskets. Just before six o'clock, as he was preparing to move on, a volley was fired from the surrounding bush and a force of Arabs appeared, preparing to rush the camp.

Cassart returned fire as best he could, hurriedly issuing the Chassepots to the unarmed porters. Hinde describes the Belgian fire as 'ill directed', which must have been an understatement considering that many of the men had never handled their weapons until that moment, but it was sufficient to check Mohara's men, who returned to cover and kept up a half-hearted fire for the next four hours. Cassart apparently kept the askaris under his direct command, and led them out on sorties to drive away any enemy who approached too near. At last the Arabs retired. It later turned out that Mohara had been wounded, and the ensuing confusion gave Cassart a respite of over an hour while his opponent reorganized his men. The Belgian officer at once struck camp and set out to rendezvous with Dhanis. The enemy rallied and pursued him, but not far away the path crossed a deep river by means of a huge tree which had been felled across it. As there was no other crossing place nearby, the askaris were able to form a rearguard and prevent the enemy following them until the loads were safely in Dhanis's camp.

Firing continued to be heard in Dhanis's rear, but that evening a soldier arrived with a report from de Wouters – and the severed head of Mohara. Not long after Cassart's escape the Arabs' camp had been located, on high ground overlooking a marshy valley. Unfortunately for the defenders tall grass and crops around the hill restricted lines of sight, and the Belgians managed to cross the swamp and get within 100 yards of the camp before they were recognized. De Wouters believed that his force had been mistaken for an expected mission from Sefu, and so the enemy was taken by surprise when the askaris charged out of the grass and opened fire. In the ensuing rout Mohara was shot down, and the camp was captured along with a large quantity of food and pack donkeys. The Nyangwe army was dispersed beyond recall, and the way cleared for an advance on the town with the aid of the captured supplies. As for Mohara's remains, the Tetela later taunted Sefu's men with the claim that they had eaten him. This may have been meant figuratively, but was quite likely the literal truth. Elsewhere Hinde describes his horror on seeing the contents of the packs which a Tetela contingent had abandoned after a repulse: among them were cooked human limbs and heads, taken along as rations for the march.

Two weeks after the death of Mohara, Dhanis's men arrived on the west bank of the Lualaba, opposite Nyangwe. But the river was 900 yards wide at this point, and unfordable. The local Wagenya boatmen were reluctant to provide their canoes for the crossing for fear of Arab reprisals, so the two sides faced each other across the river for several weeks, exchanging occasional shots. Sidney Hinde's observations on this long-range firefight are interesting. He remarks that on seeing a puff of smoke from a rifle the Arabs on the far bank had time to take cover before the bullet reached them, and that smokeless powder would have been useful in the circumstances, but none was available. Instead the Force Publique snipers lit bonfires behind them, so that the smoke from their guns would be harder to detect. They also shot at the enemy's cattle when they were driven to the river to drink, sometimes with bizarre consequences:

> The herd became enraged, and seemed further annoyed by their masters, who were returning our fire from the trenches in the neighbourhood. They charged into them, and in a very few seconds emptied the trenches. The flying soldiers, turning round and firing on the infuriated beasts, were quickly dispersed by one or two volleys from us. But for some hours afterwards we could see the cattle racing after terror-stricken wretches through the streets of the town.

Inevitably the return fire of the Arabs' smoothbore muzzle-loaders was less effective, but by loading them with huge quantities of gunpowder they did manage to hit the Belgian positions from an island 400 yards away, and even occasionally from the town itself. The irregularly shaped chunks of iron and copper which they often used can have had little velocity left at that range, but they arrived with a 'horrid shriek' that frightened Dhanis's men until they got used to them.

Eventually Dhanis decided to lure Sefu out of the town by leaking information via the Wagenya who still regularly crossed the river. Gongo Lutete and his Tetela were temporarily absent from the army, and the commandant made sure that the Arabs knew that they would not be back for a fortnight. Sure enough a few days later Sefu crossed the Lualaba a few miles downstream, and began to prepare an attack. As soon as the news reached him, Dhanis led his men out to meet him. Half of the askaris were left behind to guard the camp while the rest of the force advanced in two columns, each of approximately company strength, through the usual patchwork of dense forest and tall grass. The advance guard, under the command of de Wouters and Hinde (medical officers were not non-combatants in the Congo Free State), was accompanied by the expedition's single 75mm Krupp field gun. It was to outflank the Arab camp on the left, while Dhanis and the main body moved along the main trail to attack it frontally.

However, soon after they set out Hinde and de Wouters heard the noise of a large body of men moving through a belt of forest which separated them from the track. Assuming that it was Dhanis advancing ahead of schedule they quickened their pace, but as they entered a 'sort of cul de sac of open ground' about 400 yards across and surrounded on three sides by forest, they ran into an ambush. Sefu's scouts had informed him of Dhanis's dispositions, and instead of outflanking the enemy the advance guard was now caught between two converging Arab forces and separated from its main body by dense jungle. Hinde and de Wouters came under heavy musket fire from a range of between 30 and 100 yards, but luckily for them the Arab shooting was extremely inaccurate. In Hinde's opinion most of their shots went high and 'did more damage to each other than to us'. The Krupp gun was deployed to the front, but we hear no more of it during the action. Probably it was unable to locate many worthwhile targets in the dense vegetation. De Wouters, who was 6 feet 5 inches tall and always dressed entirely in white, was an obvious target, but miraculously he remained unscathed. Hinde says that Sefu's men, who called him the 'White Heron', attributed his survival to witchcraft. Believing that the magic was effective only against bullets, a group of them rushed out to attack him with their knives, but were shot down before they reached him.

The Free State askaris steadily returned the fire, and after an hour the Arabs on the left – furthest away from Dhanis's column – began to break and run. At that point a party of askaris arrived under Lieutenant Michaux, who had been ordered to guard the camp but had used his initiative in advancing to the sound of firing. With these reinforcements Hinde and de Wouters led a bayonet charge which drove off the enemy. Following up through the forest on a narrow path, Hinde recalled that 'the sensation of going through this undergrowth, with the enemy all the time firing apparently from out of the ground, from the tree tops and in every direction, was not a pleasant one'. But in another striking illustration of the ineffectiveness of Arab firepower, Hinde was not hit. After regrouping they moved on again, and to their surprise soon came under 'a well-sustained steady fire'. It was not until they heard a familiar drumbeat that they realized that they had been exchanging fire with Dhanis's men. The Arabs, trapped in their turn by converging enemy columns, had fled from the field. Evidently both sides had had the same intention, moving in two columns with the aim of outflanking the other, and the terrain had channelled them all into a small area so that each side had one column sandwiched between two of the enemy's. Neither commander had exercised any real control over the battle, but the steadiness and fire discipline of his askaris and white officers had given Dhanis the victory.

After this victory the Wagenya boatmen went over to the Belgians, and on 4 March 1893 they ferried them across the river in a hundred canoes. H W Wack, a contemporary American apologist for the Free State, claimed that the Arabs still had 60,000 men under arms at this point, to oppose Dhanis's 300 regulars and 2,000 Tetela auxiliaries. Understandably he described the attack as 'a bold venture', but by now the Arabs were too demoralized to do much more than stand on the defensive. After two days of fierce street fighting Dhanis's men, this time with the Tetela fighting alongside them, sacked Nyangwe and massacred the inhabitants. The Tetela fully justified their reputation for cannibalism: according to Hinde, when Dhanis eventually ordered the enemy dead to be buried for fear of disease, few of the bodies could be found. Soon after the fall of Nyangwe the same fate befell Sefu's capital, a few miles away at Kasongo. Then in May the station downriver at Stanley Falls, which had been besieged by a large Arab army, was relieved by a gunboat and a party under Lieutenant Chaltin, clearing the way for supplies to be sent by the river route.

Meanwhile the Force Publique was making contact with an unlikely new ally in the war against slavery. The French White Father missionaries had established a station at Mpala on the western shore of Lake

Tanganyika, and in 1887 a former Papal Zouave officer named Leopold Joubert arrived to set up a 'secular arm' of the mission. This was in fact a military force, recruited from local African personnel, intended to defend the missionaries against the hostile Arabs. Over the next few years Joubert became embroiled in a series of successful battles against a slaver named Rumaliza and his lieutenants. On one occasion he fought a combined operation on the lake against 400 Arabs under a chief called Rajabu, which was brought to an end by a storm which destroyed Rajabu's boats. In 1890 an anti-slavery conference in Paris voted to raise a French force to support Joubert, but Leopold refused to allow it to operate on Free State territory. Late in 1891 a Belgian expedition under Captain Jules Jacques did arrive, and in conjunction with Joubert it attacked Rumaliza's fort at Toka Toka. The attack failed, however, and in an Arab counter-attack in April 1892 a Belgian officer named Vrithoff was captured and handed over to Rumaliza's cannibal followers to be eaten. In the following year more Belgian reinforcements arrived, and Joubert was able to close in on Rumaliza simultaneously with Dhanis's advance from the west.

Nevertheless the hardest fighting of the campaign was still to come. Rumaliza's territory was defended by a number of well-constructed forts consisting of earthworks and wooden stockades. In October 1893 Dhanis resumed his advance against these with 400 regular askaris, 300 irregular tribal musketeers and the single Krupp gun. The supply situation was still difficult, and most of the spear-armed Tetela auxiliaries had been sent home as not worth the rations they consumed. The Krupp gun commenced the campaign with only forty-four shells and a dozen rounds of canister, so that it could not be used for sustained bombardment of the forts but had to be kept in reserve for emergencies. On one occasion, when an infantry assault had bogged down yards from an Arab stockade, the gun was brought up to try to suppress the enemy fire with canister. But the porters pulling it either were shot or fled, abandoning the piece 100 yards from the enemy ramparts. A group of Belgian officers managed to get it into action under heavy fire, but all they could do was provide covering fire while the askaris and then the gun itself were withdrawn. Hinde believed that it was only the poor positioning of the defenders' loopholes, which were angled in such a way that attackers lying down near the fort were beneath the line of fire, that saved the attackers from a massacre. Fortunately for the Belgians the Arabs had to expose themselves on the top of the parapets to fire effectively, making themselves easy targets.

Rumaliza was eventually forced to evacuate this fort, but retired to another position which Dhanis again unsuccessfully assaulted. Sefu was killed during this operation, but the Belgians were forced to retreat. Then in December the tide turned decisively with the arrival of captains Collignon and Rom with 180 fresh infantry, another Krupp gun and most importantly plentiful supplies of ammunition. Dhanis was now able to bombard the forts effectively before attacking, and it was not long before they began to fall, one after another. During the siege of a fort at Bena Kalunga in January 1894, a lucky ranging shot from one of the Krupps hit a powder magazine and caused an explosion which set fire to the fort, forcing the Arabs to evacuate it without firing a shot. By the end of February resistance had almost ceased, and de Wouters was able to advance unopposed to Lake Tanganyika to link up with Joubert.

Aftermath

Rumaliza escaped into the forest to the north, and eventually made his way back to Zanzibar. Tippu Tib, whose absence from the Congo had enabled him to deny any responsibility for the war, lived there in peaceful retirement until his death in 1905. The European powers had by now accepted Leopold's claim to all the territory making up his Congo Free State. Leopold was a skilled if cynical self-publicist, and the true nature of his rule did not become widely apparent until the end of the 1890s. Despite its name, the 'Free State' was never opened to free trade, and although slavery was technically abolished, in practice the entire population was virtually enslaved. The role of the State officials was to maximize production – initially of ivory, and by the 1890s also of rubber, which gained a huge new market with the invention of pneumatic tyres. They were paid generous bonuses by way of encouragement, and their methods were seldom scrutinized. These methods included the razing of villages to clear land for plantations, the seizing of women and children as hostages to force the men to collect rubber, and outright robbery. Even within 'pacified' areas the State's military forces lived mainly by plunder, so that the villagers would routinely flee into the forest as soon as a patrol approached.

It remains a puzzle how most of the missionaries and Free State employees in the Congo, drawn from all over Europe and North America, either acquiesced in or failed to notice these abuses. Stanley, for example, remained a staunch defender of Leopold. It is true that the worst conditions were not universal throughout the region, but the overall effect on the country was catastrophic. Several eyewitnesses describe significant depopulation. Ewart Grogan, who marched through the north-eastern corner of the Congo on his Cape to Cairo expedition of 1899 to 1900, and was himself by no means sympathetic to Africans, described the region as 'a howling wilderness' (Grogan and Sharp), inhabited only by terrified fugitives. He met many people who had fled into British territory to escape raids by the Force Publique. On the Lower Congo, 30,000 refugees escaped across the river into French territory. Later estimates suggest that between 1879 and 1919 the population of the Congo was reduced by half, implying the deaths by murder, warfare, starvation and disease of as many as 10 million people.

Eventually public opinion in Europe turned against Leopold, largely thanks to the revelations of an English shipping clerk named Edmund Morel, who had done his research not in the jungles of Central Africa but in the offices of his employers in Liverpool and Antwerp. He discovered that the valuable exports of ivory and rubber were not balanced by corresponding imports of trade goods; the only items routinely shipped to the Congo were rifles and ammunition, which according to international treaties could not be sold to Africans. There could be only one conclusion: wealth was being extorted from the inhabitants by violence or the threat of it. Morel faced a long struggle before the authorities in Belgium and elsewhere accepted his evidence, but in 1908 Leopold was finally forced to abandon his enterprise. The Free State was taken over by the Belgian government and became the Belgian Congo (now the Democratic Republic of Congo), though it was many years before conditions really improved.

If there was any justification at all for the Free State's abuses of power, it lay in the nature of the regime that it had replaced in the eastern Congo. Contemporary propagandists for Leopold made much of the 'crusade' against the Congo Arabs, and on the horrors of the slave trade which had underpinned their power. Some modern writers, in understandable revulsion against the Free State, have tried to present its Arab predecessor as a nascent civilization which had outgrown its early predatory phase and was beginning to learn how to coexist with the native population. They quote visitors' admiring descriptions of the size and luxury of its towns and the extent of the land which it had brought under cultivation (though ignoring Livingstone's equally enthusiastic account of the productivity of the same country twenty years earlier, when the Arabs were still newcomers). Around Kasongo, for example, Sidney Hinde and his men marched for hours through well-tended fields. In the captured town they 'slept on silk and satin mattresses, in carved beds with silk and mosquito curtains . . . . Here we found many European luxuries, the use of which we had almost forgotten: candles, sugar, matches, silver and glass goblets and decanters.' Clearly the Arab rulers had enjoyed many of the advantages of civilization, but these were never extended to the mass of the population. The Congolese, in fact, suffered two brutal conquests in succession without ever achieving liberation. Tragically, none of the succeeding regimes have had the will or the ability to undo the damage caused in those disastrous years, so that even the twenty-first-century reports from the Congo evoke not so much the luxuries of Hinde's Kasongo as Livingstone's vision of hell at Nyangwe.

Sources

Livingstone (correspondence quoted in Coupland, 1947), Cameron and Stanley (1879) all described the region in the early days of the Arab operations on the Congo. Stanley knew Tippu Tib well, and collected several of the many conflicting stories about his early career. The story of the fight with the Pygmies is related in his *Through the Dark Continent*. Hinde's eyewitness account of the Congo Arab War is invaluable for its insights into tactics and terrain, and is the principal source for the narrative in this chapter.

Chapter Seven
'A Splendid People':
The Masai and Nandi

The Masai were unique among the tribes of nineteenth-century East Africa in the awe and terror which they inspired in Europeans, Arabs and other Africans alike. Explorers as intrepid as Richard Burton and Henry Stanley planned their routes to avoid them, and in fact it was fear of their marauding war parties which kept the direct route from the coast to Lake Victoria firmly closed until the mid-1880s, forcing Uganda-bound caravans to take a long detour far to the south. Charles New, who encountered the Masai in the early 1870s, gives a verdict which may speak for most contemporary observers: 'Physically they are a splendid people; and for energy, intrepidity and dash they are without their equals in Africa; but they are cruel and remorseless to the last degree.' So who were these bogeymen, and how had they earned their reputation?

Linguistic evidence suggests that their ancestors had originated in the Upper Nile valley and migrated into what is now Masailand during the seventeenth century, replacing or absorbing the previous inhabitants, a people known as the Sirikwa. The country which they had won for themselves consisted of a high, grassy plateau bounded on the west by the Rift Valley, and on the east by the arid plains which ran down from Mount Kilimanjaro towards the Indian Ocean. Masailand was ideal country for rearing cattle, and to an even greater extent than the Zulus they relied on their herds as the economic and cultural foundation of their way of life. In fact it was possession of cattle that defined a true Masai, and related groups such as the Arusha, who adopted agriculture and lived in permanent villages, were treated as outsiders. The various clans which made up the cattle-raising Masai were bound together by a shared pride in their culture and a lofty contempt for all alternative lifestyles, but were never politically united. Four of the largest – the Kaputiei, Loitai, Purko and Kisongo – formed the core of a succession of loose and often shifting confederations, which spent as much of their time fighting against each other as they did campaigning beyond the boundaries of Masailand.

In fact by the nineteenth century the Masai were no longer expanding their territory, but devoted their energies to raiding for cattle. According to their favourite creation myth, God had originally given all the cattle in the world to the Masai. It was therefore almost a religious duty to retrieve those animals which had been lost by or stolen from their people over the centuries. In the words of the German missionary J Krapf, who left the first detailed written account of the Masai:

> When cattle fail them they make raids on the tribes which they know to be in possession of herds. They say that Engai (Heaven) gave them all that exists in the way of cattle and that no other nation ought to possess any . . . . They are dreaded as warriors, laying all waste with fire and sword, so that the weaker tribes do not venture to resist them in the open field, but leave them in possession of their herds, and seek only to save themselves by the quickest possible flight.

These raiding parties struck out from the high plateau in all directions, spreading fear and destruction throughout a huge area of East Africa. To the north they penetrated as far as the Turkana country around Lake Rudolf, and in the south they clashed with the Hehe in the highlands beyond the Ruaha River. Like the Zulus, however, the Masai fought at close quarters with spear and shield, tactics which were best suited to open country. Therefore those neighbouring tribes which could take refuge in mountainous or forested terrain usually managed to keep their cattle and survive. Some, like the Kikuyu of the Mount Kenya forests and the Kamba who lived in the hills along the eastern edge of the plateau, resisted well enough to earn the respect of the raiders. A semi–ritualized type of warfare then developed, with a chivalrous attitude of mutual respect often apparent on both sides. For others, less warlike or well defended, the Masai impact was catastrophic. According to New, for example, the Nyika people living near the coast gave up keeping livestock altogether following a great raid in 1858. 'They have not the heart to feed cattle,' he reported, 'as they say they should only be doing it for the Masai.'

Masai Warfare

In their devotion to acquiring cattle, their reliance on hand-to-hand fighting and their military dominance of an entire region, the Masai inevitably attract comparison with the Zulus. However, the basis of their power was very different. The advantages of numbers, discipline and unified command which enabled the Zulus to carve out an empire in the south were entirely lacking among the Masai. The East African highlands enjoyed less rainfall and could not support dense populations, so despite the huge area they occupied they probably never numbered more than 30,000 men of military age. Furthermore their lack of centralized leadership meant that no more than a fraction of these could ever be mobilized for a single campaign. The largest armies recorded in the field comprised no more than about 1,000 warriors.

But if they lacked discipline in the style of Shaka, the Masai did have a social system perfectly designed for success in war. Like other related Nilotic peoples, as well as the Zulus, they based their society on the 'age-set' system. All young men were initiated as warriors, or *moran*, around their late teens, at a mass ceremony which was held by each clan about every seven years. This produced an age-set which lived in its own separate *manyatta* or kraal, and shared many of the characteristics of a Zulu regiment. Cattle herding was not labour intensive and most of the work was done by the young boys and older men, so it was possible to spare the entire generation from economically productive activity, although they did have the responsibility of protecting the herds from lions and other predators. For the next fifteen years or so the new age-set would form what was in effect a professional standing army, starting as the 'left hand' or junior wing, and graduating to the 'right hand' after seven years when their successors were initiated in their turn. Eventually, at another ceremony, the group would be granted the status of elders, and would then be exempt from further military service. As *moran* the young men had no other avenue for social advancement than fighting or stealing cattle, so inevitably they would organize raiding parties on their own initiative, without any need for central command.

In another parallel with the Zulu system, each wing would adopt a name. Some of those recorded include: Il-Kupai, meaning 'the white swords'; Il-Kieku, 'the long-bladed spears'; Il-Churunye, 'those who fight by day'; Il-Ngarbut, 'the gluttons'; and Il-Meitaroni, 'the unconquerables'. Each of these groups was further subdivided into three parts, known by the standard titles of Il-Changen-opir, or 'the big ostrich feathers'; Il-Tareto, 'the helpers'; and Il-Paringotwa-lang, 'our swift runners'. This system could identify each warrior fairly precisely according to seniority, with the potential for a tactical organization based on the divisions. It is not clear, however, whether these units actually deployed and fought together in battle, or whether territorially based groupings were more common in practice.

Junior *moran* were not allowed to marry, drink alcohol, smoke or eat vegetables, though some of the dietary rules were relaxed for the 'right hand' or senior men. Warriors lived exclusively on beef, blood and milk, as other foods were believed to make them weak and cowardly. In order to discourage cautious tactics, they were forbidden to carry any missile weapons apart from clubs (though elders might use bows in defence of their homes and families if attacked), and like their Zulu and Matabele contemporaries they developed their fighting skills by hunting wild animals. Lions were common in Masailand, and were not only a threat to the cattle which needed to be controlled, but an ideal quarry for warriors wishing to hone their skills and prove their courage. A man who killed a lion (or grasped its tail while it was still alive) earned the highest honours, and was entitled to wear the beast's mane as a headdress or carry its tail on his spear on ceremonial occasions.

The leaders of Masai society were the *beijanis*, or civil chiefs, and the hereditary *laibons*, who were principally diviners and medicine men. *Laibons* might be influential in forming alliances between clans, but neither they nor the *beijanis* had a formal military role. In fact there was little in the way of a command system at all, and although the *moran* might seek the advice of respected elders, their orders were not binding. Each *manyatta* had an elected spokesman, but even he did not always lead them in war. Instead men who had gained a reputation for fighting or cattle-rustling ability would gather an informal group of followers around whom a war party would coalesce – an arrangement reminiscent of the Plains tribes of North America. Each camp had a group of *embikas*, senior warriors who acted as a sort of military police to impose rudimentary discipline in camp and on the march, but they had no powers to prevent warriors from deserting or even running away in battle. In contrast to the Zulus, cowards and malingerers among the Masai were subject to no punishment other than the scorn of their fellows, but so all-pervasive was the warrior ethos that that seems to have been enough. The Scottish explorer Joseph Thomson, who achieved the first successful crossing of Masailand in 1883, has a gruesome fictionalized account of the bloodshed which might occur when a successful raiding party divided up the spoils on its return home. If Thomson is to be believed, the warriors were simply allowed to fight among themselves, and more deaths often occurred at this point than on the raid itself. He does not, however, say that he witnessed this himself, and it is hard to believe that such an anarchic situation could have been the norm.

The men making up a war party had invariably grown up and trained together, and their style of fighting restricted them to a few tactical options, so they seem to have managed very well without any formal battlefield organization. The usual tactic in a pitched battle was for the bravest warriors to form a wedge in the centre, supported by a rearguard and a flank guard on each side, and simply break through the opposing line with a head-on charge. This formation was known as the 'eagle's wing'. Although few opponents could stand up to a Masai charge, a rapid retreat in case of need was an accepted tactic, and was apparently not seen as a cause for shame. Unlike most African armies the Masai did not use drums or other musical instruments in combat, but intimidated their opponents with chants and what the explorer Ludwig von Hohnel described as 'diabolical cries'. Psychology was an important part of the Masai approach to warfare, and the impressive ostrich-feather head-dresses which they wore were clearly designed to make the warriors look as frightening as possible. In fact von Hohnel believed that much of their reputation was based on bluff: 'There is really more pretension and im-pudence behind the self-consciousness of the "*moran*" than real courage . . . . Such an apparition strikes terror into the hearts of the natives, and at its approach they flee without coming to blows at all.'

Von Hohnel goes on to say that when the *moran* were on the warpath they would cover their spear blades with red fat or wrap them in rags to stop them catching the light, but they found it difficult to conceal their movements because of the flocks of crows and vultures which invariably followed them, anticipating the slaughter of either cattle for a feast or enemies in battle. According to Sidney Hinde (who lived among the Masai after his term of service with the Force Publique, for which see

Chapter 6), the weight of a warrior's weapons and equipment was about 15lb, and with this load he could travel up to 50 miles a day. Weapons consisted of a single spear, a short sword and one or more clubs which could be thrown at the enemy as the *moran* charged. The traditional war spear was very different from the long, slender-bladed type associated with the twentieth-century Masai. It averaged about 5½ feet long, and comprised a short wooden handle with a broad, heavy blade at one end and a long iron butt-spike at the other. It was not designed to be used as a missile, but it might occasionally be thrown: a Kaputiei warrior hurled one across a stream at one of Count Teleki's men on his 1887 expedition, though perhaps only because the obstacle prevented him coming to close quarters. Mary French-Sheldon, who travelled in Masailand in the 1890s, once witnessed a demonstration of how the broad-bladed spear was intended to be used: 'plunging forward with an upward sweep . . . describing a broad arc, yet he did not let go of the wooden centre'. This upward, underarm thrust seems to be ideally suited to the design of the blade, with its sharp edges and gently tapered point, and would no doubt have been intended to disembowel the enemy with a single blow. The weapon seems at first sight to be poorly balanced, but experiments with similar implements have shown that the metal spike on the other end balances the weight of the blade and makes it almost as easy to handle as the shorter Zulu *iklwa*.

Masai swords averaged 18 inches to 2 feet in length, and were often manufactured by grinding down old European machete blades. They were usually slightly spoon-shaped, sharp enough to thrust with but broadening out below the point to give extra weight for a cutting blow. This efficient design contrasts with that of many African swords, which were often intended as much for ritual as for war, and helps to refute von Hohnel's view that Masai war-gear was designed mainly for show. The main function of the sword, however, was to finish off or decapitate a wounded enemy. Richard Meinertzhagen, who fought alongside Masai irregulars in the 1905 campaign against the Nandi, gives a graphic description of its use in the former role: the victorious warrior would insert the sword behind his helpless victim's collar bone and thrust downwards until the point entered the bladder, causing fatal damage to the internal organs on the way. Shields were made of the hide of the wild buffalo, which is much thicker and tougher than the cowhide used by the

Zulus and Ngoni. The weight of the Masai shield, and the rough, rigid surface of the hide, made it a formidable weapon in its own right at close quarters. The *moran* believed that it could stop not only arrows, but also musket balls. This may have been true, but it did lead to dangerous over-confidence when faced with more modern firearms. A warrior who visited the explorer Samuel Teleki was unimpressed by a demonstration of breech-loading rifles, because he thought that his shield would be able to protect him. He actually agreed to allow the shield to be used as a target, only to retire disconcerted when a bullet went straight through it.

The Masai in general were contemptuous of muzzle-loading muskets and those who used them. According to Richard Burton they had once been afraid of guns, but began to appreciate their weaknesses after a battle in 1857, in which a force of 800 *moran* defeated nearly 150 Arab musketeers. The course of the engagement was very similar to the fight between Arabs and Ngoni recorded by Carl Wiese thirty years later (see Chapter 2), and suggests that the Arabs were very slow to learn from their defeats. They fired a single volley, upon which the Masai apparently fled, but when the Arabs rushed forward to round up the cattle that the *moran* had been driving away, they rallied and slaughtered them before they could reload. 'Until this year they have shunned meeting Moslems and musketeers in the field,' wrote Burton (1872): 'having won the day, they will, it is feared, repeat the experiment.' In fact it sounds as if the Masai already knew that guns took a long time to reload, and their 'flight' was probably a ruse designed to tempt the enemy to break formation. They did, however, repeat the experiment, almost always successfully. In the late 1880s the German explorer Carl Peters described their tactics against a musket-armed enemy as follows:

The Massai [*sic*] knows how to protect himself from the first shot by throwing himself on the ground, or sheltering himself behind a tree; and long before the muzzle-loader has been made ready for a second discharge, he has come bounding up, to finish the matter with a thrust of his lance . . . . Generally, in fact, the [Arab] caravans fire their guns once, and then immediately take to flight, whereupon they are regularly massacred to the last man by the swift-footed Massais.

Peters admitted that, in the battle which he fought against them at Elbejet in 1889, the warriors also showed great skill in adapting their tactics to cope with the rapid fire of breech-loading rifles: 'From tree to tree the Massais advanced, but always with caution, to cover themselves from the bullets. I may say truly, that for the next few minutes I gave up my life and all of us for lost; nevertheless, on noticing the perfect skill of their method of attack, I could not suppress a kind of admiration of my opponents.' But although they quickly learned the characteristics of the weapons used against them, unlike most African warrior peoples the Masai never adopted firearms themselves, and well into the twentieth century most preferred to adhere to their traditional ways. This can hardly have been due to the difficulty of obtaining guns, as they must have been available in their thousands on the battlefields where their owners had been slaughtered. According to Peters, for example, in 1887 a Masai army had 'cut down, to the last man, an Arab caravan numbering two thousand guns, laid all the corpses in ranks and rows side by side, and in scorn put each man's gun across his shoulder'. It is more likely that the already self-confident *moran* were not impressed by the poor showing of the Arab musketeers, and saw no reason to take up a weapon which they had so often defeated.

The Masai on the Defensive

By the 1880s both Arabs and Europeans had begun to move inland and encroach on the once inviolable Masai heartland. Opinion was divided over how dangerous the crossing of the country really was, with some observers suspecting that the early Arab pioneers had exaggerated the risks in order to discourage competitors and keep the lucrative ivory trade with the north for themselves. Some small groups of Swahili traders did make their way north to Lake Baringo and beyond – in 1888 Teleki met one such party, which consisted of only seven men – but there are also numerous reports of caravans of a thousand or more musketeers being annihilated by the *moran*. In 1877 J M Hildebrandt reported to the Berlin Geographical Society that he had been invited to join a caravan of 2,000 ivory traders travelling through Masailand to Lake Victoria, but had declined (*Proceedings of the Royal Geographical Society*, vol. 22, 1877–78). 'A year later,' he added, 'I learnt that this very caravan was attacked by the Masai, and that very few of the number escaped . . . . Generally, during the last two years nearly all the ivory caravans have been destroyed by these savage hordes.'

At the beginning of the same year Hildebrandt had been forced to turn back only three days' march from Mount Kenya because 'a short time before my arrival the Wakwafi' – by which he probably meant Masai of the Laikipiak clan – 'had to the last man destroyed a caravan of 1,500 armed men'. A decade later Teleki camped at what may have been the site of one of the massacres referred to by Hildebrandt – a spot known as Malago Mbaruk, named after a trader who was killed in 1875 or 1876, along with 400 of his men. In 1893, on his way to Uganda, Sir Gerald Portal had a similar experience when he passed the scene of a battle twelve years earlier. He was told that 300 Swahilis had held off a Masai war party for two days until their ammunition was exhausted. The warriors had then charged and killed all of the Swahilis except for three survivors. Even those parties which did eventually get through Masailand seldom did so without hard fighting. Thomson was told that the last three caravans to attempt the journey before him had each lost more than 100 men in fighting against marauding *moran.*

Thanks to his diplomatic skills (and a reputation which he had acquired as a sorcerer), Thomson got through without having to fight, but groups of warriors continually demanded gifts and imposed arbitrary fines, making it abundantly clear that they had no fear of the white men's weapons. Thomson later admitted that he had been lucky, as many of the most intransigent bands had been raiding elsewhere at the time of his visit. Nevertheless, as the Reverend J P Farler pointed out (*Proceedings of the Royal Geographical Society*, vol. 1, 1879), the Masai were not in general hostile to white men, but saved their real hatred for the Arabs. A group of Swahili merchants had once offered to go with Farler through Masailand if he would make up a caravan, but insisted that no Arabs should be taken along, because the warriors would certainly attack them. If they seldom targeted Europeans, however, it was not necessarily because of fear; as their main motivation for fighting was to acquire cattle or pursue inter-tribal feuds, they had little reason to do so. This tends to confirm the views of some British administrators in the 1890s, who felt that most of the attacks on the Arabs and Swahilis had been provoked by caravan leaders who, believing that their guns would intimidate the *moran*, allowed their men to loot the Masai villages and interfere with their women.

The Battle of Elbejet, 1889

The best recorded of the battles between white explorers and the Masai took place six years after Thomson's crossing of the country. In December 1889 a German expedition led by Carl Peters was traversing the Laikipiak Plateau on its way to Uganda. The fighting strength of the caravan was two white men, twenty-one Somali askaris and eighty-five porters, some at least of whom were armed. Nine of the Somalis were equipped with repeating rifles, while the other askaris and the armed porters had single-shot breech-loaders. Peters was one of the least sympathetic characters in the history of African exploration. A devotee of the ruthless philosophy of Friedrich Nietzsche, he was violently prejudiced against Africans, and his writings betray a pathological sensitivity to any real or imagined threat and a determination to justify even the most disproportionate use of force in response. On one typical occasion he had an African seized and flogged for allegedly hanging around his camp acting suspiciously; the man turned out to be the son of a local Gogo chief who had been sent on a diplomatic mission, and the incident provoked a clash in which Peters and his men killed hundreds of helpless Gogo. He believed that the defiant attitude of the Masai was due to lenient treatment by British explorers such as Thomson, and that it was demeaning for a white man to negotiate his passage and pay tolls. Therefore he deliberately set out to provoke conflict by firing his gun into the air – knowing that the people would object to this, as it frightened their cattle – and finally by shooting some valuable bulls on the absurd pretext that they were attacking his camp. An equally incredible allegation was that the *moran*, who possessed no firearms, had been trying to steal his cartridges.

On these dubious grounds, Peters planned an unprovoked attack on the Laikipiak village of Elbejet, which was situated on a low hill overlooking the Gnare Gobit River. He and his German colleague Lieutenant von Tiedemann collected thirty-five of the askaris and porters, and deployed them in a wood at the base of the hill. Peters commanded the right wing of this tiny force, with his Somali headman Hussein Fara leading the centre and von Tiedemann on the left. It appears from later remarks in Peters's book that von Tiedemann was armed with a repeater, while Peters himself carried his double-barrelled 'Express' hunting rifle. The attack was launched early on a cold morning, when most of the villagers were still asleep. They had obviously never expected to be attacked in the heart of their own country, and the single sentry watching over the cattle still did not realize what was happening. He called out to Peters's men to go round the herd rather than risk stampeding the beasts, and by way of reply was shot dead. The sound of firing roused the people in the village, and soon the women and children were fleeing down the far slope of the hill while the men rushed out to counter-attack. Peters describes how he fought a duel against a Masai elder with a bow, who shot three arrows at him but missed each time. Peters's first two shots also missed, but the third brought the man down. Then the defenders retired, leaving Peters in possession of Elbejet and more than 2,000 cattle.

Peters prepared to move the rest of his caravan up to this commanding position, but the Masai were by no means routed. Making use of dead ground, they swung around the base of the hill and charged his camp, forcing him to retreat from the village and concentrate his men to defend it. Although Peters does not admit as much, it seems clear from his narrative that he realized that he had lost the initiative, and that it would be impossible to make a prolonged defence, especially in view of his limited supply of ammunition. So he ordered the camp to be struck and commenced a rapid retreat. Peters went on ahead with four men, followed by the porters and livestock, while von Tiedemann and most of the Somalis formed a rearguard. They had been marching for only a few minutes through a narrow strip of forest which lined the banks of the river, when 'hundreds' of Masai were seen approaching, 'passing tree by tree to get at us'. (The writer refers to the enemy as '*moran*', but there must also have been some bow-armed elders with them, as one of his men was killed at this point by an arrow.) Peters and one Somali stood their ground, and kept the enemy at bay for a few minutes with their rapid fire until Hussein Fara and his Somalis came up to join them. Peters remarks that the Masai had never before seen repeating guns, which 'must have appeared to them supernatural'. Several times the attackers hesitated, giving the explorer time to reload, although they very quickly adapted their tactics, advancing in short rushes between patches of cover. Meanwhile the expedition's rearguard was also under attack, but held on long enough for the armed porters to deploy into line and support them. In separate incidents, both Peters and von Tiedemann were saved by their askaris at the last moment from warriors who had got within spear-thrust of them, but eventually the column fought its way clear of the forest.

Reluctantly the Masai withdrew up the hill – 'with their faces still turned towards us', admits Peters – and let them go, but a dangerous march still lay ahead of the expedition. They counted forty-three dead warriors, but they had themselves lost seven men, and most of their ammunition had gone. The nine Somalis armed with repeaters had used up 900 rounds between them, which compared with the seven rounds per man fired by the British regulars at Ulundi, for example, suggests that the fight was desperate indeed. Over the next few days Peters led a fighting retreat from the Laikipiak Plateau, shadowed all the way by large bodies of warriors. Two days after the battle at Elbejet, a Masai war party attacked the camp at night. They were only beaten back by the firing of a salvo of red and green signal rockets, which failed to frighten them off as Peters had hoped, but provided the defenders with just enough light to shoot by.

In fact, reading between the lines of Peters's account, the encounter was far from being a clear victory for the expedition. Its members did bring away some cattle, but had only saved their lives by a hurried departure from the country. On the retreat from Elbejet they passed numerous deserted kraals, and found that many areas which had been densely populated in Thomson's day were now uninhabited. The Masai had already been fatally weakened by civil war and by the wave of cattle plagues which was affecting most of East Africa at that time, and it is likely that if Peters had launched a similar rash attack only a few years before, his party would have been swiftly annihilated. However, as the Masai's first documented encounter with repeating rifles, the battle seems to have had a lasting significance. Subsequently all the clans showed a marked reluctance to fight the whites, and the shock experienced by the Laikipiaks at Elbejet may have been an important factor in this.

The Colonial Era

Joseph Thomson had been the first to notice signs of cattle disease in 1883, and although at that time the human population of the highlands was still numerous, a few years later other travellers found wide areas deserted. In 1894, in an article aimed at visiting big-game hunters, Frederick Jackson was able to describe the *moran* as 'a very much overrated individual' (Phillipps-Wolley). He still argued, however, that a caravan travelling in Masailand should include an escort of twenty-five to fifty armed men, if only to bolster the morale of the porters, who 'have a very exaggerated idea of his fighting and bloodthirsty propensities'. Gerald Portal agreed that in the early 1890s the Masai were 'no longer the dreaded, all-conquering, and triumphant "bogie" of ten years ago'. They were already slowly recovering their strength, but openly admitted that they did not want to fight the whites as they had learned to appreciate the power of their guns.

Nevertheless writers at that time still rated them as a serious potential threat to the establishment of British power in Kenya, which had been recognized as a British sphere of influence by an Anglo-German agreement in 1890. The explorer J W Gregory heard that a group of *moran* had planned to attack a Uganda Railway Survey caravan in 1893, but had changed their minds on learning that it had an escort of Sikh soldiers. The same observer described how his expedition dared not light fires at night for fear of attracting the Masai war parties which swarmed across the steppe, and even went so far as to forecast that without British intervention the country would eventually be partitioned between invading Somalis and resurgent Masai. In the event there were no major clashes between regular British forces and the Masai, although in 1894 some *moran* unsuccessfully attacked a fort at Machakos which was held by a garrison of loyal Kambas. A more serious war scare briefly followed the notorious 'Kedong valley massacre' in the following year.

This was the closest that the Masai and the British came to a major confrontation, and it was provoked by the disorderly behaviour of some British and Swahili traders. A supply caravan consisting of 105 Swahilis and about 1,000 Kikuyu porters had been sent out by the British officer in command at Fort Smith under an inexperienced Swahili headman, as no British personnel were available to command it. While passing through the Kedong valley the Swahilis abducted some Masai women, provoking an attack in which the local *moran* almost wiped out the caravan. Most of the porters had muskets and it should have been possible for a force of this size to put up some organized resistance, but instead they seem to have panicked. It is not clear whether they even managed to fire a volley before they fled, but they failed to check the Masai charge and were speared as they tried to escape. The death toll was officially put at ninety-eight Swahilis and more than 900 Kikuyu. (Seymour Vandeleur gives a figure of only 456 Kikuyu dead, but he was not an eyewitness and does not cite a source. Many no doubt fled and were reported as missing, so the true total cannot be established.) Some Masai elders tried to protect about seventy of the porters who had taken refuge with them, but were unable to prevent the excited warriors slaughtering them all.

A British trader, Andrew Dick, happened to be in the area and decided to intervene, with the help of three visiting Frenchmen and six askaris provided by the local district officer. They arrived too late to help the caravan, and the Frenchmen later alleged that Dick intended simply to take advantage of the situation to steal some Masai cattle for himself. He was a notorious troublemaker who had already been accused of provoking a Nandi uprising by cheating the tribesmen, so the charge is not implausible. He shot several Masai but then became separated from the askaris, and the Frenchmen seem to have remained aloof while the *moran* closed in and speared him to death. According to a widely repeated story he killed about 100 warriors before he died, but the source of this claim is unknown, and it seems highly unlikely; even assuming that he was a spectacularly good shot, the Masai are hardly likely to have given him the chance to fire so many rounds. In any case it was unusual for a hunter or trader to carry more than a dozen rounds of ammunition.

In terms of losses on the British side this fight was surpassed only by Isandlwana, and it was even more one-sided, as Masai casualties were negligible. But since most of the dead were local Africans, and were not even officially military personnel, it went almost unnoticed at home. The official reaction to the affair was to announce that as both the Swahilis and Dick had provoked the Masai, there was no justification for punishing the victors. However, several commentators at the time believed that this decision was made less for legal reasons than because the British authorities felt that they were still too weak to risk a full-scale war. Instead they harnessed the Masai warriors' warlike habits by recruiting them in large numbers for campaigns against other tribes, such as the Kikuyu, Kamba and Nandi. In January 1894 there were 300 Masai auxiliaries attached to the garrison at Fort Smith, and by the beginning of 1896 this number had risen to 900. These allied contingents fought under their own leaders and were usually deployed in a separate column, tasked with driving off the enemy's livestock while the British and their askaris attacked them frontally. The *moran* were not paid, but were allowed to keep most of the looted cattle as a reward for their assistance.

In contrast the Germans, who were occupying the territory south of Mount Kilimanjaro, were often on bad terms with the Masai. The Kisongo and various other groups were caught up in several punitive expeditions in the Pangani valley in 1891–92, and lost many warriors fighting on the side of the Arusha when they were defeated by the Germans in 1896 and 1900, but on the whole they tried to avoid open conflict. A band of *moran* held up a column led by the German explorer Hermann von Wissmann in 1889 and demanded that he pay a toll in return for permission to travel in the country, but when this was refused they did not press the issue. Sporadic fighting continued until 1897, but by then most of the Masai had drifted north over the border into British East Africa. In the early years of the twentieth century most of this proud warrior people were persuaded to move onto reservations and allow the bulk of their grazing lands to be given to white settlers. Perhaps because they had not been conquered in battle, they never seem to have seen themselves as subject to the British, and an attitude of mutual respect grew up between the two peoples. Even in the colonial period a Masai would address a white man not with the customary title of 'bwana', or 'master', but as 'shore', 'friend'.

The Nandi

The only other inhabitants of British East Africa who achieved the same reputation as warriors were the Nandi, one of a group of related tribes which inhabited the forested hills of the Mount Elgon region, north-east of Lake Victoria. They called themselves 'Chemwal', or 'cattle raiders'; the name 'Nandi' is in fact a Swahili insult, meaning 'cormorants' and referring to their rapacity, but by the beginning of the twentieth century the people had begun to adopt it themselves – perhaps in the same defiant spirit that led the 'Old Contemptibles' of 1914 to turn the Kaiser's jibe into a proud title. The Nandi have been in their present home since the seventeenth century or even earlier, and had been fighting the Masai for almost as long. Some time in the eighteenth century the *moran* had inflicted a severe defeat on the Nandi, but the tables were turned in the 1840s and 1850s, when the Masai were distracted by civil war. The first Nandi victory was said to have been due to a woman who distracted the enemy by dancing in front of them, while her sons drove off their cattle and hid them in the hills – an instance of the rather more subtle approach to warfare which characterized the forest people. The Nandi then took the offensive and expanded eastwards onto the open plains. Most of the border between the two tribes was demarcated by fast-flowing rivers or the crests of rocky ridges, which discouraged raids by both sides because of the difficulty of getting stolen cattle back across these obstacles. The highlands were also unpleasantly bleak for unacclimatized invaders; in the campaign of 1895 Lieutenant Vandeleur would describe conditions as 'more like being in Scotland than in Africa at this height'. However, at one point a corridor of open grassland 12 miles wide provided an easier route for raiders into Nandi territory. The Nandi had a series of look-out positions scattered across this gap on high ground, each more or less permanently manned by two or three warriors. The sentries would blow kudu horns to give warning of an invasion, giving the people time to hide their cattle in the forest.

Few outsiders visited the area before the 1880s, though some Arab or Swahili traders may have arrived a generation earlier, as the name 'Wa-nandi' was reported as early as 1854. The Nandi were not interested in trading for foreign goods, however, and saw the caravans as a source of plunder. 'Kapchumba', or 'place of the Swahili', became a common place name in the country, and was said to commemorate locations where the foreigners had been lured into ambushes by the promise of ivory and then massacred. In 1882 a report to the Royal Geographical Society mentioned 'a tribe called Wananda, never visited on account of their ferocity' (*Proceedings of the Royal Geographical Society*, vol. 4, 1882). Joseph Thomson was warned about the Nandi a year later on his crossing of Masailand, but he skirted the edge of their grazing grounds without making contact. The first Europeans did not visit them until the early 1890s, and at first the self-confident warriors laughed at them as 'women', because unlike Nandi men they were fully clothed.

Organization and Tactics

The total fighting strength of the Nandi has been estimated at slightly less than 5,000, but the population was very fragmented by the wooded and rocky nature of their country, and no army of anything like this size ever took the field. Like the Masai they were organized into age-sets, with the younger adult male sets forming the warrior class, but their military organization was more sophisticated than that of the Masai *moran*. Every seven years or so a ceremony was held at which responsibility for the defence of the tribe was formally handed over from one age-set to another. The main political subdivision of Nandi society was the district or *pororiet*, of which there were fifteen, each ruled by a council of elders. Each district raised its own regiment of warriors, which was called a *luket* (meaning literally 'a raid'), and undertook its own military operations, either alone or in alliance with other districts. A *luket* was divided into a varying number of subunits, or *siritaiik*, of between twenty and fifty men each, depending on the size of the *pororiet*. Each subunit was commanded by a leader with the title of *kirkit*, or 'bull'. Parallel to but distinct from this territorial organization was another system based around seventeen clans or families, each of which was associated with a particular totem animal. Some of these clans had traditional military roles. Members of the lion clan, for example, always deployed on the right wing in battle. The hyena clan was responsible for providing a rearguard to cover a retreat if this became necessary, and for blocking the tracks through the forest to delay an invader.

The Nandi had once been forest hunters, and although by the nineteenth century they had long ago adopted the cattle-herding culture of their Masai neighbours, hunting was still a significant part of their way of life. Probably for this reason they continued to use bows and poisoned arrows alongside the spears, shields and swords which they borrowed from the Masai. Despite their small numbers they had a formidable reputation as fighters, and regarded less warlike peoples with contempt. According to the anthropologist G W B Huntingford, who interviewed many veterans in the early years of the twentieth century, they regarded warfare as 'a form of sport, the only kind on a large scale that they understood, which gave them something real and exciting to live for' (Huntingford, 1953). They had little need to expand their territory, and traditional military operations were restricted to small-scale raids for cattle and prisoners. Prisoners of war were usually ransomed for cattle, but captured Masai warriors were respected for their fighting abilities and were often adopted into the tribe.

An important strength of the Nandi military system was the role of the *orkoiik* (singular *orkoiyot*), who first came to prominence in the mid-nineteenth century. These men combined the roles of prophets and war leaders, and were directly inspired by the Masai *laibons*. The office was hereditary within a single family, which was probably of Masai origin, and the whole Nandi people recognized the authority of a single *orkoiyot*, or at most two at any one time. They were feared and respected for their magical powers, and made use of this fact to impose an unprecedented degree of cohesion on the tribe. This may be one reason why, despite their lack of formal political unity (and in contrast to the Masai), the Nandi are never known to have fought among themselves. It was necessary for a group of young men who wished to form a raiding party to first ask the *orkoiyot* for permission. If this was granted, a kudu horn would be blown to summon the warriors, who were given a club blessed by the *orkoiyot* to be carried at the head of the war party as a symbol of his authority. The *orkoiyot* was sometimes referred to by the title of *kipsetmet*, or 'one whose head goes to war'. This was an allusion to the belief that he could detach his head from his body and send it to keep an eye on the performance of the warriors in battle – a belief which was said to be an important factor in maintaining discipline. A man who showed cowardice might also be beaten or even killed by his fellows.

Just as they are today, the inhabitants of the Nandi country were famous for their speed and stamina as long-distance runners, and raids were regularly carried out against targets as far as 100 miles away. Fellow Nandi, as well as the closely related Kipsigis, were off-limits to raiding parties, but other related peoples such as the Suk, Sapei and Terik, who were less well organized militarily, were frequently targeted. So were the Masai and the Bantu tribes of Kavirondo on the shore of Lake Victoria. Not all of these raids were successful, and a major defeat was suffered in 1890 when an army of 500 warriors was ambushed in Kavirondo, leaving only two survivors. The *orkoiyot* Kimnyole received the blame for this, and was put to death by his fellow tribesmen. The men of one small district of only fifty warriors, Cheptol, were notorious for their pride and over-confidence. Tradition recalled how they were so certain of success before one raid that they slaughtered and ate all their cattle in a huge feast, only to go hungry when they had to return home without capturing any. On the other hand, the reputation of the Nandi and the inaccessible terrain of their homeland made them virtually immune to counter-raids. Before the arrival of the British, only the Masai are known to have undertaken offensive operations against them.

The preferred time for campaigning was in the dry season, which began in October. Traditional raiding tactics relied heavily on surprise. A war party would send out scouts in advance to determine the location of the enemy warriors and their cattle, and the best approach and escape routes. When the patrol returned the main body was mustered by sounding the kudu horn, but the approach to the enemy village was made stealthily and in silence, in single file, and making use of cover. Ideally scouts would have located a spot where the warriors could deploy unobserved within easy reach of the target, in which case they preferred to wait until after dark before attacking. The war party would then split into three groups. One had the task of creating a diversion, while the second broke into the enclosure where the cattle were kept and drove them out. Most of the Nandi's neighbours had learned to keep their animals inside kraals protected by thorn hedges or mud walls, so this task often involved demolishing a section of wall or hedge, which was likely to alert the enemy. This second party would then deploy to cover the withdrawal against the inevitable counter-attack, while the third group, consisting of the least experienced warriors, herded the cattle away. Loot was distributed according to an orderly system. Every warrior would normally receive at least one cow, though if there were not enough to go round, the *orkoiyot* and the senior warriors got their shares first. Then a victory dance was held, after which every man who had killed an enemy had to undergo four days of ritual purification. It was also customary to drink the blood of enemies washed from their spear blades, in order to give the killers courage.

War with the British

It was the naivety of the Nandi concerning outsiders, combined with their location on the flank of the main route to Uganda, which eventually brought them into conflict with the British authorities. They began by damaging the telegraph line which was being built close to their territory because they valued the wire as ornaments for their women, and later they stole the heavy iron bolts which secured the rails of the Uganda Railway for use as war clubs. A C Hollis, writing in 1909, laid the blame for the first outbreak of hostilities in 1895 on the provocative behaviour of two British traders, Andrew Dick and Peter West. Dick had flogged two Nandi for allegedly rustling his cattle, and in retaliation the tribe slaughtered a mail caravan and attacked West's camp at night, killing him and stealing his guns. Dick escaped his just deserts on this occasion, only to be speared later by the Masai.

The first British punitive expedition against the Nandi was mounted at the end of 1895. It took the field as several independent company-sized columns with orders to quarter the country and round up the cattle. Vandeleur, who fought in the campaign, provides an invaluable eye-witness account of the Nandi tactics at an encounter on the banks of the Kimonde River. A patrol had been sent out across the river, and Vandeleur's No. 4 Company of Sudanese askaris, supported by a Maxim machine gun and a few Baganda irregulars, was deployed to cover its return. The country was mostly grass with patches of forest, and sloped steeply down to the river, which was crossed by what the lieutenant refers to as a 'native bridge'. Suddenly 500 Nandi warriors appeared over a ridge on the far bank and charged them. Vandeleur describes them as 'apparently excellently organised, and formed in three sides of a square, above which a dense thicket of long-bladed spears flashed in the sunlight'. The Maxim, which was deployed beside the river, opened fire and they wheeled away from it to their left, then 'charged with tremendous dash' at No. 4 Company. The warriors caught and wiped out a group of four-teen men who were detached from the column, and must also have come perilously close to overrunning the Maxim, because one of the gun detachment was also among the casualties. They got to within 30 yards of Vandeleur's firing line before being broken by the fire of the Martini-Henry rifles, and suffered further losses from the Maxim as they retired across the bridge.

Vandeleur believed that had his troops been surprised while in column of march they would have been annihilated, and commented that 'This charge was a revelation to us, after fighting the cautious Wanyoro . . . and at once accounted for the warlike reputation . . . which the Wa-Nandi possessed.' Nevertheless the Nandi had learned from their defeat, and two days later they changed their tactics and attacked the British camp at night. This time they reached the thorn fence which had been built to protect the camp, but were unable to scale it in the face of intense rifle fire, and were again repulsed. Subsequently they contented themselves with shadowing the column, killing stragglers, shooting arrows from ambush and rolling down boulders from cliffs above the track. The

British sacked a few villages, drove off the Nandi cattle, and proclaimed the area pacified. In fact three more expeditions were required, in 1900, 1903 and 1905, before the tribe admitted defeat, making the Nandi Wars as a whole the most serious opposition which the British encountered in Kenya.

Sources

The Masai were a popular subject among nineteenth-century explorers and travel writers. Thomson (1885), von Hohnel and Peters had the closest acquaintance with them, and their accounts are the principal contemporary sources. The Hindes (1901) and Hollis also collected a great deal of anthropological material at the beginning of the twentieth century. Hollis and Huntingford did the same for the Nandi and provide us with most of our information on their military organization, while Vandeleur is the main source for the campaign of 1895.

Chapter Eight

'He Fears the Spear, but Not the Big Guns': The Hehe and the Kaiser

In taking over the southern portion of East Africa while leaving the Kenya Highlands to the British, the Germans seem to have got the worst of the bargain. Despite their proximity to the equator, the highlands around Iringa in what is now southern Tanzania are not very productive for agriculture, and can be surprisingly cold and bleak. Several early European explorers complained of the incessant cold and rain when crossing this district. The population has always struggled to support itself from its own resources, and in the early nineteenth century the people were known to the outside world mainly as cattle thieves. In the 1840s the hills became a refuge for people driven off the plains by Ngoni and Masai invaders, including elements of the Sango, Bena, Gogo and Kimbu tribes. The first two of these had adopted some of the Zulu-inspired weapons and tactics introduced by the Ngoni, but most of the highland peoples remained militarily insignificant until the 1860s, when a Sango warrior named Munyigumba organized them into a formidable private army. He led them first against the Bena, who were defeated in a battle at Mugoda Mutitu and driven out of the highlands altogether, then turned against the Sango and forced them in turn to withdraw north-westwards into the Kimbu country.

Munyigumba's army appears to have been the foundation of what became known as the kingdom of the Hehe. Before this time the Hehe were probably not a distinct ethnic or political group at all; their name is not recorded until the 1860s, and is said to be derived from a war-cry: 'Hee! Hee! Vatavagu twihoma! Ehee!' (Reusch). The German anthropologist E Nigmann, writing in 1908, admitted that there was no such thing as a 'pure' Hehe, and other twentieth-century scholars identified twenty-nine once-independent tribes which made up the confederation. It seems that the defining characteristic of the Hehe was allegiance to the dynasty established by Munyigumba (to which he gave the name of 'Vamuyinga', after a legendary founder named Muyinga), and that it was not until the colonial period that a cohesive Hehe 'nation' really came into being. This process is by no means unusual in African history, and we have already seen how similar melting pots gave rise to the Zulus, Matabele and Ngoni (see Chapter 2).

Under Munyigumba the Hehe, like Shaka's Zulus, quickly gained a formidable reputation out of all proportion to their numbers. Joseph Thomson, who visited them in 1879, says that they were once 'a very insignificant tribe' (Thomson, 1881), but they had already made an impression on Verney Cameron, who encountered a group of Hehe warriors in 1873 during his crossing of the continent. 'Such is their reputation for courage and skill in the use of their weapons,' he wrote, 'that none of the tribes on whom they habitually make their raids ever dare to resist them.' Not long before his death in 1879 Munyigumba fought his last campaign against the dreaded Ngoni, who had sent a raiding army into the heart of Hehe territory. There, at the Battle of Nyamulenge, the invaders were defeated and their chief Chipeta, a man notorious for his cruelty, was killed. The German missionary Richard Reusch records a Hehe tradition that Munyigumba personally killed the enemy commander in single combat. 'This fight of the two chiefs was so grand,' he says, 'that both hosts stopped to watch it in deadly silence, until it was over and Chipeta fell down with the sword of his great enemy in his heart.'

The Organization of the Hehe Kingdom

Munyigumba's new kingdom was well organized, and subject to a strict code of laws. During his reign he established his authority over at least fifteen neighbouring chiefdoms, whose rulers either accepted his overlordship or were replaced with Hehe appointees. The plateau of Wota on the northern edge of the highlands, which was inhabited by refugees from further south who had settled there early in the century, was also occupied and placed under an appointed governor. This official seems to have had the extra responsibilities of reporting on events along the caravan route from Zanzibar, and of defending the northern frontier against the Masai. The Hehe king, or *mutwa*, owed his pre-eminence partly to his real or alleged royal birth, and partly to his role as an intermediary with the spirits of dead chiefs. He was also believed to possess a powerful magic charm, the *amahomelo*, which protected him in battle and helped him to defeat his enemies. It seems that this charm may have been regarded as an essential part of the king's authority to rule, and his success in war strengthened his legitimacy by proving the effectiveness of the magic. Whatever the true reasons, the kingship established by Munyigumba seems quickly to have gained the sort of prestige which inspired the notoriously individualistic highland warriors to fight and die for it.

There are no reliable figures for the total manpower available to the Hehe kings. After the German conquest in 1898 it was estimated that the 'nation' numbered about 50,000 people altogether, but this does not include many non-Hehe who had been incorporated into the realm, and who sometimes fought in their own styles alongside the Hehe proper. The army fighting in Usango in 1877, for example, included a high proportion of Bena auxiliaries who were armed and equipped like Ngoni. Subordinate chiefs known as *vanzagila* were responsible for raising their own regiments in time of war. Like the king himself, many of them maintained small standing armies. These consisted of two categories of warriors: older men known as *vatambule*, or veterans, who served as subordinate officers, and the young men in training, or *vigendo*. Munyigumba also introduced the practice of establishing military colonies of young men of between twelve and twenty years of age in the territories of subjugated tribes. These various regular units formed the permanent cadres of regiments or *majinga*, often named in Ngoni style, into which all the unmarried men could be enrolled in time of war.

As among the Zulus and Ngoni, each regiment was formed from the men of a particular age group, who were not allowed to marry until they had proved themselves in combat. One senior unit, the Vatengelamutwa ('those who stand firm by their chief'), acted as a royal bodyguard in battle. Regiments were further divided into companies, known as *fipuka*, though their tactical role, if any, is not clear. Men who particularly distinguished themselves were additionally rewarded with gifts of cloth, slaves and cattle, while cowards were humiliated by being forced to work as porters. Food production, supply columns and even medical services were also well organized. Several German observers described this system as identical to that of the Zulus, but it is not known whether it was directly inspired by the Zulu example (perhaps transmitted by the Ngoni) or was simply a development of local practice. Some Hehe regimental names were identical with those known among the Sango, so it is possible that these rather than the Ngoni may have been the model for the Hehe regimental organization.

The life of the Hehe soldier, as recalled by veterans interviewed in the twentieth century, has echoes of the Viking sagas. Between campaigns they caroused in beer halls, singing and boasting of their past and future exploits. Munyigumba's successor Mkwawa also employed a professional praise singer of Sango origin, who made speeches to inspire the men before a battle. Many warriors adopted picturesque praise names or *noms de guerre* describing their achievements or ambitions. Recorded examples include Mudenye-wa-ndembo, or 'breaker of elephants'; Muhayanga-danda-ya-tangu, 'drinker of his enemies' blood'; and Mugopisala-amandusi-sinagope, which meant, perhaps prophetically in view of the events of Mkwawa's reign, 'he fears the spear, but not the big guns' (Redmayne).

The Reign of Mkwawa and the Arrival of the Germans

After Munyigumba's death a struggle for power erupted between his son Mkwawa and his son-in-law Mwambambe. Hehe tradition describes Mkwawa as tall and well built, 'with the neck of a bull and the muscles of a lion' (Reusch), but it was not so much his physical strength as his persistence that won him the throne. At one point he was forced into exile, but eventually he returned and drove out his rival. Mwambambe in turn fled, and was given refuge among the neighbouring Kimbu. In 1881 Mkwawa turned on the Ngoni and defeated them again, forcing them to agree to a truce until the sons of the current warriors had come of age. This truce was faithfully observed until the arrival of German rule, which prevented any attempt to resume the war. Meanwhile Mwambambe had returned with an army which included many men armed with muskets. Although Mkwawa's warriors had very few guns, they defeated the invaders in a bloody battle at a place later known as Ilundamatwe, 'the place where many heads are piled up'. Mwambambe and most of his supporters were killed, leaving his rival unchallenged. In the early 1880s the Hehe clashed with a horde of Masai, probably members of the Parakuyo clan which had been defeated and displaced in the Masai civil wars. According to Hehe oral tradition the invaders collected a large herd of stolen cattle, but as they were returning home the Hehe attacked and drove them into a patch of quicksand, where many Masai perished.

Another story describes a battle between the Masai and a Hehe army led by Mkwawa's sister, Mtage. Allegedly both armies were almost annihilated, only three men remaining alive at the end according to one version. This is obviously unlikely, but a hand-to-hand fight between Hehe warriors, who were trained to use stabbing spears in Zulu style, and the similarly equipped Masai may well have been bloody enough for the carnage to leave an indelible impression on both sides. Masai tradition, however, claims that the Hehe were frustrated by their failure to defeat them, and resorted to trying to terrorize them by roasting prisoners alive. The *moran* retaliated in kind until both sides tired of the slaughter and made peace. It is not clear whether all these accounts refer to the same campaign, but it is clear that the Masai ceased to threaten Mkwawa's possessions after 1883, when two stone pillars were erected to mark a permanent border between the two tribes' spheres of influence. Meanwhile Mkwawa continued to expand his kingdom in other directions. The main trading route inland from Zanzibar was regularly attacked by Hehe raiding parties based in Wota. In the course of the fighting many of the villages along the route were burnt and plundered, depriving the caravans of supplies. European observers in the late 1880s frequently complained that the trade route was almost closed by the combined depredations of Mkwawa, the Masai and a notorious Kimbu warlord named Nyungu-ya-Mawe. But this activity was to bring the Hehe into conflict with a far more formidable enemy than any they had encountered so far.

In 1884, as the European powers began their 'scramble' for colonial possessions in Africa, an unofficial action by a party of adventurers (including the notorious Carl Peters), backed by the Society for German Colonization, brought the chaotic hinterland of Zanzibar into the sphere of international power politics. Travelling in secret, and with no authority from their government, they persuaded or bribed ten local chiefs to sign treaties accepting German protection. Legally the chiefs were not free to make treaties as they were all subjects of the Sultan of Zanzibar, who in turn was under British protection. It seems unlikely, in fact, that they understood what they were signing; one man put his name to a document declaring that he had never heard of the sultan, even though he lived so close to the island of Zanzibar that it could be seen from his village. Nevertheless, despite the risk of provoking an incident with Britain, Kaiser Wilhelm I agreed to grant the society a *Schutzbrief*, or charter, which automatically granted German protection to any territory which it acquired. The British government was not particularly interested in the unproductive interior, and eventually agreed to accept the Kaiser's claims in return for a free hand elsewhere. In 1885 an Anglo–German agreement conceded to Germany the entire hinterland of Zanzibar as far west as Lake Tanganyika, and the sultan had no choice but to accept the situation when a German naval squadron threatened to bombard his palace.

Authority in the new territory was vested in a commercial company, the Deutsch Ost-Afrika Gesellschaft or German East African Company, and its first years were turbulent. The local Arabs resented the Germans, who imposed restrictive laws and generally behaved as if they were in a conquered country. In 1888 fighting broke out when the German commander at the port of Pangani, Lieutenant von Zelewski, chopped down a pole bearing the all-red Zanzibari flag, despite an agreement that it should be flown side by side with the black, white and red German tricolour. This officer was already hated for his severity, which had earned him the Swahili nickname of 'Nyundo', 'the hammer', but this did not prevent his rapid promotion during and after the ensuing war. The conflict was known to the Germans as the 'Abushiri Rebellion' after the main Arab leader, although technically it was not a rebellion at all, as few if any of the participants had ever given their allegiance to Germany. German authority was eventually restored in 1890, but the discredited East African Company was replaced by direct German government control. In the following year a regular army was established, with the title of imperial *Schutztruppe* or 'protection force'.

The *Schutztruppe*

This quickly established itself as one of the most professional armed forces in Africa. All the officers, NCOs and military specialists were white, and the other ranks exclusively African. At first many of the latter were enlisted in the Sudan, Somalia and Mozambique, the last-named including some Shangaan who had passed themselves off as Zulus and were formed into what became known as the 'Zulu company'. As time went on these men were supplemented by increasing numbers of local recruits, mostly from tribes with well-known military reputations such as the Hehe, Ngoni and Nyamwezi. The askaris were trained with characteristic German professionalism, well treated and well paid. In 1898, for example, a private soldier received 30 rupees a month, compared with 16 rupees in British East Africa. Each man was also provided at government expense with a servant to carry his kit and cook his food. The result was that although German rule was unpopular with the mass of the people, morale in the *Schutztruppe* was extremely high and there was never any shortage of volunteers. In contrast, several European visitors remarked on the poor quality of the junior officers and NCOs seconded from the regular army. All too often these were men whose superiors were happy to be rid of them, and like their equivalents in the Congo Free State (see Chapter 6) they were given too much freedom of action without supervision in isolated posts. Inevitably they robbed and otherwise oppressed the local people, and failed to discipline their askaris if they did the same. Senior officials such as Zelewski and the former explorer Carl Peters (see Chapter 7) also set an example of indiscriminate brutality.

Unlike the British, who usually equipped their askaris with obsolete weapons discarded by the white soldiers, the Germans issued the same weapons as those used by the army in Germany. By 1891 these included the Model 1871/84 11mm rifle – a magazine conversion of a single-shot breech-loader – and the improved 7.92mm calibre 1888 Commission model, which was a modern bolt-action rifle using smokeless powder cartridges. This was at a time when the East African Rifles, precursor of the King's African Rifles, still carried single-shot Sniders which had been replaced in British front-line service more than twenty years previously. In fact the Model 71/84 remained in use until the First World War, not for want of anything better but because its large 11mm calibre round was considered to be better for bush fighting than its 7.92mm replacement because of its greater stopping power. The Germans were slower than the British to adopt machine guns, and the Maxim gun was not officially taken into service by the army until 1899. However, individual officers were usually able to acquire such weapons from unofficial sources, and contemporary accounts describe Maxims in action with German forces in Africa as early as 1889.

In 1890, with the war against Abushiri concluded, the new governor of German East Africa, Freiherr von Soden, wished to extend German influence further inland by peaceful means. He established forts at Mpwapwa and Kilosa to protect the caravan route and proposed negotiations with Mkwawa to bring Hehe raids to an end, but this initiative was pre-empted from an unexpected quarter. Zelewski, 'the hammer', far from being disciplined for his role in starting the recent war, was now commander-in-chief of the *Schutztruppe*, with the rank of *Hauptmann* or major. In June 1891 he led an expedition out of Kilosa to the border of Hehe country to pacify a band of Ngoni who had been raiding for slaves in association with some renegade Hehe. Zelewski's force consisted of five companies, each comprising about ninety askaris, plus three field guns and two Maxim guns. One company, the 8th, was commanded by a young half-Scottish lieutenant named Tom Prince and was composed of 'Zulus', the rest of the rank and file being Sudanese. There were also about 170 locally recruited porters. The Ngoni easily avoided contact with Zelewski, who contented himself with burning a few Hehe border villages. He then advanced up the Kitonga gorge towards the highlands, probably aiming for a fort which Mkwawa had built at Kalenga, of which he had been informed by the Arabs. Zelewski had no orders to invade Mkwawa's kingdom, and because he did not survive to give an account of his actions it is impossible to be sure whether or not he intended to provoke another war. Certainly, though, he shared with his colleague Peters both a firm belief in the use of ruthless methods, and a deep contempt for the fighting qualities of Africans. According to Lieutenant Prince he had been advised that the Hehe were dangerous, but had dismissed the warning on the grounds that as they did not possess firearms they could not seriously threaten a well-equipped expedition.

The Hehe Army

In fact Zelewski had been misled by his anonymous informant on two counts. The Hehe were by no means ignorant of firearms, but even if they had been they would still have been formidable opponents. Early in the twentieth century Nigmann interviewed Hehe veterans of the ensuing war about the tactics which Mkwawa's armies had employed. Unlike many native forces they were accustomed to fight in both the dry and wet seasons, and Hehe armies often campaigned in several theatres simultaneously. According to Joseph Thomson, the warriors could travel at a trot for days without food. An expedition would be preceded by scouts or *vatandisi*, who might operate several days ahead of the main body. Then came an advance guard, the *vandagandaga*, which was strong enough to carry out surprise raids or pursue a fleeing enemy on its own, and could be quickly supported by the main body in the event of serious resistance. This main body would consist of one or more regiments and the supply train. Large numbers of prisoners of war accompanied the armies as labourers and porters. Munyigumba's duel with the Ngoni Chipeta notwithstanding, a commander was not normally expected to lead the army into battle in person, but remained in the rear with his bodyguard. The reason for this was that the Hehe believed that the body of a chief was almost sacred, and it was feared that the troops would be demoralized if they saw his blood spilt.

The most interesting aspect of the tactics used against the Germans is that they seem to have represented a deliberate reversion to traditional methods. The main striking force of the army consisted of the *majinga* regiments, which advanced to battle in dense formations, culminating with a charge to close quarters. According to Cameron and Thomson, writing in the 1870s, each man was equipped with a heavy Zulu-style spear with a short shaft and a long narrow head, for use as a thrusting weapon at close quarters, and between six and eight lighter throwing spears or assegais. Cameron claims that these missiles were accurate up to 50 yards. They seldom appear in battle accounts of the German war and may have largely gone out of use by this time, although in 1898 Tom Prince was wounded by a spear thrown from ambush. A short sword of Masai type, or what Thomson (1881) describes as 'a hybrid article, between a billhook and an axe', was sometimes carried as a sidearm. Shields were also similar to the Zulu type but could be very large, occasionally as tall as a man. The warriors seen by Cameron in 1873 carried huge bull-hide shields, up to 5 feet high by 3 feet wide, with a piece of wood running down the centre as a stiffener and curved outwards in the middle to act as a handgrip. It seems that at least in Mkwawa's day units could be distinguished by the colours or patterns on their shields, and Tom Prince's wife, Magdalene, who accompanied him on the campaign, recorded that at least one of the Hehe regiments in the war of the 1890s carried plain white shields. Following the Zulu precedent, this might have indicated elite status, but this cannot be confirmed from contemporary sources.

If the warriors were armed with muskets, they would usually fire a single volley at close range before charging. But according to the testimony of the explorer J F Elton, who had been an eyewitness of Munyigumba's campaign against the Sango in 1877, this had not been the practice at that time. Instead Elton describes a Hehe war-party besieging a fortified village for several days, trading abuse and long-range musketry, advancing cautiously and only under cover, and even entrenching themselves for protection against the defenders' bullets. Each night they lit fires, apparently to make the enemy think that they had burnt their temporary huts and left. After a few days they really broke off the siege and retired, pursued by the Sango. It may be that this unsuccessful record in siege warfare encouraged the Hehe in their reliance on their own fortifications like those at Kalenga in their struggle against the Germans. Guns seem always to have been in short supply and were mostly hoarded by the chiefs, who distributed them when required to favoured followers. In a group of warriors encountered by Lieutenant Tettenborn in the early 1890s a minority carried muskets, while the rest had only spears. Several hundred German rifles were captured in the battle at Lugalo, but it is not clear how many of them were used against their former owners. Mkwawa appears to have collected most of them in the fort at Kalenga, where they were recaptured after its fall in 1894. Magdalene Prince refers to others being returned to the Germans in 1896. Mkwawa himself owned a German army revolver, presumably captured, with which he is said to have committed suicide in 1898. After his death he was also found in possession of an old carbine, 'considerably cracked at the muzzle' (Iliffe), and a half-filled cartridge belt.

The Battle of Lugalo, 17 August 1891

There are several widely differing accounts of what happened in this battle, which is perhaps inevitable in view of the fact that none of the Germans who were heavily engaged survived to tell their story. Lieutenant Prince and the 8th Company were left to hold the ford over the River Ruaha while Zelewski pressed on towards Kalenga, which was about 15 miles further on. The Germans had already shown their hostile intentions by firing on a group of Hehe – who according to one story were part of a peace mission from Mkwawa – and burning some huts at the village of Image. Towards the top of the Kitonga gorge, where dense bush on both sides of the trail provided cover for an ambush, an army of 3,000 warriors under the command of Mkwawa's brother Mpangile was lying in wait. At dawn on 17 August the Germans set out in a long column through an area of dense bush, with Zelewski at the head riding on a donkey and Lieutenant Tettenborn's company bringing up the rear. Some accounts suggest that Zelewski was totally unprepared for any opposition, but as he had already deliberately provoked the Hehe such carelessness is inexplicable. There appear to have been no scouts deployed, the artillery and the Maxim guns were being carried dismantled on pack animals, and some of the askaris had not even loaded their rifles. Just before 7.00 am they halted to allow stragglers to catch up, then moved on again, advancing towards a hill covered with large rocks and thick vegetation.

Then a single shot was fired. It is not clear who fired it – some Hehe witnesses said that Zelewski took a snap-shot at a bird – but it seems to have either deliberately or accidentally triggered the Hehe ambush. (Another Hehe version says that the signal was supposed to be for their leader to imitate the cry of a bird, but a real bird call caused them to attack prematurely.) Some German accounts speak of a volley of musketry, but it seems better to rely on the recollections of the Hehe themselves, who were the only survivors in this sector of the battlefield. In 1907 a veteran of the battle stated that 'the Hehe shot one gun; they all moved quickly and fought with spears' (Redmayne). Tettenborn and Reichard also imply that only one shot was heard from the Hehe side (quoted in Redmayne). Then the warriors charged out of the bush, only thirty paces from the head of the German column. It appears that the leading companies were overwhelmed almost at once, and probably from several directions, because Hehe veterans said that Zelewski was speared in the back as he fired at another group of attackers. His killer was a boy of sixteen, who received three cows from Mkwawa as a reward. But because the ambush had been launched sooner than intended, those at the rear of the German column were able to organize some resistance.

According to one account the medical officer, Dr Richard Buschow, and a handful of askaris got one of the Maxims into action and fought off their assailants from the shelter of a hut until nightfall, when they made their escape. But this appears to be an example of colonial myth-making. In reality Buschow was killed in the ambush, and his name is listed among the fallen 'heroes' of the battle on the Lugalo Memorial which still stands on the site. Tettenborn, commanding the rearguard, retired to a small hill and formed a defensive position there, which was not seriously threatened. He waited for two days to collect any survivors, then retreated to Mpwapwa, leaving the dead unburied. (Peter Rutkowski, on the basis of the differences between Tettenborn's version and others, has suggested in an unpublished account that Tettenborn was not an eyewitness of the battle at all; either his company had been detached before the ambush, or he retreated as soon as the fighting started and later invented a story to justify himself. However, contemporary sources contain no criticism of Tettenborn, and it is quite possible that his own account, which attributes his survival to the premature triggering of the Hehe ambush, is correct.)

According to Rochus Schmidt, the bodies left on the battlefield included ten Europeans (Zelewski, three other officers and six German NCOs), 250 askaris and around 100 porters. Assuming that the three leading companies averaged ninety men each, this would imply that they were virtually annihilated. Many of the wounded had crawled into nearby cover to hide, only to be burnt to death when the victorious Hehe set fire to the grass. All the artillery was also lost, including the Maxims, which the Hehe later set up at Kalenga. Schmidt remarks that the dead men were among the best and most experienced in the whole *Schutztruppe*; in fact they made up almost a fifth of the force's total manpower at that time. Only one lieutenant from the forward companies, though wounded, managed to escape and rejoin Tettenborn. The latter claimed that the Hehe lost around 700 men, but this is unlikely in view of the fact that few of the askaris can have had time to fire more than one shot. Tom Prince's estimate (Iliffe) was more realistic: he believed that about sixty of the enemy had been killed on the battlefield, and perhaps another 200 died of their wounds later. If Dr Buschow really did get the Maxim into action this may have been the cause of most of the Hehe casualties, but he was obviously too late to affect the outcome of the main battle. The shortage of accurate information about the course of the fight has subsequently led to confusion even about the fate of the main protagonists. An account published after the First World War in the British *Handbook of Tanganyika* (ed. Moffett) states incorrectly that Zelewski survived, even though his name heads the list of dead on the German memorial.

Tettenborn even listed Mkwawa himself among the dead. In fact Mkwawa was almost certainly not present, although one of his leading commanders, Ngosingosi, was killed at Lugalo.

This defeat temporarily threw the Germans onto the defensive throughout their East African territories. The remaining *Schutztruppe* units were too weak to mount another expedition, so all that could be done was to deploy 150 men to protect the loyal population of the neighbourhood from Hehe raids, and enlist the Holy Ghost missionaries to act as intermediaries in opening peace negotiations with Mkwawa. No agreement was reached, and in October 1892 a Hehe army destroyed a trading caravan at Mukondoa and attacked the fort at Mpwapwa. In the following year they ravaged the lands of a chief called Mudgalula who had co-operated with the Germans. However, Mkwawa seems to have deliberately avoided contact with German-led forces, no doubt aware that his victory at Lugalo was due partly to Zelewski's mistakes, and was unlikely to be repeated if he met riflemen on equal terms in the open. The Hehe king's main strategy was to develop his base at Kalenga into an impregnable stronghold in preparation for the inevitable counter-attack.

The Fall of Kalenga, October 1894

Despite their success at Lugalo, and the raids which they were in the habit of launching against native enemies, Hehe strategy seems to have been essentially defensive. Oral tradition describes their immense confidence in the fort which Mkwawa had built at Kalenga, of which the people sang that 'there is nothing which can come in here, unless perhaps there is something which drops from the heavens' (Redmayne). It had originally been surrounded by a simple wooden stockade, but the king had sent an officer called Mtaki to the coast to study the Arab fortifications there, and – inspired by his report – had ordered it to be rebuilt in stone. Work began about 1887, and by 1894 the whole site – nicknamed 'Lipuli', or 'Great Elephant' – was surrounded by a stone wall about 2 miles long, 8 feet in height and up to 4 feet thick. The garrison was 3,000 strong and included the two Maxim guns captured at the Lugalo. However, the Hehe did not know how to operate these, so they played no part in the siege and were eventually recaptured intact by the Germans.

With hindsight Mkwawa's confidence in this fort seems incomprehensible. The impressive perimeter was too long for the garrison to hold in strength, and there was no operational artillery to counter the German field guns, which had already destroyed stone forts at Isike and elsewhere in East Africa. Mkwawa must have been aware of this, because his garrison had been joined by a group of anti-German Nyamwezi who had survived the fall of Isike. Tom Prince, who fought in the siege, believed that if they had made a stand outside the fort the Hehe would probably have won another victory, but their ruler would not allow this. To make matters worse, Mkwawa still had his arsenal of 300 rifles under his personal control, and had only issued 100 of them when the attack came. According to Hehe tradition he had temporarily lost his wits, ordering his warriors to load their guns with blank charges, and placing his reliance on magic charms placed on the paths to deter the German advance.

So when the long-awaited German invasion force came, it encountered no resistance as it approached Kalenga and built a stockaded camp only 400 yards from the walls. The column was commanded by the provincial governor, Freiherr von Schele, and comprised three companies of askaris and a number of field guns. For two days the artillery battered the defences, then on 30 October a storming party under Tom Prince scaled the walls and broke into the fort. The walls themselves proved to be only lightly held, while the main body of the defenders was hidden among the huts inside, those with firearms shooting from concealed positions on roofs and in doorways. According to von Schele's report (Schmidt), every house inside the stronghold had been specially prepared for defence, complete with loopholes and reinforced walls. But after four hours of fighting Mkwawa realized that the fort was lost: he allegedly tried to blow himself up inside one of the houses, but was led away to safety by his officers. At this point resistance collapsed and the Germans took possession of Kalenga with its stores of gunpowder and ivory. One German officer and eight askaris had been killed, with three Germans and twenty-nine askaris wounded. Von Schele claimed that 150 Hehe died in the fighting or were burnt to death when the attackers set fire to their huts. If correct this figure would represent only 5 per cent of the garrison, which does not imply a particularly determined defence: perhaps the Hehe were demoralized by the ease with which Prince's men had surmounted the supposedly impregnable wall, or possibly Mkwawa's departure had persuaded them that further resistance was useless.

But Hehe morale was quickly restored, and resistance continued in the hills outside the fort. On 6 November a force estimated at 1,500 warriors charged von Schele's marching column on its return journey to Kilosa. They broke through the line of porters, but were stopped by the rifle fire of the askaris and retreated, leaving twenty-five dead behind. Once again the authorities tried to open talks with Mkwawa, but he wisely refused, no doubt aware of the German habit of arresting their enemies during negotiations. He continued to avoid attacking regular troops, while raiding the neighbouring tribes who had submitted. So in 1896 Prince was sent with two companies of askaris, each 150 strong, to establish a forti-fied post at Iringa, a few miles from the ruins of Kalenga. In an attempt to divide the Hehe, Prince recruited Mpangile, the victor of the Lugalo battle, who had recently surrendered to the Germans. He was given the title of 'sultan', and set up as a puppet ruler over the pacified Hehe villages. Mpangile gained nothing from his defection, however. In February 1897 Prince became suspicious that he was secretly ordering attacks on German patrols, and despite a lack of concrete evidence summarily executed him.

The war dragged on for two more years, but there were no more major engagements. The Hehe resorted to guerrilla warfare, ambushing isolated patrols and caravans and raiding the villages which were under German control. Prince sent his askaris out on regular patrols to hunt down hostile bands and burn the villages which sheltered them. On several occasions they came near to capturing Mkwawa, and gradually their scorched earth tactics bore fruit. Drought and famine intensified the pressure, and in the first half of 1897 more than 2,000 warriors came in and surrendered. Now only a hard core of loyalists remained around Mkwawa. In January 1898 one of Prince's columns surprised the Hehe chief's camp. Once again he got away thanks to a rearguard action by his followers, but many other warriors – described by Prince as 'mere skeletons' – were taken prisoner. Soon afterwards Mkwawa organized his last successful operation: an attack on a German outpost at Mtande, which took the thirteen-man garrison by surprise and annihilated it. The governor of German East Africa, General von Liebert, now offered a reward of 5,000 rupees for his head.

In July a patrol under a *Feldwebel* Merkl was following up information received from a local tribesman when it intercepted Mkwawa's trail near the River Ruaha. The patrol followed it for four days, and eventually captured a boy who claimed to be Mkwawa's servant and offered to lead them to where he was hiding. Near the village of Humbwe, Merkl was shown two figures lying on the ground, apparently asleep. It is an indication of how wary the Germans still were of their opponents that the *Feldwebel* made no attempt to take the men alive. Instead, obviously fearing a trap, he opened fire from cover. One of Merkl's bullets struck Mkwawa in the head, but it was clear from the subsequent examination that both of the Hehe had already been dead for some time. Tired and ill, the king had first shot his companion and then himself. With his death all Hehe resistance ceased, but his surviving people continued to revere him, and in 1904 the Germans sent his sons into exile on the grounds that they were the focus of a potentially inflammatory cult honouring their father.

There was a further bizarre postscript to Mkwawa's career. When the British took over Tanganyika in November 1918 at the end of the First World War, they received a request from the Hehe elders for the return of their king's skull, which they said had been taken as a trophy by the Germans twenty years earlier. The German authorities continued to deny all knowledge of it, but the British governor of Tanganyika, Sir Edward Twining, continued to pursue the matter. He finally located the relic in 1953, in a museum in Bremen. It was formally identified by a German forensic surgeon from the bullet wounds, and in 1954 it was returned to Mkwawa's grandson Chief Adam Sapi. It remains in the custody of the Hehe, as a memorial to their country's finest hour.

Sources

Cameron, Thomson and Elton all have eyewitness accounts of the Hehe during Munyigumba's reign. Redmayne's article, based largely on anthropological fieldwork among the Hehe, provides a comprehensive overview of the history and organization of the kingdom. The main source for the war from the German side is Schmidt.

Chapter Nine

'No Law but Blood for Blood':
British East Africa's Northern Frontier

In the summer of 1886 a wealthy Hungarian aristocrat, Count Samuel Teleki von Szek, was planning a big-game hunting expedition to Lake Tanganyika. Rashly, perhaps, he mentioned his plans to his friend Crown Prince Rudolf of Austria, who incidentally was the son-in-law of the Belgian King Leopold. Possibly with a view to acquiring for Austria a slice of what Leopold had once called 'this magnificent African cake' (Pakenham), the prince asked Teleki to take along a young naval officer on his staff, Lieutenant Ludwig von Hohnel. Von Hohnel lacked the means to visit Africa himself, but had been fascinated by exploration from an early age and had become a self-taught expert on the continent's geography. With the prince's backing, he persuaded Teleki that his time and money would be better spent exploring one of the few remaining blank spots on the African map. So the count found his quiet hunting trip transformed into one of the largest privately funded exploring expeditions ever to operate in Africa. It was also one of the very last to traverse totally unexplored country and make geographical discoveries of the first magnitude. In July 1887 Teleki and von Hohnel marched north from Taveta, at the base of Mount Kilimanjaro, in search of a vast lake which was said to lie somewhere to the north. With them were 200 armed Zanzibaris, and 450 porters carrying supplies for two years.

Beyond the plains of Masailand they discovered that the land fell away northwards towards the Chalbi Desert, an extension far inland of the arid steppes of Somaliland. In this great desert depression lay the mysterious lake, which Teleki named Lake Rudolf (now Lake Turkana) in honour of the prince, and beyond that rose the hills bordering the Ethiopian plateau. Teleki's powerful caravan had some skirmishes with the local people, but found most of the country virtually uninhabited, and suffered far greater hardships from lack of food and water than they did from hostile tribes.

Like several subsequent expeditions they found that this remote region had other unique perils. The rhinoceroses which abounded in the denser bush had never been hunted, so they were often extremely aggressive and charged without warning. Von Hohnel was seriously injured by a rhino on a later trip, whose leader described the return journey as 'a nightmare of continuous horror' due to the constant attacks by the short-tempered creatures. The lions were also particularly voracious, and it was rare for a caravan not to lose several of its members to them during the course of an expedition. The people whom Teleki and his companion encountered were semi-nomadic pastoralists, who migrated over great distances with their herds of cattle, sheep and camels in search of water and grazing. They included the Suk, whom von Hohnel calls 'the terror of the neighbourhood'; the Samburu, distant relatives of the Masai; and their camel-herding allies the Rendille. On the fringes of the region lived other peoples who regularly raided into the desert zone in search of livestock. These included the Laikipiak clan of the Masai, who had lost out in the Masai civil wars and retained only a vestige of their former power, but still ranged almost as far as the Ethiopian frontier. From the east came the Somalis, and to the north the Borana, both peoples who fought on horseback with spears.

The Turkana

In the far west, beyond Lake Rudolf, lived the most dreaded of all these desert raiders, the Turkana. During the nineteenth century they had expanded south and eastwards at the expense of the Samburu and others, and had even raided as far as Lake Baringo, where they clashed with the Masai. In spite of the extensive territory which they conquered, the Turkana themselves claimed that this was not their main aim: their campaigns were launched to capture cattle to replace their losses in the frequent droughts, but they were so successful at this that their victims eventually moved away to escape the raiding parties, evacuating new grazing lands which the victorious bands then occupied. They continued to clash with an almost equally formidable people, the Karamojong, along the Turkwel River on the border with what was to become Uganda, and sporadically with the Samburu in the east, but elsewhere Turkana expansion had virtually stopped by the 1890s, though this would change early in the twentieth century, when the tribe became a focus of resistance to the British.

By 1900 the Turkana numbered around 30,000 people spread across an area of 24,000 square miles, a population density so low that they were no longer able to muster and feed large armies. The aridity of this territory made it of little interest to potential invaders, so that there was no reason to maintain standing armies for defence. Turkana warfare had become a matter of skirmishing and sudden raids rather than pitched battles. The traditional age-set system gave way to a more locally based organization, and the authority of the elders declined. Life in the desert was so precarious that there was little energy to spare for show and bravado; one twentieth-century informant described the campaigns of his predecessors in strictly practical terms: 'the Turkana fought to get food' (Lamphear, 1976). According to a traditional saying, the secret of success in war was 'not power, but knowledge'. In their painstaking use of reconnaissance, their emphasis on surprise, and the desire to minimize their own casualties while maximizing material gain, the Turkana could perhaps be compared to the Apachès. Captain John Yardley, who fought them in the Northern Frontier District of Kenya during the First World War, describes their tactics as follows:

> Like most of their kindred tribes, and in contrast to the Abyssinians, the Turkana had no knowledge of any military formations or movements. They did not need any. Their intimate acquaintance with their own country, where every rock was familiar to them, and every mountain track as easy to find by night as by day, made preconcerted movements superfluous. Even if they had been well drilled, they were far better off when they bolted from one ridge or hollow to another in their own time and by their own route.

The Turkana were very dark-skinned, and did not paint their bodies. Therefore they referred to themselves as 'black people', as opposed to the 'red people', who included whites as well as the Samburu and Masai, who were naturally paler and painted themselves with red ochre. In the late nineteenth century the Turkana were often believed to be giants, although von Hohnel – the first European to describe them – described them as 'of middle height only', though 'very broad and sinewy, in fact, of quite a herculean build'. Turkana war gear reflected their ruthlessly practical attitude. The spear or *akwara* was considerably longer than the weapons used elsewhere in the region. An average length was 8 feet, but one 'giant' chief seen by Captain Wellby in 1899 carried a spear 'twice his own length' – which must have made it more than 12 feet long. The blade was protected when not in use by a leather sheath to keep it sharp. On their right wrists most men wore a circular iron wrist knife or *ararait*. This peculiar weapon – basically a bracelet with the outer edge kept razor-sharp – could be brought into action almost instantly. In an emergency it could be used without the warrior having to drop his spear or anything else he was carrying, and could inflict serious wounds when grappling at close quarters. Like the spear blades, these knives were usually kept covered by a leather sheath to prevent injury to the wearer. Yardley describes this weapon as 'the most murderous kind of knife I have ever seen . . . . After throwing their spears, they slipped the scabbard off in a fraction of a second and closed with their enemy. One well-directed gash at the throat would wellnigh decapitate a man, or an upward thrust entirely disembowel him.' Variants of this type of knife were popular over a wide region of north-east Africa, and in some places they were also worn by women. It was said that Arab slavers would always shoot a woman seen wearing a wrist-knife rather than attempting to capture her, as it was so dangerous to approach her. Other Turkana weapons were wooden clubs and throwing sticks. Their buffalo-hide shields were fairly small and light, befitting the mobile skirmishing tactics which the Turkana preferred, but were solid enough to be used as weapons in their own right if necessary.

In 1895 the British government took over the territories formerly administered by the bankrupt Imperial British East Africa Company. These included what was to become the Northern Frontier District of Kenya, but at that time the frontier had not been surveyed. Since 1891 an agreement had existed with the Italian government, which laid claim to southern Somaliland and to a protectorate over the kingdom of Ethiopia (then commonly known as Abyssinia). However, in 1896 the Ethiopian Emperor Menelik decisively defeated an Italian army at Adowa, securing his country's independence for the next forty years. It suddenly became necessary for Britain to deal with a power which it had until then disregarded, especially as Ethiopian expeditions soon began to penetrate into the desert south of the escarpment in search of ivory and slaves.

The Fight at Lumian, 1901

The nature of warfare against the Turkana was epitomized by the fate of the Austin expedition. In October 1900 a survey party was dispatched to the Ethiopian border region under the command of Major H H Austin of the Royal Engineers, who had served with Macdonald on his campaign in the far north of Uganda during the war against Kabarega (see Chapter 4). Austin left Khartoum with three British officers, twenty-three Sudanese soldiers seconded from the Egyptian army, and thirty-two 'Gehadiah', former followers of the Mahdi. Both these contingents were armed with Martini-Henry rifles, though in the words of Austin's second-in-command, Major Bright of the Rifle Brigade, the ex-Mahdists were 'most indifferent' shots. This expedition was dogged by misfortune almost from the start. Its members floundered for months in the Nile swamps, and when they emerged near Lake Rudolf they found food and water scarce, and the local tribes, who had mostly welcomed previous visitors, hostile to all outsiders as a result of Ethiopian raids.

Austin made a detour to a Turkana village at Lumian, which was believed to be still friendly, in search of supplies. Having arrived near the village late in the day, he camped in the angle formed by the junction of two small, almost dry river beds. While the camp was still being set up, two soldiers and the cook were ambushed and speared to death by Turkana warriors who quickly vanished into the surrounding scrub. It was now nearly dark, so there was no time either to move the camp or to build a thorn-bush *zeriba* to protect it. Austin therefore ordered the sentries to keep their rifles loaded, and the rest of the soldiers to sleep at their posts with fixed bayonets. After dark, according to Major Bright's account, the 'giant Turkana' crept close to the camp along the river beds, 'without the slightest noise'. Then, around midnight, they attacked: 'Rising as from the ground they rushed with blood-curdling yells on the unprotected camp. They came from three sides, but were met with a steady and rapid rifle fire which appeared to surprise them, for they threw a few spears into camp and then fled. For the remainder of the night we were left unmolested.'

But the Turkana continued to harass the expedition as it marched southwards along the western shore of Lake Rudolf. Large bodies of tribesmen shadowed them just out of rifle range, but 'when they approached too near they were dispersed with a few well-directed shots'.

It soon became clear, however, that smaller groups were keeping them under observation from much closer range, although they were seldom seen. Bright relates how one of the Gehadiah was killed within 100 yards of the camp when he crept out to scavenge some meat from a dead camel. One night a corporal guarding the animals was speared within earshot of his companions by a band of Turkana, who escaped into thick bush before a shot could be fired. After one march, during which no enemy had been sighted all day, a soldier waded across the Turkwel River to bring in a missing donkey, carelessly leaving his rifle on the bank to avoid getting it wet. As soon as he reached the far bank, a group of warriors emerged as if from nowhere and stabbed him to death. By the time the expedition reached safety, it had lost forty-five men from Turkana attacks and exhaustion due to starvation. Only one of the Gehadiah survived the march.

The Somalis

Further east, towards the shores of the Indian Ocean, the frontier region was dominated by another famous warrior people, the Somalis, who were regarded by many Europeans with something close to awe. They differed from most of their neighbours in being Muslims, and in relying mainly on their herds of camels, which replaced cattle in the most barren stretches of the desert. The southern part of Somaliland, which overlapped the Northern Frontier District, was more fertile than the north, but the peculiarities of terrain and climate made its inhabitants unusually difficult for the colonial administration to deal with. Inland lies an elevated plateau known as the 'Haud', which has extensive pastures fed by seasonal rain, but no permanent water. The rain that falls here, and in the Ethiopian highlands further north, soaks through the porous rocks and percolates down to feed wells in the arid coastal zone, which consequently has water but no pasture. This unusual situation forced the Somali herdsmen to migrate constantly between the two regions even after they were partitioned between British Kenya, which claimed most of the plateau along the border with Ethiopia, and the Italian territory on the coast.

A fundamental feature of Somali society was its emphasis on genealogy and family relationships. It was divided into six major clan groups, each of which was subdivided into countless individual lineages which were often mutually hostile, but were bound by long-standing custom to join together against any third party who was less closely related. The resulting combination of clannishness and political fragmentation, together with a sense of national unity against foreign intervention, was seldom understood by Europeans, who interpreted the Somalis' constantly changing allegiances as a tendency to treachery. They were also addicted to the pursuit of blood feuds, and never allowed an injury or insult to go unavenged. In the words of Sir Bartle Frere, writing in the 1870s, they 'knew no law but blood for blood' (*Proceedings of the Royal Geographical Society*, vol. 17, 1873). Furthermore, being strongly individualistic and immensely proud of their ancestry, they were not impressed by the white man's technological superiority and resisted all attempts to make them change their way of life.

Frederick Jackson, whose opinions on the Masai have already been noted (see Chapter 7), felt that by the 1890s the country south of Lake Baringo had been sufficiently pacified that an expedition of fifty armed men would be fairly safe from attack. Further north a force of eighty to 100 would be preferable, as the tribes had less experience of firearms and so were less wary of attacking caravans. He concludes, however, with the warning that, 'If the trip should be extended further north into the Somali country, it would not be worth while running the risks of entering the country of such grasping, treacherous, religious fanatics as the southern Somalis are with an escort of fewer than a hundred and fifty rifles' (Phillipps-Wolley). Jackson may have been exaggerating the risks: certainly expeditions much smaller than that did traverse the Somali country and survive, but his view of the people's character is supported by many other sources. According to Vincent Glenday, an officer who fought alongside them before and during the First World War, the Somalis were 'temperamental, treacherous, cruel and as fighting men . . . marks above any other tribe' (Hunter and Mannix).

Like the Masai, the Somalis sometimes attained the stature of bogeymen who were believed to be capable of astounding feats. The Kikuyu of the Mount Kenya district preserved a tradition that at some time around the middle of the nineteenth century an invading Somali army had penetrated as far south as the Kenya Highlands and attempted to settle there, requiring the combined efforts of the three most powerful local tribes, the Kikuyu, Kamba and Masai, to drive them out. One British governor even suggested that without European intervention the Somalis and the Zulus might eventually have partitioned the whole of East Africa between them. Another indication of British preoccupation with the Somalis was the frequent recurrence of rumours that they were holding a number of sailors who had been shipwrecked on the coast – a parallel to the 'missing in action' issue in the USA after the Vietnam War. It was often suggested that naval landing parties should be sent in search of these men, but in fact there seems to have been no solid evidence that the Somalis ever held any British prisoners.

The Fight at Berbera, April 1855

A revealing insight into Somali fighting methods is provided by a minor but well-known incident which took place near Berbera in April 1855. Four British explorers and their local escort were camped on a ridge over-looking the port. Two of the men were later to become famous in the story of African exploration: they were Richard Burton, fresh from his visit to the 'forbidden city' of Harar, and John Hanning Speke, who later identi-fied Lake Victoria as the source of the Nile. Their companions were Lieutenants Stroyan and Herne, both surveyors with experience in India. The party was engaged in what was essentially a peaceful geographical expedition, but the Somalis suspected them of being spies sent by the British government with a view to suppressing their slaving activities. Furthermore Speke had managed to offend a respected local family by having one of its members, his guide on an unsuccessful trip to the Wadi Nogal, thrown into prison for theft. One night about 350 local tribesmen surrounded the camp, and in the early hours of the morning they attacked, using the traditional stratagem of cutting the tent ropes in the hope that the falling canvas would entangle their victims. Luckily for the explorers an alert sentry gave the alarm just in time, but then most of the friendly Somalis fled, leaving them to their fate.

According to the account given by Speke (1864), as he stepped out of his tent he was pelted with stones, one of which struck his knee and nearly knocked him down. He ducked under the fly of the tent and stooped down so that he could better see the attackers silhouetted against the skyline as they looked over a row of boxes. Other Somalis, meanwhile, were doing the same in an attempt to spot him. At this point Burton shouted out 'Don't step back, or they will think we are retiring' (Burton, 1856). Speke, offended by what he took to be a suggestion of cowardice on his part, strode forward firing his revolver into the mob. The warriors in front of him fell back, but he found himself surrounded, and at this critical point the cylinder of his gun jammed. One man snatched the useless gun from his hand, while another knocked him down and winded him with a blow from behind. Quickly he was tied up and searched: he experienced a bad moment when they felt for a hidden dagger between his legs, fearing that they belonged to a clan notorious for castrating their prisoners, but at first he was not harmed. Later, however, when he was tied up in the Somali camp, the man standing guard over him began to threaten him, and eventually stabbed him several times in the legs. So Speke, fearing for his life, managed to get to his feet, knock down his assailant with his bound hands and escape, dodging the spears hurled after him as he ran. He finally reached safety despite receiving a total of eleven spear wounds.

Burton meanwhile had been struck in the face by a thrown spear, but he and his local overseer defended themselves with their sabres and also reached the seashore and safety. So did Lieutenant Herne, despite what Burton describes as 'sundry stiff blows from the war club', but Stroyan was cut off from his companions and fatally speared in the heart and abdomen. The British government put pressure on the local chiefs, and the man who claimed to have killed Stroyan was eventually surrendered, but most of the attackers went unpunished. This minor affray may have had a significant influence on the history of African exploration, because it appears that Speke never forgave Burton for what he saw as his insulting remark. By the standards of the irascible Burton it was a fairly mild rebuke and it is likely that he quickly forgot all about it, but years later, on their famous joint expedition to Lake Tanganyika, Speke became delirious with fever and brought it up again, accusing his companion of calling him a coward. As Speke put it, they were all 'highly disgusted with our defeat', but the incident did not reflect very well on the fighting abilities of the Somalis either. Despite having the advantage of surprise and outnumbering their victims by almost a hundred to one, they had failed to kill three out of four of the white men. Both Speke and Herne remained in action despite multiple wounds inflicted at close range.

Burton carried the scar from his spear wound for the rest of his life, but was scathing about the men who had inflicted it. He argued that they always preferred to avoid a fight on equal terms, and that most of the slaughter in Somali warfare was inflicted by surprise attacks on women and children. 'In their great battles,' he observes, 'a score is considered a heavy loss; usually they will run after the fall of half a dozen.' He considered that the shortage of visible battle scars among the Somalis was proof of their lack of martial spirit (though the Somalis themselves might have regarded it as proof of intelligence): 'amongst a Kraal full of braves who boast a hundred murders,' he says, 'not a single maimed or wounded man will be seen, whereas in an Arabian camp half the male population will bear the marks of lead and steel.' Elsewhere he recommends that when travelling in the desert an explorer should challenge any horsemen he sees approaching, and fire on them if they fail to stop: 'when two saddles are emptied, the rest are sure to decamp'. The American explorer Dr A Donaldson Smith, who travelled in Somaliland in the 1890s, concurred with this view. Dismissing their reputation for ferocity, he argued that the Somalis would never attack unless the odds were heavily in their favour. Although impressed by a demonstration of spear-throwing from horseback, he also felt that they were poor horsemen: their bits were too harsh, and they continued to ride their ponies even though their backs were 'a mass of sores'. They were, however, good marchers when on foot, and remarkably resistant to thirst.

The typical Somali spear was about 7 feet long, with a blade of what Burton (1856) calls 'coarse bad iron'. Normally two were carried, one to throw and one to keep in the hand for emergencies, though some warriors might have up to four. The poor quality of the metal is confirmed by Speke, who recalled that the man who attacked him after his capture failed to put his spear through his leg until he took a run up and threw his whole weight behind it. A warrior would often make the blade of his spear quiver before throwing by slapping it with his palm; this was believed to increase accuracy in the same way as spinning a rifle bullet, by ironing out minor irregularities in the shape and balance of the missile. F L James, who visited Somali country in 1884, says that these spears could be thrown accurately up to 25 yards, but Burton experimented with a target consisting of a pair of slippers planted upright in the ground, and found that the average proportion of hits at 12 yards was only one in three. He concluded that the throwing spear was too easily avoided in the open in daylight, but could be 'terrible in night attacks or in the "bush", whence it can be hurled unseen'.

The Somalis used small round shields of ox or antelope hide to catch or deflect an opponent's missiles. When their own spears were used up they would fight at close quarters with wooden clubs, and short swords or daggers with blades about 18 inches long. According to Burton the Arabs were 'far more skilful' in close combat than the Somalis, who did not know how to use their shields to defend against sword cuts. This judgement is confirmed by James, whose expedition doctor beat all comers in a fencing contest using wooden sticks, because the Somalis 'knew nothing about the outside wrist cut and guard', and were hit on the forearm every time they attempted to strike a blow. Interestingly, however, Burton approved of the Somali method of stabbing overarm with their swords, with the blade held downwards, in an attempt to get behind an opponent's shield. Although this goes against all the tenets of European sword and knife fighting, Burton – who was himself an expert fencer and had written a book on bayonet drill – argued that an underarm thrust with such a short blade would be too easy to stop simply by seizing the attacker's arm.

As might be expected from these less than flattering assessments of their fighting capabilities, the Somalis of the Northern Frontier District never attempted to engage the British in a pitched battle, and most of the operations in which they were involved were police actions aimed at recovering stolen livestock or preventing them from massacring each other in pursuit of blood feuds. Early in the twentieth century the situation was to change dramatically when a charismatic individual named Sayyid Muhammad Abdullah Hassan rallied the clans in the Ogaden, a region claimed by the Ethiopians, to resist foreign domination. By 1901 he had 6,000 armed followers, whom he equipped with large numbers of imported rifles and subjected to sometimes ferocious discipline. The British agreed to joint action with the Ethiopians against Sayyid Muhammad, who had become known as the 'Mad Mullah', and so became involved in an unnecessary war which lasted for two decades. Under their new leadership the Somalis displayed unprecedented determination, and at Gumburu in 1903 they actually broke a British square, killing nearly 200 men. Sayyid Muhammad received support from the Turks in the First World War, and was finally defeated in 1920 with the aid of air power, which takes his career rather beyond the scope of this book. Nevertheless his achievement in transforming a nation of lightly armed nomadic raiders into a force capable of sustaining such a protracted war is worthy of note.

Karamoja

The Karamojong, like their enemies the Turkana, came originally from the region north of Mount Elgon, not far from the Nandi country. They had probably separated from the Turkana as recently as 1720, and continued to share many of their attitudes to warfare. By the nineteenth century the Karamojong were occupying a stretch of dry, hilly country west of Lake Rudolf, living on the tops of the ridges which flanked the few watercourses. They engaged in limited agriculture, but the arid climate of what was to become known as Karamoja was not very suitable for crops, and so they relied mainly on their cattle. The young warriors spent most of their time in nomadic stock camps, driving the herds around the country in search of grazing. This was the chief motivation behind Karamojong warfare, as they were often obliged to move onto grazing grounds claimed by neighbouring tribes. The first outsiders to appear in Karamoja were Swahili elephant hunters who arrived during the 1880s. They introduced a few guns, as well as human and livestock diseases which weakened the local tribes, but trade was on a very small scale and did not lead to any change in methods of warfare until after the beginning of the twentieth century. The people's first contact with Europeans came as late as 1897, when Major Macdonald's column from Uganda passed through. The Karamojong did not resist him, but instead allowed the caravan to purchase food. Evidently, however, their warriors made an impression on Macdonald, as he later described them as 'the best fighters in Equatoria'. Their homeland was eventually allocated to the British colony of Uganda, but the government's policy at this time was to avoid conflict with the 'wilder tribes' of the region, so the Karamojong remained independent until the establishment of a formal administration in 1916, and despite their warlike reputation they never clashed seriously with the whites.

Like most of the cattle-herding peoples of this region they had little in the way of political or military organization. They were divided into clans which consisted simply of the occupants of a particular ridge, controlled loosely by councils of elders. The usual age-set system divided the male population into two major 'generations' – warriors and elders. All the men who were initiated as warriors within the same five- or six-year period formed an age-set, of which five made up a generation. It is not clear to what extent these sets served as military units: oral tradition suggests that Karamojong armies fought as a disorderly mob, with no formal division into units and no proper system of command. The elders exercised a form of authority over the warriors by their power to bless or curse their raiding parties before they set off on the warpath, but otherwise had no direct military role. There were warriors known as 'fierce men', who rose to prominence because of their fighting prowess, but they had no real authority over other individuals, who were free to follow any leader they chose. No man was considered fit to marry until he had killed a member of an enemy tribe, but the victim did not have to be a warrior, and nor was it necessary for them to be killed in battle. A woman or child, or a man murdered in his sleep, was equally acceptable as a trophy. Karamojong armies, like those of many other African peoples, were often accompanied by boys too young to fight, who carried supplies of water and helped to drive off any captured cattle.

No accurate data is available on the size of nineteenth-century armies, but in 1911 the total number of warriors in Karamoja was estimated at 6,000. The population was no doubt larger before the smallpox epidemic which struck in the early 1890s, but as their clans were never united, the Karamojong probably never mustered an army stronger than 4,000–5,000. We have few contemporary descriptions of their methods of fighting, but they appear to have been remarkably successful against the Arab slaving expeditions which began to penetrate the country around the turn of the century. The elephant hunter 'Karamoja' Bell, whose name commemorates his association with the area around the same time, says that on at least three occasions the Karamojong had ambushed and annihilated Arab caravans without any loss to themselves. Bell was not an eyewitness and so we have no details of the tactics used in these battles, but another visitor, Major Powell-Cotton, described Karamojong warriors advancing in a series of rushes, kneeling behind their shields for cover when they halted, then throwing their spears when close enough to the enemy. Battle formations were open and flexible, with the emphasis on fighting at a distance, evading the enemy's missiles with dodging and bobbing movements. These movements were taught and practised by means of war dances, and young boys also practised for war by throwing spears at a rolling hoop. Spears were light and designed mainly for throwing, and could be up to 8 feet long. Heavy wooden clubs with sharpened edges were also used, and wrist-knives similar to those of the Turkana could be worn on the right arm. Shields were made from the hide of thick-skinned animals such as elephant, buffalo, rhinoceros or giraffe, the latter being the most sought after, as it was both strong and light.

Karamojong warriors plastered their hair with clay, which dried to form a 'helmet' which could provide useful protection against blows from clubs. Bell once seized a club from a hostile warrior and struck one of his companions on the head with it: 'I was fairly hefty, in good training, and meant all I knew,' he recalled. 'To my astonishment the native turned on me with a smile instead of dropping dead or at least stunned, while the club flew to atoms. I had hit his shock-absorbing periwig . . . I might as well have hit a Dunlop Magnum.' White ostrich feathers were often worn on top of the head; their number apparently reflected the rank or seniority of the wearer, and so might have been used to distinguish between age-sets in battle. According to Bell a man who had killed an enemy was entitled to wear a feather 'dipped blood-red', and to tattoo his body on the right side if his victim was a man, on the left for a woman.

The Borana

The Borana, like the Oromo and other related peoples of the Ethiopian borderlands, are generally referred to in nineteenth-century accounts by the rather vague term 'Gallas'. Like the Somalis many of them fought from horseback, though their spears were longer and heavier and were used mainly for thrusting rather than throwing. In the late nineteenth and early twentieth centuries the Borana suffered badly from drought, live-stock diseases and Ethiopian raids, and replenished their herds by ferocious mounted raids on their pedestrian neighbours such as the Rendille and Samburu. One of the first acts of the British administration when it arrived was to confiscate most of their horses, which quickly put an end to these incursions. They fought only one major battle against the whites, and that was against not a military expedition but a well-armed exploring party led by the American Dr Donaldson Smith. Like Teleki he was a wealthy adventurer who equipped a caravan at his own expense, and wishing to make some contribution to African exploration he undertook to map the Ethiopian border region on behalf of the Royal Geographical Society. His armed escort consisted of fifty-five experienced Somalis, fifteen of whom were armed with Winchester repeaters and the rest with breech-loading Snider rifles.

The Ethiopians, suspecting the doctor's British connections, refused him entry to the territory which they claimed. This forced him to detour through the land of the Borana, even though they were known to be hostile to outsiders – a hostility which Donaldson Smith attributed to the aggressive behaviour of two earlier Italian expeditions. Early in 1895, while marching through the hills north-east of Lake Rudolf, the expedition began to encounter large numbers of armed tribesmen. At first they shadowed the caravan at a distance, but after a brief clash which led to the spearing of two of the expedition's members and the shooting of a Borana warrior, they became bolder and made several attempts to run off the party's pack camels. One evening the explorers pitched camp in the middle of an open plain to reduce the risk of being surprised, but woke up to find themselves surrounded by 'great masses' of Borana on the surrounding hills. These turned out to be the followers of an eminent local 'king' named Abofilato, and the explorer estimated their numbers at 2,000–3,000, more than 1,000 of them being mounted. Most of them wore ostrich feathers in their hair, a sure sign that they were on the warpath. But they still did not attack, even when the caravan struck camp and began to march off. Instead two warriors rode down, making signs indicating peace and offering their services as guides.

Both sides now made some inexplicable mistakes. Donaldson Smith must have realized that the Borana were unwilling to risk fighting in the open where the expedition's guns would have a clear field of fire, but he allowed the guides to lead him into an area of thick bush. The guides tried to persuade him to camp there, but he admits that this 'rather raised my suspicions', so he insisted on continuing until they reached a more open spot, some 200 yards away from dense cover. Hurriedly the explorer dispatched his men to cut bushes and bring them to build a *zeriba* around the baggage. This was a poor obstacle, as (unusually for Africa) there were no thorn bushes in the vicinity and it had to be constructed of ordinary brushwood. The *zeriba* had just been completed and the defenders placed in position when a group of Borana cavalry appeared. At the same time other warriors on foot emerged from the nearest patch of bush and charged towards the camp. It appears that the tribesmen had not had the men in place to ambush the expedition before they could complete their defensive preparations, but now they launched their attack with part of their force while the main body was still far behind. Donaldson Smith suspected that the younger warriors, eager for loot and the social status to be gained from killing the invaders, had charged prematurely in order not to have to share the glory with their seniors.

The explorer himself opened fire on the cavalry with his Winchester, leaving the nearer targets to be dealt with by his askaris. The first rush was quickly halted, and Donaldson Smith had the satisfaction of seeing the cavalry, who had obviously not realized that they were vulnerable at a range of 200 yards, gallop hastily for cover. But the rest of the enemy force regrouped and made a desperate rush at one side of the *zeriba*. Their casualties were heavy – they could be seen holding up their large round shields to stop the bullets, a futile gesture which only made them better targets – but they reached the obstacle and tried to force their way through it, partly concealed by the clouds of powder smoke from the defenders' rifles. The expedition's pack animals, alarmed by the firing, stampeded through the *zeriba* and escaped, adding to the confusion. 'The smoke became so thick,' Donaldson Smith reported, 'we could hardly distinguish our enemy, when suddenly their long thrusting spears loomed up among us.' But he had had the foresight to call up the men who had been stationed on the unengaged side of the camp, and at the crucial moment these arrived and fired a volley into the enemy at point-blank range. The Borana broke and fled, leaving their dead behind. The next peace mission proved to be genuine: the tribesmen had learned the futility of attacking men armed with guns, and subsequent expeditions found them less aggressive. They even returned the lost animals, enabling Donaldson Smith to make his escape. Whether the Borana would have learned a different lesson if they had planned their ambush more carefully, or had waited until they could muster an overwhelming force against the sketchy *zeriba*, we can only speculate.

The Suk, Samburu and Rendille

The Suk – better known nowadays as the Pokot – were a pastoral tribe who roamed the arid country south of Lake Rudolf, between the territories of the Turkana to the north and the Nandi to the south. They had apparently once been farmers, but during the early nineteenth century they had expanded into areas formerly held by peripheral groups of Masai and adopted their herding lifestyle. According to Ludwig von Hohnel they were divided into two groups: the sedentary Suk and the nomads. He describes the latter as 'very bold raiders, the terror of the neighbourhood, even the Masai standing in some awe of them'. Joseph Thomson (1885) confirms this, saying that the Suk were 'described as very warlike, and generally quite a match for the Masai, in whose country they frequently make raids'. In the 1850s and 1860s they became friendly with the Turkana, and joined with them in raiding the Samburu and the farming communities around Lake Baringo. Then in the 1870s the two tribes fell out, and the Suk forced the Turkana to withdraw from some of the southern portions of their range, before themselves falling victim to the series of cattle epidemics which swept through East Africa in the 1880s. Writing in 1894, Frederick Jackson listed the Suk – along with the Masai, Nandi and Somali – as one of only four tribes in Kenya which were still considered dangerous to whites. He describes them as 'not only very treacherous, but much more fearless of firearms than other tribes' (Phillipps-Wolley). In practice, however, they did not pose a serious threat to European expeditions. Teleki had little trouble with them in 1888, and at the very end of the century the members of the Austin expedition, arriving exhausted and helpless after their running fight with the Turkana, also found them friendly.

The Samburu and their Rendille allies inhabited the dry pasturelands to the east of the Suk country, where they seem to have lived peacefully in a sort of symbiosis during most of the nineteenth century. The cattle-herding Samburu occupied the wetter pastures, especially those around their forested strongholds on mounts Kulal and Nyiro, while the Rendille grazed camels in the more arid regions. The Samburu derived their name from a leather bag, the *samburr*, in which the warriors carried their possessions. They were closely related to the Masai, and their existence as a distinct tribe dated only from the first half of the nineteenth century. Additional groups of Laikipiak Masai were absorbed during the 1880s and 1890s, either as refugees from the Masai civil wars or from among Laikipiak warriors captured in battle. The Rendille were related to the Somalis, but had adopted so many elements of Samburu culture that their warriors were virtually indistinguishable.

The Samburu and Rendille were both pushed out of the region around the southern shore of Lake Rudolf by the Turkana in the 1830s. The Samburu continued to suffer from Turkana raids until the 1890s, but their best-recorded campaigns were fought against the Laikipiak Masai. In 1879–80 the Samburu and Rendille joined together to resist a large army of Laikipiaks who had been driven out of their usual grazing grounds by rival Masai. The Samburu fought two battles at Longosori and Susukh, east of Mount Marsabit, but were eventually forced to take refuge in the mountains. The Rendille beat off an attack on their settlement at Kurikude-Intargeta, but nevertheless retreated westwards in order to avoid further raids. Despite this, the Laikipiaks continued to harass them throughout the 1880s.

The Battle of the Merille River, 1890

In 1890 a major confrontation took place between the Rendille and the Laikipiaks, who attacked a village while the Rendille men were away hunting. The invaders captured many women and children, as well as goats and camels, and then decided to relocate the entire village into their own territory. When the Rendille hunters returned, they found their families camped along the Merille River as virtual prisoners of the Masai. They challenged the Laikipiaks to a formal pitched battle, the challenge was accepted, and both sides held a feast of meat in preparation for the fight. The Rendille deployed beside the river and sent out champions to taunt their enemies, calling out: 'You women; the Rendille are waiting for you. Come and fight!' (Spear and Waller). The Laikipiaks charged them, but were lured onto the Rendille main body, and after a confused hand-to-hand battle the invaders were decisively repulsed and fled. The Masai lost eighty killed and many others captured, compared to only five dead on the Rendille side. This victory secured relative peace for the Rendille, but in 1892 the Laikipiaks launched another attack on the Samburu on Mounts Kulal and Nyiro. The Laikipiak leader, Loldapash, planned a two-pronged assault which broke into the Samburu positions on both mountains, only to meet with disaster. At Mount Nyiro a warrior called Lentumunai killed Loldapash, and his followers fled. The second column was also repulsed from Mount Kulal after its leader, Lesanchu, was captured by the Samburu.

Both the Suk and the Samburu employed an age-set system which was very similar to that of the Masai, although the Samburu elders are said to have enjoyed rather more authority over their *moran* than was usual in Masailand. By the end of the century the Rendille were also organized into age-sets, which they may have borrowed from their Samburu allies. Donaldson Smith, who visited them in 1896, says that the Rendille numbered about 8,000 warriors in total, and that they had often defeated the Somalis as well as the Laikipiaks, but they were hampered by the fact that their arid environment did not permit them to gather in large bands. The Suk and Samburu fought in a similar manner to the Masai, but – perhaps because of their reliance on mountain hideouts in a region where the plains were occupied by stronger enemies – they placed much more emphasis on defensive tactics, notably the use of archery from ambush. 'Their dread of raids from the Turkana and Suk,' says von Hohnel, led the Samburu 'to live with their herds in the highest portions of the mountain.' According to the Samburu themselves, the forests on Mounts Nyiro and Kulal were ideal defensive positions because 'the paths are small and good to kill enemies'. Von Hohnel says that most Samburu weapons were 'of inferior quality', but that their buffalo-hide shields were larger than those of their neighbours. The Suk used very similar equipment, but they did not possess iron arrowheads, relying instead on fire-hardened wooden points. The Rendille were similar in many respects, but they possessed a small number of horses, probably acquired from the Borana, which may have been ridden in battle. At the Merille River at least one man rode up to the Laikipiak line to hurl insults at the enemy. In defence of their villages the Rendille warriors would first make a collective vow never to turn their backs on the enemy, and then draw up in three concentric circles around the stockade, where an ox or a camel was tied to the gate as a rallying point. The women and children would take refuge inside, but would flee into the bush if the defensive circles were broken.

The British Response
Following the partition of Africa among the European powers, Britain had found itself in control of the territory which came to be known as the Northern Frontier District, but the area appeared to be economically worthless and there was no great enthusiasm for occupying it. Gradually, however, during the first decade of the twentieth century, frontier posts

were established, officials were appointed and the region was brought under effective control. But for the first two decades of British rule there was no permanent military presence in the NFD, and operations were limited to punitive expeditions against Ethiopian raiders and tribes which preyed too blatantly on those who claimed imperial protection. The nature of this warfare was well described by Captain Chauncey Stigand of the Queen's Own Royal West Kent Regiment, who in 1907 published his observations in *Scouting and Reconnaissance in Savage Countries*, based on five years' experience in Somaliland and elsewhere on the northern frontier. Typically, he wrote, a punitive expedition would be sent out against a tribe which was guilty of raiding another group which was under British protection, but had 'not the slightest conception of the powers or resources of the government'. Ninety-nine times out of a hundred the resulting campaign would be 'a poor enough show', as the enemy would flee on the expedition's approach, and the only casualties would be a couple of stragglers taken unawares. Some cattle would be rounded up, a village or two burnt, and the column would return to base. However, occasionally a tribe would be motivated to resist, perhaps by an exceptional leader, or simply because of ignorance of the power of the white man's guns. 'On the hundredth occasion all starts as before, but either the strength or the courage of the enemy has been underrated, or a small column becomes detached. Nothing is seen of the assailants except a few flying men. Suddenly there is a rush in thick grass or bush and the little column gets massacred.' Ironically, the captain had described with uncanny accuracy the circumstances of his own death twenty years later. By then governor of the Anglo-Egyptian Sudan's Mongalla province, he personally led a punitive expedition against the Aliab Dinka tribe, who had already attacked another British-led force, in November 1919. All his scouting skills could not prevent the soldiers walking into just the sort of ambush in thick grass which he had described. The column formed a square and eventually extricated itself, but it was badly cut up, and three of its officers and twenty-two other ranks were speared to death in the initial rush. Among the dead was Stigand.

Sources

Burton (1856) and Speke (1864) are the sources for their own skirmish with the Somalis at Berbera. Von Hohnel, Wellby, Donaldson Smith,

Bright and Bell all described their experiences among the tribes of the region later in the century. Yardley, though writing about a slightly later period, has some perceptive views on the nature of Turkana warfare. M Brown offers a comprehensive modern survey of the history of the NFD, from the first explorers to the establishment of British authority after the First World War. The campaigns of the Laikipiak Masai are discussed in Spear and Waller, while Lamphear's studies of the Turkana provide details of their military organization.

Chapter Ten

Conclusion:
'The White Men Beat Everyone Now'

When Carl Peters marched into the Arab settlement at Kamasia at the end of 1889 after his retreat from Masailand (see Chapter 7), he naturally represented his fight at Elbejet as a victory, to the delight of the locals who had their own reasons for hating the Masai. 'That is very fine!' one elderly Arab remarked to Peters. 'The white men beat everyone now.' It seems, when reading of the events of the last decade or so of the nineteenth century, that he was right. There is a new air of inevitability about the progress of imperial armies. Journeys which early explorers took years to complete at the cost of terrible privations are routinely undertaken in weeks by a junior officer and a few dozen askaris. The once terrible Matabele are machine-gunned by armed civilians under the control of a commercial company. Remote fastnesses such as the Ruwenzori Mountains, unseen by outsiders since the days of Ptolemy, are now scaled by adventurous tourists. Some of the reasons for the success of the colonial armies were obvious even at the time; in Hilaire Belloc's famous words, 'We have got the Maxim Gun, and they have not.'

Other factors, however, are identifiable only with hindsight. It could be fairly argued that the contest between African and European military systems was not fought on equal terms. Apologists for imperial expansion regularly cited the political chaos and endemic violence in most of Africa as a justification for intervention. But to a large extent it was interference from outside that had created these conditions in the first place. Another contrast which strikes anyone reading explorers' accounts from the second half of the nineteenth century is between the generally admiring verdicts of the earliest observers of African societies and the contemptuous dismissal which was fashionable by the 1890s. Of course some of this was due to the growing influence of 'scientific' racism in Europe, and to the arrival of increasing numbers of officials, big-game hunters and others who had no sympathy for unfamiliar cultures and ways of life. But it is also clear that many sophisticated African societies had suffered serious damage in the intervening years, both to their material prosperity and to their self-confidence.

In addition to all the external military and political pressures, the late nineteenth century saw a series of environmental disasters across the tropical regions of the world. By the 1880s exploring expeditions and the growth of trade routes had already begun to introduce deadly cattle diseases such as rinderpest into Africa, and to spread human ones, such as smallpox and sleeping sickness, into new regions where the populations lacked immunity. Mortality was often catastrophic. In Uganda, for instance, where sleeping sickness appeared around the end of the century, more than a third of a million people died in a single year. The 1890s were also a time of widespread drought, which combined with the cattle mortality to cause severe famine throughout East Africa. The once-prosperous Kambas of Kenya lost many thousands to disease and starvation, and unburied bodies were a common sight along the route of the Uganda Railway, which the British were building through their country at the time. (As if this was not enough, it was probably the easy availability of corpses which gave the notorious man-eating lions of Tsavo their taste for human flesh.) These disasters weakened many African societies at the very time they were under attack from increasingly self-confident European-led forces, equipped with improved weaponry and benefiting from the latest advances in medical science.

It was particularly unfortunate for many Africans that their geographical isolation from the outside world had insulated them from conflict with Europeans when the technological gap had still been small enough to be bridged. Many Native Americans, for instance, had been in contact with white traders, if not with soldiers and settlers, for centuries before the decisive clashes came. They had time to adapt to innovations such as guns and horses, and to win a few victories over opponents whose weaponry was not decisively superior to their own. Likewise in China and Japan, large populations and well-organized states were able to adapt before they were overrun. But for many African societies the first outside contact was with Europeans already equipped with breech-loading rifles and machine guns, weapons beyond the abilities of untrained men to operate, let alone manufacture for themselves. Some Africans, conditioned by a long-standing warrior ethos which enabled them to accept heavy losses without denting their sense of superiority, could rise to the challenge. But for many it is not surprising that the initial clashes with the white man produced serious demoralization, further reducing their chances of resisting. The victims of this collapse of confidence included some who had previously enjoyed a reputation among fellow Africans as fearsome fighters. The predatory Bemba (or Awemba) of Northern Rhodesia (now Zambia) were an extreme example. They used to boast that they had forgotten how to cultivate their fields, as they made a better living from plundering their terrified neighbours. In alliance with the Arabs they had become predominant in the slave trade in the north-east of the country, and so were a prime target when the British South Africa Company took it over in the late 1890s, following its conquest of the Matabele (see Chapter 2). In 1896 the newly appointed Administrator, Major P W Forbes, concluded in his report that although the territory was mainly quiet, 'There is, however, one power that should be broken, and that is the Awemba' (Brelsford).

This was achieved with unforeseen ease in two minor skirmishes in 1897 and 1899, in which a single white man played the role of a one-man army. 'Bobo' Young was an ex-Scots Guardsman serving with the British South Africa Police. In 1897 he was the only white policeman in the Chambezi district, in charge of fifteen sketchily trained local recruits. When this tiny force encountered a combined Bemba and Arab war party, Young sensibly decided not to rely on the steadiness of his men, so he went forward and stationed himself in a tree with his rifle. Firing from cover, he single-handedly killed between twenty-five and thirty of the enemy and put the rest to flight. Young was clearly a brave man and an expert shot, but given the superior range and rate of fire of a breech-loading rifle over the smoothbores used by the Bemba there is nothing particularly surprising in this feat. Yet the tribesmen had apparently identified Young and came to regard him as invincible. Two years later, during an attack on a fortified village held by a chief named Ponde, Young was part of a force led by an officer named Mackinnon. According to the latter's account (in Brelsford), he left Young in charge of half the force to give covering fire while the rest crawled through a swamp in front of the village, making full use of cover. Then he signalled the policeman to follow him, covered in turn by the advance party. Young, however, 'walked upright over the plain', and then had himself carried through the swamp on the shoulders of the tallest askari, in full view of the enemy. Despite this obvious target Ponde's men did not fire, and the village was taken without loss. Mackinnon was in no doubt that it was Young's reputation alone that had cowed the Bemba: 'By such means was this powerful and wonderfully organized tribe brought within the British Empire with hardly a shot ever fired.' His commander regretted that Young was not eligible for the Victoria Cross, as he was no longer a member of Her Majesty's Armed Forces, but instead recommended him for a substantial pay rise.

It is obvious from our survey of the nineteenth-century campaigns that for those who did fight back there was no universal magic formula for victory. There was one formula which did work, at least for a time, but few African societies were in a position to put it into effect. It is obvious enough with hindsight that the dominance of the white man was based not – as all too many contemporary Europeans persuaded themselves – on innate racial superiority, but on access to a particular set of advantages. A long-established state with the resources and manpower to support a strong, centralized government, and to muster large armies and keep them in the field, with access to overseas trade and the wealth to buy in modern armaments, and above all with the self-confidence and cultural cohesion which comes from a proud history, could, given time, transform itself into a power able to resist the conquerors. In all of Africa there was only one state which met all these criteria. The Zulus had the confidence but lacked the wealth; the Arabs had the wealth but not the manpower; the Ashanti and other West African peoples had strong government and manpower, but were either cut off from the sources of armaments or, like Dahomey or the state founded by Samori Touré in Guinea (both victims of the French), were not given time to complete the transformation of their economies or their armies. Hence on the eve of the First World War there remained only one independent African power: Ethiopia.

We saw in Chapter 9 how in 1891 the British government was content to demarcate the northern frontier of its East African possessions by agreement with the Italians. Although at that time Italian possessions in the region were limited to a handful of outposts along the coast, it was recognized in Europe that Ethiopia lay within Italy's claimed sphere of influence, and it was confidently expected that the claim would be made good over the next few years. There was therefore no point in entering into negotiations with the Ethiopian Emperor Menelik II, as he and his people would shortly become Italian subjects. Menelik had no intention of allowing this to happen. It was true that he had signed a treaty with Italy at Wichale in 1889, but (in spite of a diplomatic wrangle caused by a deliberately inaccurate Italian version of the text) he was emphatic that this had not compromised his country's independence. He had already circulated to the great powers a letter in which he set out the boundaries which would be acceptable to him, and warned that: 'Ethiopia has been for fourteen centuries a Christian land in a sea of pagans. If Powers at a distance come forward to partition Africa between them, I do not intend to be an indifferent spectator' (M Brown).

Needless to say, Menelik was not taken very seriously. The French and the Russians supplied him with guns and advisers, but their main aim was to frustrate the expansionist aims of the Italians and British: the big strategic prize in north-eastern Africa was control of the Upper Nile, and Ethiopia was regarded mainly as a means to that end. Menelik was certain to be forced to accept the 'protection' of one of the powers; the question was simply which one? The Italians moved first. The governor of Italy's coastal colony of Eritrea, General Oreste Baratieri, marched into Ethiopia at the head of more than 20,000 men. Of these, 10,000 were Italian regulars, organized into three brigades and armed with modern Vetterli magazine rifles. Supporting them was a similar number of Eritrean askaris, armed with single-shot breech-loaders, and no fewer than fifty-six field guns. This army has been disparaged by most writers on the subject, and with some reason. Most of the Europeans were conscripts recently sent out from Italy, and few of the officers had any experience of colonial warfare. There was very little strategic or logistic planning, the staff and the government in Rome apparently believing that the army's firepower could negate any advantage which the enemy might have in generalship or numbers. But there were some very professional units present, including detachments of the elite Bersaglieri and Alpini light infantry. Armament was as up to date as that deployed in Africa by any other colonial power, and the logistic arrangements were no worse than those with which the Portuguese in Mozambique had recently destroyed the empire of the Gaza Nguni. Anywhere else in Africa, this host would have been a sledgehammer to crack a nut.

Baratieri's real problem was that he had underestimated his enemy. In February 1896 a force of around 100,000 Ethiopians under the command of Ras Makonnen, accompanied by Menelik and his empress, Taytu, advanced to meet him near Adowa in the north of Tigre province. This was no tribal horde. Patriotism, loyalty to the emperor and to their Orthodox Christian religion, and a national pride just as deep-rooted as the 'myth of Rome' of the Italians, gave the Ethiopians great courage and resilience in battle. In a previous engagement at Amba Alagi an Italian officer had been horrified to see how, when artillery shells burst in the middle of the enemy columns, the survivors just closed the gaps, stepped over the dead and kept advancing. Some 30,000 of Menelik's men were traditionally armed warriors bearing swords, spears and shields, but the rest were equipped with modern repeating rifles. Their forty-six artillery pieces were mostly French quick-firers, more advanced than the old Italian mountain guns, and there were even a few machine guns. The troops were organized into formal units with a sophisticated chain of command. Writing in 1898, Count Gleichen described a hierarchy of officers from the Emperor down to 'captains' of units of 1,000, 500, 100 and 50 men. There were permanently appointed brigade and divisional commanders, and even specialist transport and engineer officers, though logistics were not a strong point of the Ethiopian army. Although this was not a permanent standing army (which could not have been fed for long by the struggling peasantry), many of the troops were veterans of wars against the Mahdists and other opponents, and displayed at least as much cohesion and *esprit de corps* in combat as the hastily trained Italians. This system of organization had not been invented by Menelik, but was a tried and tested arrangement with a history longer than that of several European armies; the Scottish explorer James Bruce had described a very similar hierarchy in the 1770s.

Despite their numerical strength Menelik and Ras Makonnen were reluctant to attack Baratieri frontally, but attempted to outmanoeuvre him and force him to retreat to Eritrea. Baratieri was no more keen to fight, but was being bombarded by messages from Rome ordering him to take the offensive, and by the criticisms of his own brigade commanders who refused to believe reports of the size of the enemy force. By the end of February both sides were running out of supplies, and Menelik was actually on the verge of disbanding his army to avoid starvation. But it was the Italians' resolve which broke first. On the evening of 29 February Baratieri's brigades moved out under cover of darkness, aiming to occupy some high ground between the opposing camps and launch an attack from there in the morning. The terrain was formidable: an open, arid plain was broken by a tangle of hills and ridges running in several directions, and it soon turned out that the Italian maps contained serious inaccuracies. Two of the three advance brigades ran into each other in the dark and were delayed for several hours, while another, under General Dabormida, became completely lost and diverged far to the right of its designated axis of advance.

When dawn broke on 1 March, Baratieri's brigades were all out of position and separated by wide gaps. On the left flank, the askaris of Albertone's brigade were on a hill 3 miles in front of the feature they had been ordered to occupy, unsupported and in close proximity to the enemy army. Dabormida was still too far to the right, while Arimondi, in the centre, was lagging far behind. The Ethiopians, by contrast, were still concentrated and had plenty of warning of the impending attack. (One observer claimed that discipline in the Italian camp was so poor that enemy agents could come and go at will, and that some of the guides employed for the night march were actually Menelik's spies.) They had a screen of cavalry scouts out in front, and were soon aware of the weakness of the Italian dispositions. Ras Makonnen was summoned from a church service, obviously convinced that his prayers had been answered, and ordered an immediate attack. Pinning Dabormida with a feint assault, he concentrated his main force against Albertone.

The Eritreans fought well, and it took four hours to break them. Several Ethiopian attacks were repulsed at different points along the line, but eventually the askaris were outflanked, and the survivors abandoned the hill and fled. Arimondi and the reserve brigade were still struggling forward to make contact with the isolated units in front, and were taken by surprise when Albertone's men ran past them, pursued by the Ethiopians. They were outflanked in turn and pushed back, leaving Baratieri's headquarters surrounded. About noon the Italian commander ordered a retreat, abandoning Dabormida to his fate. The tactics employed by the Ethiopians in this battle were an interesting combination of indigenous and up-to-date European methods. They advanced in a crescent formation to encircle the enemy in a manner which would have been familiar to the Zulus, Ashanti and many other traditional African armies. But instead of closing in a mass rush they operated as individual skirmishers, making use of cover and keeping up a continual fire from their breech-loading rifles. This sounds very much like the tactics prescribed for the British regulars in 1914, but the Ethiopians despised regular European-style drill and volley firing, telling the Italians 'you fight like a herd of slaves' (Berkeley).

As the battle began to swing their way and they realized that the white men were not invincible, the confidence of Menelik's soldiers soared, and they started to run up as close as 10 or 15 yards from the Italian firing lines before firing their rifles at point-blank range. Then as the enemy wavered they charged in with swords and spears to complete their destruction. This recklessness naturally increased the proportion of casualties on both sides, and by the end of the day the Ethiopians had lost as many as 7,000 killed and another 10,000 wounded. The Italian army, however, was effectively destroyed. With nearly 7,000 dead (more than 4,000 of them Italians), it had suffered a loss of 43 per cent killed and wounded (the wounded were in fact only a small proportion of the total). Another 4,000 were taken prisoner. The survivors were shocked and demoralized, and the army was clearly incapable of further offensive action. The defeat caused the fall of the government in Rome, and in October its successors signed a new treaty with Menelik renouncing their claim to his country. The white men, after all, did not beat everyone.

In conclusion, however, it should be emphasized that even at the height of the 'scramble for Africa' not all relations between Africans and Europeans were based on hostility. Like the Italians, the Portuguese deployed metropolitan regulars for their campaign against the Gaza kingdom in 1895, mainly because – like Sir Garnet Wolseley in 1874 – they felt that the enemy had hitherto known white men mainly as traders and officials, and doubted their ability as soldiers. But in tropical regions white troops remained at risk from climate and disease, and were accustomed to levels of supply which the poor communications in the interior could not sustain. So, north of the Limpopo at least, most of the colonial wars were fought and won by Africans in European employ. Naturally the quality of these native troops varied, largely depending on how well they were treated and rewarded by their employers. Where they were conscripted by force or trickery, inadequately fed and motivated mainly by the whip, as in the Congo Free State, they were prone to desert, or even to murder their officers and mutiny. Even in more professional armies, things could go wrong. The Sudanese veterans recruited in Uganda by the British revolted when they were sent to fight the Nandi – not from fear of the enemy, but due to resentment of the actions of a tactless officer, and the discovery that they were being paid far less than raw recruits from Kenya.

At their best, though, African soldiers proved to be as good as any in the world, and some of the relationships which began in the colonial wars lasted well into the twentieth century. In German East Africa the askaris were encouraged to consider themselves a social elite, and they repaid their masters by the fight which they put up against overwhelming odds in 1917–18. At the same time the Tirailleurs Sénégalais of French West Africa were serving in large numbers on the Western Front, where their reckless courage appalled the Germans. The various units serving in British East Africa were formed in 1902 into the King's African Rifles, which was later to serve with distinction as far afield as Burma and Malaya. During these campaigns was forged an attitude of mutual respect between black and white soldiers, some of which persists into the twenty-first century. In 2008 the ex-servicemen's association of the King's African Rifles announced the raising of £300,000 for their 'Askari Appeal' in aid of elderly and destitute former askaris. This is the legacy of the African Wars which, it is to be hoped, will remain long after the bloodshed and suffering have been forgotten.

Sources
The career of 'Bobo' Young is discussed by Brelsford. The account of the Adowa campaign is based mainly on Berkeley.

Glossary

abakumba Azande term for senior, married warriors.

Albini Belgian version of the *Snider rifle*.

askari A term widely used in East and Central Africa for native troops in European service, from an Arabic and Swahili word for a soldier.

assegai A term popularly used nowadays for the short stabbing spear of the Zulus and related peoples, derived from a North African word for a spear. In the nineteenth century its usage was often quite different, referring to any light throwing weapon.

batakari An Ashanti 'war-shirt', covered with sewn-on packets containing charms and believed to provide magical protection.

boma In East and Central Africa, a defensive stockade or thorn-bush hedge for protection against wild animals or human enemies. This may be a permanent construction, or a temporary ring of thorn branches surrounding a campsite.

Dane gun A West African term for a long-barrelled smoothbore muzzle-loading musket. Danish merchants were the first large-scale suppliers of these guns, though by the nineteenth century most were of British manufacture.

Force Publique The armed force of the Belgian King Leopold II's 'Congo Free State'.

Gatling gun An early machine gun, first introduced during the American Civil War, and widely used in Africa during the 1870s and 1880s. It had six barrels which rotated and fired in rapid succession, operated by a hand crank. Ammunition was .45in. calibre, the same as that for the *Martini-Henry rifle*. Rate of fire was theoretically very high, but was not sustainable for long owing to operator fatigue and the difficulty of supplying ammunition, which in most models was fed in by gravity via a hopper. Maximum practical range was about 900 yards. Other hand-operated machine guns included the Nordenfelt and Gardner guns, which worked on a different system using multiple fixed barrels, but were similar in performance.

ibutho (pl. amabutho) Zulu or Matabele regiment, normally recruited from the members of a single age-set.

iklwa (pl. amaklwa) A broad-bladed Zulu stabbing *assegai*, said to have been introduced by Shaka.

impi Zulu or Matabele term for a military formation or task force of any size.

induna (pl. izinduna) Zulu or Matabele commander or senior military official.

iviyo (pl. amaviyo) Zulu company of between fifty and 150. Subdivision of an *ibutho*.

kpinga A multi-bladed Azande throwing knife.

kraal An Afrikaner term for a stockaded African town or village. A similarly fenced enclosure for cattle.

laager Afrikaner word for a camp, generally used in South Africa for a defensive ring of wagons used to protect the camp against attack.

Martini-Henry rifle The British Army's first purpose-designed breech-loading rifle, issued in 1874. Fired a .45in. calibre round and was sighted to 1,450 yards. Reports from the Zulu War confirmed its great penetration and destructive effects on personnel. Although theoretically more accurate at long range than its predecessor the *Snider*, the Martini-Henry was seldom issued to hastily trained African troops because it was liable to go off accidentally if handled carelessly. It was also notoriously prone to jamming, especially in sandy or dusty conditions.

Maxim machine gun The first fully automatic belt-fed machine gun, developed by Hiram Maxim in 1883. The action was powered by the chemical energy of the rounds rather than by a crank or lever, giving a faster rate of fire and greater reliability. (Rates of fire up to 600 rounds per minute are often quoted, though the British Army's official handbook of 1901 gives 450 rounds per minute for rapid fire, and 70 rpm if using deliberate aimed fire.) Officially adopted by the British Army in 1891, it had first seen action in 1888. Originally used the same .45in. calibre ammunition as the *Martini-Henry* rifle, later converted to .303in. Normally mounted on a tripod and carried by porters, but some were fixed onto light wheeled artillery carriages.

moran   A Masai warrior.

Snider rifle   The first standard-issue breech-loading rifle of the British infantry. It was originally a conversion of the older muzzle-loading Enfield design. It used a heavy .577in. bullet, and could fire ten rounds a minute. It saw action in the Abyssinian campaign of 1868 and in the Ashanti War of 1873–74, before being phased out in favour of the *Martini-Henry*. The Snider and its variants continued to equip the bulk of African troops in European service until the end of the century.

wajinga   A regular regiment of the Hehe army, usually armed in Zulu style with shields and stabbing spears.

zeriba (or zariba)   Alternative term for a *boma*, commonly encountered in north-east Africa and the Sudan.

Bibliography

Contemporary Accounts

Capt C H Armitage and Lt Col A F Montanaro, *The Ashanti Campaign of 1900*, London, 1901

Maj Ashe and Capt E V Wyatt Edgell, *The Story of the Zulu Campaign*, London, 1880

S Baker, *The Albert N'yanza, Great Basin of the Nile*, London, 1866

——, 'Experience in Savage Warfare', *Journal of the Royal United Services Institution*, 1873 (reprinted Kent, 1995)

——, *Ismailia: A Narrative of the Expedition to Central Africa for the Suppression of the Slave Trade*, London, 1874

W D M Bell, *The Wanderings of an Elephant Hunter*, London, 1923

G F-H Berkeley, *The Campaign of Adowa and the Rise of Menelik*, London, 1902

T E Bowdich, *Mission from Cape Coast Castle to Ashantee*, London, 1819

Capt H Brackenbury, *The Ashanti War*, London, 1874

R G T Bright, 'Among the Soudan Swamps', *Wide World Magazine*, vol. 9, London, 1902

British Parliamentary Papers. Colonies: Africa. Vols 57 and 58. Ghana, 1850–1874, Shannon, Ireland, 1970–71

H Brode, *Tippoo Tib*, London, 1907

R Brown, *The Story of Africa and its Explorers*, London, [no date, *c*.1896]

Capt G Burrows, *The Land of the Pigmies*, London, 1898

R Burton, *First Footsteps in East Africa*, London, 1856

——, *The Lake Regions of Central Africa*, London, 1860

——, *Zanzibar: City, Island and Coast*, London, 1872

——, *Two Trips to Gorilla Land and the Cataracts of the Congo*, London, 1876

Cmdr V L Cameron, *Across Africa*, London, 1877

C Chaille-Long, *Central Africa*, London, 1876

F E Colenso and Lt Col E Durnford, *History of the Zulu War and Its Origin*, London, 1881

H Colville, *The Land of the Nile Springs*, London, 1895

A Donaldson Smith, *Through Unknown African Countries*, London and New York, 1897

P B du Chaillu, *Explorations and Adventures in Equatorial Africa*, London, 1861

——, *A Journey to Ashango-Land*, London, 1867

Lt Col A B Ellis, *A History of the Gold Coast of West Africa*, London, 1893

W A Elmslie, *Among the Wild Ngoni*, London, 1899

J F Elton, *Travels and Researches Among the Lakes and Mountains of Eastern and Central Africa*, London, 1879

W Finaughty, *The Recollections of an Elephant Hunter*, Bulawayo, 1980

M French-Sheldon, *Sultan to Sultan: Adventures in East Africa*, Boston, 1892

H F Fynn, *The Diary of Henry Francis Fynn*, ed. J Stuart and D Malcolm, Pietermaritzburg, 1969

E J Glave, *Six Years of Adventures in Congo-Land*, London, 1893

A E W Gleichen, *With the Mission to Menelik, 1897*, London, 1898

J A Grant, *A Walk across Africa*, Edinburgh and London, 1864

J W Gregory, *The Great Rift Valley*, London, 1896

E S Grogan and A H Sharp, *From the Cape to Cairo*, London, 1900

W M Hall, *The Great Drama of Kumasi*, London, 1939

W C Harris, *Wild Sports of Southern Africa*, London, 1838

G B Hill (ed.), *Gordon in Central Africa, 1874–1879*, London, 1881

S L Hinde, *The Fall of the Congo Arabs*, London, 1897

—— and H Hinde, *The Last of the Masai*, London, 1901

Lady Hodgson, *The Siege of Kumasi*, London, 1901

A C Hollis, *The Masai, Their Language and Folklore*, Oxford, 1905

——, *The Nandi, Their Language and Folklore*, Oxford, 1909

Lt Gen Sir E Hutton, 'Recollections of the Zulu War', *Army Quarterly*, April 1928

N Isaacs, *Travels and Adventures in Eastern Africa*, London, 1836

Sir F Jackson, *Early Days in East Africa*, London, 1930

F L James, *The Unknown Horn of Africa*, London, 1888

W P Johnson, *My African Reminiscences, 1875–1895*, London, 1924

H H Johnston, *British Central Africa*, London, 1897

——, *The Uganda Protectorate*, London, 1902

——, *The Nile Quest*, London, 1903

——, *George Grenfell and the Congo*, London, 1908

W Junker, *Travels in Africa, 1875–1886*, trans. A H Keane, London, 1891 and 1892

J Krapf, *Travels, Researches and Missionary Labours*, London, 1860

F D Lugard, *The Rise of Our East African Empire*, Edinburgh and London, 1893

——, *The Story of the Uganda Protectorate*, London, [no date, *c*.1900]

J R L Macdonald, *Soldiering and Surveying in British East Africa*, London, 1897

Col J W Marshall, *Report: Operations in Timini Country*, London, 1898

R Meinertzhagen, *Kenya Diary, 1902–1906*, Edinburgh and London, 1957

M Merker, *Die Masai*, Berlin, 1904

B Mitford, *Through the Zulu Country: Its Battlefields and Its People*, London, 1883

R Moffat, *Missionary Labours and Scenes in South Africa*, London, 1842

E D Morel, *Red Rubber*, London, 1906

C New, *Wanderings and Labours in East Africa*, London, 1873

E Nigmann, *Die Wahehe*, Berlin, 1908

C L Norris-Newman, *In Zululand with the British throughout the War of 1879*, London, 1880

C Peters, *New Light on Dark Africa*, London, 1891

J Petherick, 'The Arms of the Arab and Negro Tribes of Central Africa', *Journal of the Royal United Services Institution*, vol. 4, 1861

——, *Egypt, the Soudan and Central Africa*, Edinburgh and London, 1861

—— and K Petherick, *Travels in Central Africa*, London, 1869

C Phillipps-Wolley (ed.), *Big-Game Shooting*, London, 1894

G Portal, *The British Mission to Uganda*, London, 1894

Maj P H G Powell-Cotton, *In Unknown Africa*, London, 1904

M von Prince, *Eine Deutsche Frau im Innern Deutsch-Ostafrikas*, Berlin, 1908

Proceedings of the Royal Geographical Society, vols 1–22, 1857–78, and new series, vols 1–6, 1879–84 [reports by various authors]

R Schmidt, *Deutschlands Kolonien*, Berlin, 1898

G Schweinfurth, *The Heart of Africa*, London, 1873

F C Selous, *Travels and Adventures in South-East Africa*, London, 1893

——, *Sunshine and Storm in Rhodesia*, London, 1896

J H Speke, *Journal of the Discovery of the Source of the Nile*, Edinburgh, 1863

——, *What Led to the Discovery of the Source of the Nile*, Edinburgh, 1864

H M Stanley, *How I Found Livingstone*, London, 1872

——, *Coomassie and Magdala*, London, 1874

——, *Through the Dark Continent*, London, 1879

——, *In Darkest Africa*, London, 1890

C H Stigand, *Scouting and Reconnaissance in Savage Countries*, London, 1907

A J Swann, *Fighting the Slave Hunters in Central Africa*, London, 1910

J Thomson, *To the Central African Lakes and Back*, London, 1881

——, *Through Masai Land*, London, 1885

E Torday, *On the Trail of the Bushongo*, London, 1925

Lt S Vandeleur, *Campaigning on the Upper Nile and Niger*, London, 1898

L von Hohnel, *Discovery of Lakes Rudolf and Stefanie*, trans. N Bell, London, 1894

H W Wack, *The Story of the Congo Free State*, New York, 1905

H Waller (ed.), *Livingstone's Last Journals*, London, 1874

H Ward, *Five Years With the Congo Cannibals*, London, 1890

J H Weeks, *Among the Primitive Bakongo*, London, 1914

M S Wellby, *'Twixt Sirdar and Menelik*, London, 1901

C Wiese, *Expedition in East-Central Africa 1888–1891*, trans. D Ramos, ed. H W Langworthy, London, 1983

C T Wilson and R Felkin, *Uganda and the Egyptian Soudan*, London, 1882

W Winwood Reade, *The Story of the Ashantee Campaign*, London, 1874

FM Visc Wolseley, *The Story of a Soldier's Life*, New York, 1903

Sir E Wood, *From Midshipman to Field Marshal*, London, 1907

Capt J H R Yardley, *Parergon, or, Eddies in Equatoria*, London and Toronto, 1931

Modern Works
P Abbott, *Unknown Armies: British East Africa*, Leeds, 1988
R W Beachey, 'The Arms Trade in East Africa in the Late Nineteenth Century', *Journal of African History*, vol. 3, 1962
J H M Beattie, *Bunyoro: An African Kingdom*, Stanford, California, 1960
——, 'Bunyoro: An African Feudality?', *Journal of African History*, vol. 5, 1964
M Boucher, 'Frederick Hitch and the Defence of Rorke's Drift', *Journal of the South African Military History Society*, vol. 2, no. 6, Johannesburg, 1973
W V Brelsford, *The Story of the Northern Rhodesia Regiment*, Bromley, Kent, 1954
M Brown, *Where Giants Trod: The Saga of Kenya's Desert Lake*, London, 1989
The Cambridge History of Africa. Volume 5: c. 1790 – c. 1870, ed. J E Flint, Cambridge, 1976
——. *Volume 6: c. 1870 – c. 1905*, ed. R Oliver and G N Sanderson, Cambridge, 1986
Y M Cibambo, *My Ngoni of Nyasaland*, London, 1942
Sir R Coupland, *Livingstone's Last Journey*, London, 1947
——, *Zulu Battle Piece: Isandhlwana*, London, 1948
G L Dodds, *The Zulus and Matabele: Warrior Nations*, London, 1998
Sir E E Evans-Pritchard, *The Azande: History and Political Institutions*, Oxford, 1971
L H Gann and P Duignan, *The Rulers of German Africa*, Stanford University, 1977
A Greaves, *Rorke's Drift*, London, 2002
——, *Redcoats and Zulus: Myths, Legends and Explanations of the Anglo-Zulu War*, Barnsley, 2004
J Guy, *The Destruction of the Zulu Kingdom: The Civil War in Zululand, 1879–1884*, London, 1979
D Headrick, 'The Tools of Imperialism', *Journal of Modern History*, vol. 51, 1979
I Hernan, *Britain's Forgotten Wars*, Stroud, 2003
A Hochschild, *King Leopold's Ghost*, New York, 1998
J A Hunter and D Mannix, *African Bush Adventures*, London, 1954
G W B Huntingford, *Nandi Work and Culture*, London, 1950
——, *The Nandi of Kenya*, London, 1953
J Iliffe, *A Modern History of Tanganyika*, Cambridge, 1974
M S M Kiwanuka, 'Bunyoro and the British', *Journal of African History*, vol. 9, 1968
——, *A History of Buganda*, London, 1971
I Knight, *Brave Men's Blood: The Epic of the Zulu War*, London, 1990
——, *The Anatomy of the Zulu Army*, London, 1995
——, *Great Zulu Battles, 1838–1906*, London, 1998
——, *Great Zulu Commanders*, London, 1999
——, *Companion to the Anglo-Zulu War*, Barnsley, 2008

J Laband, *Rope of Sand: The Rise and Fall of the Zulu Kingdom*, Johannesburg, 1995

J Lamphear, 'Aspects of Turkana Leadership', *Journal of African History*, vol. 17, 1976

——, 'The People of the Grey Bull: The Origin and Expansion of the Turkana', *Journal of African History*, vol. 29, 1988

W L Langer, *The Diplomacy of Imperialism, 1890–1902*, New York, 1960

D Levering Lewis, *The Race to Fashoda*, London, 1988

A T Matson, *Nandi Resistance to British Rule*, Nairobi, 1972

L Maxwell, *The Ashanti Ring*, London, 1985

J P Moffett (ed.), *Handbook of Tanganyika*, Dar es Salaam, 1958

D R Morris, *The Washing of the Spears*, New York, 1966

F Myatt, *The Golden Stool*, London, 1966

J W Nyakatura, *Anatomy of an African Kingdom: A History of Bunyoro-Kitara*, New York, 1973

M Page, *A History of the King's African Rifles*, London, 1998

T Pakenham, *The Scramble For Africa, 1876–1912*, London, 1991

C J Peers, *Armies of the Nineteenth Century: East Africa*, Nottingham, 2003

M Pegler, *Powder and Ball Small Arms*, Marlborough, 1998

M Read, *The Ngoni of Nyasaland*, London, 1956

A Redmayne, 'Mkwawa and the Hehe Wars', *Journal of African History*, vol. 9, 1968

R Reusch, *History of East Africa*, Stuttgart, 1954

R Robinson and J Gallagher, *Africa and the Victorians*, London, 1967

T Saitoti and C Beckwith, *Masai*, New York, 1980

E Smith and A M Dale, *The Ila-Speaking Peoples of Northern Rhodesia*, London, 1920

Lt Col M Snook, *How Can Man Die Better: The Secrets of Isandlwana Revealed*, London, 2005

T Spear and R Waller (eds), *Being Maasai: Ethnicity and Identity in East Africa*, London, Dar es Salaam and Nairobi, 1993

C Spring, *African Arms and Armour*, London, 1993

R Summers and C W Pagden, *The Warriors*, Cape Town, 1970

J Sutherland and D Canwell, *The Zulu Kings and their Armies*, Barnsley, 2004

O von Sydow, 'Deutsch Ost-Afrika', *Savage and Soldier*, vol. 10, nos. 2–4, 1978

B Vandervort, *Wars of Imperial Conquest in Africa, 1830–1914*, London, 1998

R Waller, 'The Masai and the British, 1895–1905', *Journal of African History*, vol. 17, 1976

J Wellard, *The Great Sahara*, London, 1964

G White, 'Firearms in Africa', *Journal of African History*, vol. 12, 1971

Index